Object Relations and Intersubjective Theories in the Practice of Psychotherapy

‖‖‖‖‖‖‖‖‖‖‖‖‖‖‖‖‖‖‖‖
I0083885

The evolution of psychoanalytic/psychodynamic psychotherapy has been marked by an increasing disconnect between theory and technique. This book re-establishes a bridge between the two. In presenting a clear explanation of modern psychodynamic theory and concepts, and an abundance of clinical illustrations, Brodie shows how every aspect of psychodynamic therapy is determined by current psychodynamic theory.

In *Object Relations and Intersubjective Theories in the Practice of Psychotherapy*, Brodie uses the theoretical foundation of the work of object relations theorist D.W. Winnicott, showing how each of his developmental concepts have clear implications for psychodynamic treatment, and builds on the contributions of current intersubjective theorists Thomas Ogden and Jessica Benjamin. Added to this is Brodie's vast array of clinical material, ranging from delinquent adolescents to high-functioning adults, and drawing on nearly 40 years of experience in psychotherapy. These contributions are fresh and original, and crucially demonstrate how clinical technique is informed by theory and how theory can be illuminated by clinical material.

Written with clarity and detail, this book will appeal to graduate students in psychology and psychotherapy, medical residents in psychiatry, and young, practicing psychotherapists who wish to fully explore why psychotherapists do what they do and the dialectical relationship between theory and technique that informs their work.

Bruce R. Brodie received his B.A. from the University of California, Berkeley, and his Ph.D. from the University of Chicago. He worked for 20 years at a secure residential treatment center for delinquent adolescents. He was adjunct faculty at the California School for Professional Psychology for 20 years and has been affiliated with the Saturday Center for Psychotherapy and Training for 35 years. He is currently in private practice in Santa Monica, CA. He is the author of *Adolescence and Delinquency: An Object Relations Theory Approach*.

Object Relations and Intersubjective Theories in the Practice of Psychotherapy

Bruce R. Brodie

Routledge
Taylor & Francis Group

LONDON AND NEW YORK

First published 2020
by Routledge
2 Park Square, Milton Park, Abingdon, Oxon OX14 4RN

and by Routledge
52 Vanderbilt Avenue, New York, NY 10017

Routledge is an imprint of the Taylor & Francis Group, an informa business

© 2020 Bruce R. Brodie

The right of Bruce R. Brodie to be identified as author of this work
has been asserted by him in accordance with sections 77 and 78 of the
Copyright, Designs and Patents Act 1988.

All rights reserved. No part of this book may be reprinted or reproduced or
utilised in any form or by any electronic, mechanical, or other means, now
known or hereafter invented, including photocopying and recording, or in
any information storage or retrieval system, without permission in writing
from the publishers.

Trademark notice: Product or corporate names may be trademarks or
registered trademarks, and are used only for identification and explanation
without intent to infringe.

British Library Cataloguing-in-Publication Data
A catalogue record for this book is available from the British Library

Library of Congress Cataloging-in-Publication Data
A catalog record for this book has been requested

ISBN: 978-0-367-42879-2 (hbk)
ISBN: 978-0-367-42877-8 (pbk)
ISBN: 978-0-367-85569-7 (ebk)

Typeset in Times New Roman
by Apex CoVantage, LLC

I am a part of all that I have met.
Tennyson, *Ulysses*

Contents

PART III
The depressive position, intersubjectivity,
and the discovery of external objects   169

Acknowledgments

This book owes a huge intellectual debt to three giants of psychological theory: two living and one long dead. The two living are Jessica Benjamin and Thomas Ogden. Both have shaped and informed my thinking in ways I cannot give justice to. The third is the great D.W. Winnicott who has informed so much of modern psychodynamic theory.

A number of people read and provided helpful feedback to different drafts of my manuscript. Of these, I want to single out in particular Samoan Barish for her characteristic insight and encouragement and Maureen Mahoney for her painstaking reading, sage advice, and unflagging support. I also want to thank Christine Ashe, Lina Dicken, Nic Harbeck, Brian Henley, James Kalivas, Erica Krakovitz, Cindy May, Rincy Mathew, Bahar Moheban, Jennifer Mozel, Diem Nguyen, Katy O'Donnell, Laura O'Loughlin, John Peloian, Owen Petersen, Chrystal Rahmani, Afrouz Shay, Timothy Wong, Milla Zeltzer, and Nicole Zokaeem for their time and helpful feedback.

I want to reiterate my thanks and appreciation to my students, interns, and – especially – my clients who allowed their personal stories to be used as illustrative vignettes in this book. This is no small thing! Not only are these often intensely personal stories, the type of intimate details of one's life that are only told to a therapist, but there is an inherent distortion involved that comes with the transformation of a story told to bear one's soul to one told to illustrate a clinical concept. It is always a rude shock to see oneself so used. I am deeply appreciative and grateful.

I want to thank my sons and my daughters-in-law, Jedediah, Nathaniel, Olga, and Kelly, for their love and loyalty and my grandchildren, Joaquin Raven, Fiona Wren, and Niko Peregrine, for the joy and inspiration they provide. Most of all, I want to express my love and my thanks to my wife,

Janet, for her constant love, her patience and support and, not incidentally, her exquisite copyediting. She worked tirelessly to save me from my addiction to the passive voice.

Preface

The birth of our first child was difficult. Labor had been induced which meant that my wife went into powerful contractions when her cervix was still only minimally dilated. To compound matters, the baby was big (well over eight pounds), he was in an "anterior presentation" (which meant that he was pushing out with the broadest part of his head instead of the narrowest), and . . . Brodie babies have big heads. I was my wife's "Lamaze" coach.

In our Lamaze classes we had been taught not to use the word "pain." "Discomfort" was the preferred word. In hindsight, this seems to have been an early attempt at "positive psychology." If you think of childbirth as painful you will feel pain. If you think of childbirth as discomfort, you will feel discomfort instead of pain. Not true!

By the end of 22 hours of intense, powerful, fruitless, and *painful* contractions my wife was physically and emotionally exhausted. During the last of the contractions (before the doctors went in with an epidural and forceps), my wife and I would do the breathing exercises that we had been taught, our eyes inches from each other. Looking into her eyes I saw the desperation with which she was holding onto my gaze and I suddenly realized that my gaze was the only thing between her and a screaming insanity. I was – my eyes were – the only thing she was still holding onto. I realized that I was, in that moment, absolutely essential to her.

But I got no pleasure from that realization. To the contrary, here was the person I loved more than anyone else in the world, in agonizing pain, and I was completely helpless to take any of that pain away from her. In that moment I felt – simultaneously – absolutely essential and utterly useless. These two opposing feelings seemed to coexist completely independently of each other. My feeling essential did not mitigate my feeling useless. And my feeling useless did not detract from my feeling essential. I felt both.

I have since come to see that experience as a metaphor for what it is like to be a therapist. Clients come into therapy in some sort of discomfort, and with our help they gradually get in touch with the buried pain of which the discomfort is but the tip of the iceberg. I doubt very much whether there is any psychotherapy client who does not wonder, at some point, if the process is worth it and, more to the point, if the as-yet still buried pain might not be, in fact, unbearable.

New therapists have to learn that they cannot take away their clients' pain and that they do their clients a huge disservice if they attempt to do so. Yet they also have to learn that, in spite of this, they become essential to their clients. A therapist's two-to-three-week vacation can be a well-deserved respite for the therapist and a re-traumatizing abandonment for a client.

How do therapists understand, how do they deal with, how do they negotiate this paradox? In what way do they become essential to their clients if they cannot (and should not attempt to) take away their clients' pain? And is being essential a good or a bad thing? Are we talking about a healthy dependency here (as with my wife's momentary use of me as a last tie to sanity) or a pathological dependency in which a client metaphorically attaches himself, leech-like, to his therapist's "breast?" And how do we know the difference?

The answers to these, and countless similar questions, are found in more-or-less systematic bodies of thought that are called *clinical theories*. Without a theoretical foundation, therapists are not just babes-in-the-woods, not just babes-in-a-pitch-dark-woods, they are babes-in-a-minefield. Worse yet, they are babes trying to help another human being, someone who is paying them, trusting them, counting on them to have *some* idea of what the hell they are doing and where the hell they are leading them.

When I retired from The California School of Professional Psychology after more than 20 years as adjunct faculty, the School was in the midst of a curriculum change. The three core courses on clinical theory (psycho-dynamic, cognitive-behavioral, and systems) were out. In their place were a series of how-to courses (how to do therapy with adults, therapy with children, therapy with families, etc.). I realized with horror that an entire generation of clinical psychologists may end up "doing therapy" without any theoretical understanding of what they are doing, why they are doing it, beyond "this procedure works; that doesn't." This is "evidence-based practice" carried to its most insane extreme. Indisputably, to blindly follow the dictates of a particular theory despite evidence that it is not helping or even harming a client is the height of irresponsibility. But it seems equally irresponsible to me to assert that clients are best served by pro-grammed robots. Jessica Benjamin (1998, p. 15) quotes Gallop (1985) as saying, "No one wants to be unlocked by a skeleton key." I think that it is even more profoundly obvious that no one wants to be (or can be) nurtured by a robot.

This book aims to provide a link between two overlapping theories – object relations theory (as elaborated in particular by D.W. Winnicott) and intersubjectivity (as formulated primarily by Thomas Ogden and Jessica Benjamin) and clinical technique. The last part of the book's title, "*in the Practice of Psychotherapy*," should by rights be, "and why we do what we do as therapists," (though that would have been a bit unwieldy as a book title). As psychotherapists, we need to be intelligent and we need to be empathic. And we need to be informed. But we cannot allow our "being informed" to be limited to what the latest research data indicates about "what works and what doesn't." We need to be informed about *why* what we do works, about *how* it works, about how and why it affects the client in the way it does, about who the client is (beyond a set of diagnostic criteria), about what changes the client needs to make (beyond thinking more like the therapist does), and about how and why the client seems to have to go through so much pain to achieve those goals.

That is the goal of this book.

Introduction

The issue that this book addresses – the relationship between theory and therapy – was noted by psychoanalyst Jay Greenberg over 30 years ago. Greenberg wrote: Few issues in psychoanalysis are quite so muddled, or tend to generate so much confusion in the mind of the clinician, as the relationship between theory and technique (Greenberg, 1986).

This book comes out of almost 20 years of teaching graduate students in psychology. What I found in the process is that there are basically two kinds of textbooks: books on theory and books on technique. There are excellent books in both categories. But I find a paucity of books that try specifically to bridge the gap between theory and practice. What is it exactly that we do as psychodynamic psychotherapists and why is it that we do these things? How does theory inform our practice and how does our clinical work reflect back on our theory?

Cognitive Behavioral therapists have it relatively easy. Aron Beck's (1979) theory, for example, is simple, elegant, and easily understood: *psychopathology is the result of "cognitive distortions."* And the theory inexorably points to clear therapeutic interventions: *Correct cognitive distortions.* But psychodynamic theory (theories) is (are) much more subtle (unclear?), nuanced, and ambiguous in their implications. And the fact that psychodynamic theory has undergone over a century of evolution, diversification, and contestation among practitioners has not added to its simplicity or clarity.

Freud's (1916–1917) original theory was as simple and elegant as any: *the psychoneuroses arise out of an excess of repression.* And his theory points to a clear path of intervention: *remove the repression.* To be sure, this turned out to be no easy task. Freud's early difficulties in meeting this goal led to significant changes in both his theory and his technique. The evolution of psychoanalytic theory has proceeded dramatically since Freud's time, such that the master would hardly recognize what is practiced today under the name of "psychoanalysis." The role of instincts in general and sexuality in particular have shifted from a central to a marginal focus. What is valued in a psychoanalyst (psychotherapist) has flipped from objectivity to subjectivity. Fundamental concepts such as the unconscious and transference have undergone serious rewriting and the concept of countertransference has shifted from being described as problematic in analysis to being an invaluable psychoanalytic tool.

It is not the goal of this book to detail the history of, and the justifications for, these changes. The changes have been overwhelmingly positive and have kept psychoanalytic theory intellectually relevant in the twenty-first century and psychoanalytic practice clinically effective (see Schedler, 2010). Rather, my goal is to address a critical problem resulting from this profound evolutionary change: the loss of a clear, simple link between psychoanalytic theory and technique. Freud's original theoretical formulation (neurosis arises from an overabundance of repression) led to a clear and direct prescription for a treatment technique (remove repression!). But that original conceptualization of neurosis bears little resemblance to our modern views of psychopathology. So, we are left with some huge questions: What does the current state of the "psychoanalytic dialog" (Ogden, 1990) tell us about the nature of psychopathology and how does that inform our clinical technique? Put simply, what do we do as therapists and why do we do it?

In this book I try to address those questions. To do so, I will focus on a branch of psychodynamic theory, *object relations theory* (and the theories of D.W. Winnicott in particular), that I have found particularly useful, and on a relatively recently melding of philosophy and psychology known as *intersubjectivity*. In doing so I will try first of all to show how object relations theory and intersubjectivity can be seen as simply two versions of, or two facets of, the same overall theory or belief system. Second, I will attempt to show how that theory or belief system leads implicitly to a set of behaviors and interventions that produce "therapeutic change."

At this point I need to clarify some of my terms. In doing so, I make no claim to actually giving *definitions* of object relations theory and intersubjectivity. Rather, I will attempt to simply give as clear an idea as possible of what it is that I am talking about when I use these terms.

Object relations theory

Object relations theory is difficult to define because there is no single, dominant figure, no establisher-of-orthodoxy. There is no single Freud one can look to and quote to define "classical psychoanalysis," no Jung to define "Depth Psychology," no Kohut whose writings one can quote to define and understand "Self Psychology." This is a help as well as a hindrance. The absence of a central, defining figure in a theory makes the theory obviously harder to define (although even with someone like Freud one always has to ask whether one is dealing with earlier or later Freudian theorizing). But the absence of an "arbiter-of-orthodoxy" also allows a theory to be continually cross-pollinated, to be forever infused with new blood. Orthodoxy contributes simultaneously to clarity and to stagnation.

Object relations theory refers to an amalgam of theoretical material to come out of a group of psychoanalytic writers between the 1920s and the 1960s, most of whom were then referred to as comprising the "Middle School" of British psychoanalysis (called "middle" in part because they were caught in the middle between, and arbitrated between, the personal feud/war-of-orthodoxy battle between Anna Freud (classical psychoanalysis/Ego Psychology) and Melanie Klein (Kleinian psychoanalysis). The Middle School theorists all owed a strong intellectual debt to Melanie Klein but were never bound by her orthodoxy. They also maintained a profound respect for classic Freudian thinking (and to its then current iteration, "*Ego Psychology*"), but were united in their rejection of Freud's (and for that matter, Klein's) adherence to "drive theory." The names most often included in this group are Ronald Fairbairn, Donald W. Winnicott, Wilfred Bion, John Bowlby, Michael Balint, and Harry Guntrip. Otto Kernberg (1976, 1984) recombined object relations theory with Freudian theory, suggesting that they were complementary rather than divergent theories, each being more appropriate to a different developmental level of pathology. More recently, the American psychoanalyst Thomas Ogden has synthesized his own version of object relations theory that neatly morphs into a theory of intersubjectivity.

If defining classical psychoanalysis is complicated by having to differentiate between early Freud and late Freud, this is nothing compared to having to define object relations theory by compiling a list of only partially-in-agreement theorists. Thomas Ogden (1990) lists Bion as a major contributor to object relations theory, but Mitchell and Black (1995) call Bion a definite Kleinian. John Bowlby, a clear member of the then "Middle School," is more commonly known as the founder of his own theory: "Attachment Theory." Otto Kernberg who, in my mind, is one of the major American contributors to object relations theory, is listed by Mitchell and Black (1995) as a "Post-Freudian." To make matters even less clear, in my statement that object relations theory has evolved or morphed into intersubjectivity, it needs to be pointed out that one of the major intersubjective thinkers, Robert Stolorow, whose name is most commonly associated with intersubjectivity, came out of a Kohutian, Self Psychology tradition rather than an object relations tradition at all and Stolorow makes scant references to object relations theory in his writings.

Clearly, names, or a collection of names, are not particularly helpful in defining a theory. Let me try and outline the basic components of what I am referring to as an object relations theory. First, object relations theorists share a common rejection of the kind of drive theory that served as a foundation for both Freud and Klein. More specifically, they reject libido theory as an all-encompassing explanation of human behavior. In this they differentiate themselves from the Ego Psychologists who wrote in the same era, but who tried to tweak and modify drive theory in an attempt to preserve it as a fundamental explanatory concept. This is not to say that object relations theorists completely rejected the role of biology or even of instinct in human psychology. But they clearly downplayed these factors. Winnicott (1968a), for example, acknowledged that anger, rage, and aggression may have some genetic/instinctual component, but he argued that the primary cause of these reactions was likely to be situational frustration.

Instead of Freud's hydraulic-modeled libido theory, object relations theorists suggest a less specific but equally powerful need for human contact (object relatedness). *Homo sapiens*, they suggest, are biologically programmed to live in groups, to form and value social contacts, and to focus especially on the mother-child relationship. Like all primates, Homo sapiens are social animals. Were we felines, we would be like African lions which live together affectionately in prides, rather than like the American mountain lion which seems to thrive on solitude.

What I refer to in this book as "object relations theory"[1] is a model of the psyche primarily crystallized around Melanie Klein's concepts of the paranoid-schizoid position and the depressive position.[2] These concepts, however, have evolved significantly since the time of Klein's own writings. Klein seems to have envisioned both positions as fundamentally intrapsychic processes. In both positions, she saw the individual as dealing with internal objects, which were then projected onto external objects (as a slide would be projected onto a screen). The difference between the two positions was that in the paranoid-schizoid position one dealt with split (or part) objects while in the depressive position one was dealing with internal whole objects.

Part objects will be discussed in detail in Chapter 4. For introduction purposes, they are internal (psychological) constructs representing real, external objects, which are marked by a uniformity of affect. A part object is felt to be all good or all bad, all desirable or all repulsive, all safe or completely threatening. Part objects abrogate the need for ambivalence. Whole objects (like real people) have good qualities and bad qualities, are sometimes loving and sometimes hating, are at times brave and at times cowardly.

In Ogden's more contemporary version, the paranoid-schizoid position remains essentially unchanged from Klein's version (or at least from Klein's later version as influenced by Fairbairn). In this version, what are internalized are not simply objects but *object relationships*. That is to say, it is more of a *dialog* that gets internalized than simply an object. And each internal dialog has two components: the voice (not literally heard as an internal voice) of the object (person) that has been "internalized," and the corresponding voice of the individual (the self) that completes the dialog. These dialogs are internal (intrapsychic) and generally unconscious. As a result, they tend to be cut off from external influence and therefore don't change easily. They are endless-loop tapes that play in our heads over and over again. In this position these internal dialogs get projected out onto the world, onto "external objects" (real people), who then have the disconcerting experience of being seen not as themselves but rather as a fill-in for some earlier, unknown soul. In object relations theory this kind of projection is seen as the mechanism for what Freud called "*transference*."

Building on Winnicott's (1968a) contribution, most modern object relations theorists reject altogether Klein's notion of internal whole objects. Internal part objects are an extremely useful psychological mechanism for dealing with the world. But internal whole objects have no such useful function. They add nothing to the experiencing of the reality of an external whole object (there is no such thing as an external part object. All external objects are whole). Thus, rather than seeing the depressive position as simply a more advanced platform for projection and projective identification, Winnicott, Ogden, and others sees the depressive position as the mind's mechanism for dealing with external objects, with real people and the real world. In this way, Ogden melds object relations theory with intersubjectivity.

Relational psychoanalysis and intersubjectivity

Like object relations theory, intersubjectivity is made more difficult to define (but also enriched and unfettered) by the absence of a single, proprietary voice. The person who claims credit for introducing the term to psychology (from philosophy) and the name most commonly associated with the term is that of Robert Stolorow who comes out of a Kohutian, Self Psychology tradition. Other seminal names in intersubjectivity are those of Jessica Benjamin and Thomas Ogden, both of whom cite a more object relations background. My own bias is strongly for the object relations foundation. Object relations theory, after all, is basically about the relationships between people and either other people or the internal representations of other people, in other words, about intersubjectivity. Self Psychology, on the other hand, arose out of an exhaustive study of Narcissism.

To make things even less clear, the term "intersubjectivity" is poorly differentiated from the term "relational," as in "Relational Psychoanalysis" (cf. Mitchell (1988, 2000), Wachtel (2008)). What is meant by "intersubjectivity" (and the difference in meaning between intersubjective and relational) depends on whom one asks. Stolorow (2013) uses the term in the context of a specific theory (Intersubjective-Systems Theory) that he and his colleagues (Atwood, Orange, and others) have been devising. Intersubjective-Systems Theory, says Stolorow, is characterized as being "contextual" (the self is defined exclusively in terms of its relational context) and phenomenological (focusing on the emotional experience).

Jessica Benjamin uses the word intersubjectivity to refer specifically to that state of developmental achievement in which the "other" is recognized as a separate, autonomous, subject. In contrast to Benjamin, who appears to use the term to reflect a heightened state of consciousness, Brown (2011) says that essential to the "intersubjective experience" is a kind of direct, unconscious to unconscious communication. Ogden (1994, 2004) uses the term in both senses. He says that there are "innumerable forms" (1994, p. 4) of intersubjectivity but that only the highest forms (those in the depressive position) achieve the levels demanded by Benjamin's criterion. Lesser forms of intersubjectivity (e.g., a "subjugating" form of intersubjectivity) characterize the paranoid-schizoid position.

For the purposes of this book I will refer to intersubjectivity in both a broad and narrow sense, as involving all levels of interpersonal engagement but with various levels of real connectedness, culminating in the *conscious awareness of mutual subjectivity* as described by Benjamin (1998, 1990, 2004). I add one criterion to those listed previously in an attempt to differentiate what I see as intersubjectivity from my reading of what others refer to as relational psychoanalysis. Intersubjectivity, as I will use the term, implies a dialectical relationship between the intrapsychic and the interpersonal. As I read them, "interpersonal" writers argue (correctly, I believe) that psychoanalytic theory historically has focused too myopically on the intrapsychic. But, to my mind, they tend to throw the baby out with the bathwater in their consequent diminished focus on the intrapsychic.

The essential question in object relations theory is how one gets from the paranoid-schizoid position to the depressive position. The parallel question in intersubjectivity is how one gets from the experience of self and other as *object* to the experience of self and other as *subject*. As I have indicated, I believe that these are the same question. As Ogden (1884, 1990, 1994) has painstakingly demonstrated, the experience of self in the paranoid-schizoid position is that of object. The corresponding experience of self in the depressive position is that of subject. But as Klein indicated, the depressive position is never fully achieved. There is always a dialectical tension between the two positions. We seesaw back and forth between them. And, as Ogden (1990) has pointed out, fully achieving the depressive position wouldn't be that wonderful an accomplishment anyway. As the paranoid-schizoid position is essentially one of intrapsychic functioning and (the modern conceptualization of) the depressive position is one of interpersonal functioning, then we must be willing to consider a constant seesawing, a constant dialectical tension, between the intrapsychic and the interpersonal.

Intersubjectivity, defined as any interaction between two subjects, of course begs the question of what constitutes a "subject?" A "subject" is defined dialectically in contrast to an "object." The easiest and most direct way of understanding these terms is in reference to grammar. In grammar, the subject of a sentence is the performer of an action and the object of the sentence is the one to whom the action is done. In the sentence, "Dick hit Jane," Dick, the doer of the vile deed, is the subject and Jane, the innocent to whom the nefarious deed was done, is the object of the sentence. What intersubjectivity adds to grammar is consciousness: in intersubjectivity *subjects* are those with some awareness of their agency, their ability to take action, to affect their environments. *Objects* are people who experience themselves as things to which actions are done. The experience of self as object is frequently reflected in the way people speak. "That guy made me mad." "I got caught up in something." Or, in the words of a teenage boy explaining how he got his girlfriend pregnant, "Something just came up." When one asks people in the paranoid-schizoid position "Who are you?" they will answer with a recitation of everything that has happened to them or that has been done to them. "They" are the sum-total of everything that has happened to them. Other than that, there is no "they." *Subjects* (people with depressive position functioning), on the other hand, tend to begin the answer to that question with the words "I am . . ." They experience a sense of *self*, a sense of *identity*, that transcends a simple listing of life experiences. They are aware that life events have shaped who they are, but they have an entirely different experience of who they are as opposed to what has happened to them.

Ogden emphasizes one crucial aspect of subjectivity, of experiencing oneself as a subject, that I want to focus on here. If being a subject is defined as being an agent, an actor, as opposed to being the one things are done to, then one of the most important "acts" a subject does is to create meaning. If one experiences oneself as an object, then meaning is "done to you" as much as anything else is: "It is what it is." People who experience themselves as objects (people in the paranoid-schizoid position) are likely to say "It is hot today!" as though it being hot was an objective fact. People who experience themselves as subjects (people in the depressive position) might use the same words, but for them the statement is short for, "I find it hot today," recognizing that heat is a subjective experience and that different people may have different standards of "hot."

This is what makes an intersubjective encounter such a profoundly important and such a deeply disturbing experience. When I, as a subject, encounter another subject, I am encountering another *subjectivity*, another way of attributing meaning to the universe. Two people experiencing themselves as objects may get into an argument about which of them possesses the "true" (objective) viewpoint. But two people experiencing themselves as subjects have a more difficult and potentially much more growth-enhancing experience: each must come to terms with the fact that another being exists who may see the world profoundly differently from the way he or she sees it.

The Question, in intersubjectivity, is how one gets, developmentally, from experiencing oneself and others as objects to experiencing oneself and others as subjects. And to find an answer to this Question, Ogden looks to object relations theory, and in particular to D.W. Winnicott, for how one progresses from the paranoid-schizoid position to the depressive position.

This book is an act of intersubjectivity. In it I present the work of two major intersubjective theorists, Jessica Benjamin and Thomas Ogden, and the work of their joint inspiration, object relations theorist D.W. Winnicott. I do not simply *present* their theories, or even give *my understanding* of their theories. Rather, I attempt to interact intersubjectively with each of them. Winnicott, of course, is long dead, and I do not have a collaborative relationship with either Ogden or Benjamin. Nevertheless, I cannot help but to have formed a mental dialog with each of them, a meeting of the minds between my own psyche and the words that these theorists have expressed in print. The result then, is something new, something that is neither entirely mine nor entirely theirs, but something that has been created in the "intersubjective third" that has arisen between us.

Of course, the intersubjective dialog between me and these three thinkers becomes frozen the moment I put my (co-created) thoughts into print. But it is replaced (unfrozen) by a new intersubjective dialog between my words in print, and the thoughts and reactions of you, the readers. This dialog began long before this book actually went to press. It began in my mind as a dialog between me and hypothetical readers, as I imagine various readers scratching their heads, wondering what such-and-such means, nodding in agreement, or shaking their heads in disagreement. And these fantasized reactions help shape my words and my thoughts.

I imagine younger, relatively inexperienced therapists shaking their heads and muttering, "What the hell is he talking about?" And I imagine older, more experienced therapists shaking their heads and muttering, "He doesn't know what the hell he is talking about." And with both sets of readers I ask that you join me in an intersubjective dialog, much like the one I engaged in with Ogden, Benjamin, and Winnicott.

If you do so, my ideas, co-created with Ogden, Benjamin, Winnicott, Freud, and Klein, will interact with the ideas and reactions of you, the readers, and a new set of ideas will be co-created as you interact cognitively and emotionally with the words printed on these pages but that are now spoken with your voices, inside your heads. None of you will read my words purely cognitively. To the extent that they are useful to you, it will be because they touch and influence an intuitive understanding that each of you already has.

This is how it worked for me. I worked for 20 years in a locked, residential treatment center for severely delinquent adolescents. And on a daily basis I would scratch my head and struggle to understand the psyches of those kids. And as I gradually discovered object relations theory and intersubjective theory, I began to formulate an understanding. These theories did not *explain* anything to me. Rather, they gave form and structure to my previously unformed or inarticulate intuitions. "Oh yes," I would exclaim, "that could be how it makes sense."

April was a third-generation gang member who helped disillusion me from any glorification of gang life that I might have been prone to. She had grown up living in a series of cheap motel rooms, sleeping on floors crowded with extended family members. She remembered one time her father slapped her for smiling. "Gangsters don't smile," he barked. She knew he was doing this for her own good.

In her early teens she formed an intense, Romeo and Juliet type of relationship with a boy, Marco, from an enemy gang. Although Marco was willing to violate the one cardinal rule of gang loyalty, he was in every other respect a hard-core gangster. He had the kind of nearly paranoid jealousy that is common among male gangsters, and this jealousy was exacerbated by his frequent drug use.

April became pregnant and began to show. One night Marco came home high on methamphetamines and nearly psychotic with jealousy. "That's not my baby," he told her, and he began to beat her, and her stomach in particular. A few days later, April miscarried.

April told me this story with neither anger nor hatred. Although everything in me was appalled and horrified, somehow I recognized that she was telling me a love story. "He loves me that much!" she was trying to tell me. "He loves me so much that I can drive him crazy with rage and jealousy. He loves me so much he would kill his own unborn child out of love for me."

But, of course, April was not *telling* me a love story. She was telling me a story of violent abuse and killing. Her problem was that she didn't feel abused. She felt loved. More accurately, she didn't know what she felt, nor how to make sense of her own story – any more than I knew how to make sense out of her confused and conflicted account. The fact that it was a love story she was telling me was arrived at intersubjectively: it was co-created.

An outline for this book

The chapters of this book follow a semi-developmental progression based on the developmental contributions of D.W. Winnicott. I say "semi-developmental progression" because Winnicott's developmental schema is not strictly linear. Certain developmental lines parallel each other, while others seem to leapfrog one another. In any case, Winnicottian developmental concepts are presented in as linear a fashion as I can, and the clinical implications of each developmental issue is discussed. At the end of the book there is a shift in theory from object relations theory (Winnicott) to intersubjective theory, although, as with the earlier chapters, even this shift is not strictly linear.

A brief précis of each chapter follows. These summaries are repeated at the beginning of each chapter.

Chapter 1

Commencing a semi-developmental structuring of this book, Chapter 1 reexamines Winnicott's concept of the "holding environment" in terms of both the mother/infant and the therapist/client relationships. The holding environment is commonly thought of as a unidirectional communication: the mother/therapist communicating safety and caring to the infant/client. I argue that Winnicott actually presented a two-way communication model wherein both the mother/therapist and the infant/client communicate to the other and, in doing so, learn about themselves. As such, the holding environment becomes not a precursor to therapy but a prototype of therapy.

Chapter 2

Although quite similar, the holding function and the "mirroring function of the mother" are different in terms of the experience of both the infant and the mother. The holding function begins before the infant has learned to differentiate between self and non-self (environment or object). The mirroring function begins when the infant is beginning to be able to identify the mother as a separate object. It is the infant's first intersubjective experience.

Chapter 3

Winnicott's "mother-infant unit" may be seen as another kind of prototype for therapy, but a different kind from the holding environment. In the mother-infant unit, the infant learns about itself and others by the use of the mother as a surrogate ego or, more specifically, through the fantasy that its own ego and its mother's ego are fused. The fantasy of fused egos also becomes a part of the psychotherapy relationship and allows for the repair of early ego damage.

Chapter 4

"Potential space" is one of the least understood and most ignored of Winnicott's concepts. But I argue that it is crucial for the understanding of the goals of psychotherapy. Potential space is the space "in which we live." If potential space is empty our lives are empty. If potential space is full, our lives are full. The task of the therapist is not to try and fill the client's potential space. Rather, it is to discover and repair potential space damage that stems from disruption of the early separation/individuation stage of development.

Chapter 5

The "paranoid-schizoid position," along with the "depressive position," is one of Melanie Klein's two modes of emotive-cognitive functioning. The paranoid-schizoid position is defined by the use of "splitting." Splitting happens for emotional reasons, but it leads to certain cognitive consequences. I argue in this chapter that splitting leads to a complex, interwoven, and consistent logical system: what I call "the logic of splitting."

Chapter 6

Fairbairn contributed an important modification to Klein's original conceptualization of the paranoid-schizoid position. Rather than consisting simply of "internal objects," the psyche in the paranoid-schizoid position consists of "internal object relationships." These are not of the voices of internalized objects but of the internal dialogs between the self and significant objects. Kernberg coined the term "Object Relation Units" (ORUs) to described paired substructures of the psyche representing the internal object, the self in relation to that object, and the characteristic affect that defines that particular relationship. Ogden argues that internal objects are not simply representations of unfinished business from the past. They represent structures of the psyche; they constitute who a person is. Either component (self or object) can be projected out onto others. This makes the analysis of the transference much more immediately important, and much more complex, than in the traditional Freudian paradigm.

Chapter 7

In Chapter 5 I argue that the paranoid-schizoid position can be seen as the template for the notoriously unstable Borderline Personality Disorder. In this chapter I present a long vignette that demonstrates how extremely stable character structures can also occur in the paranoid-schizoid position.

Chapter 8

Chapter 8 reexamines the Freudian concept of "resistance" in light of object relations theory. This, in turn, leads to a reanalysis of the entire concept of the unconscious. In this chapter I argue that while in Freudian theory the unconscious is defined primarily by its contents, object relations theory tends to think in terms of unconscious processes. This leads to a significant difference in how the task of the therapist is conceptualized in terms of working through the resistance.

Chapter 9

Chapters 9 through 15 deal with the problem of how one leaves the paranoid-schizoid position and enters the depressive position and, in the process, how one disavows internal objects and discovers external objects. Chapter 9 shifts out of object relations theory and into intersubjectivity theory long enough to discuss the concept of the "psychological third." Relational and intersubjective theory argue that the only way out of the binary relationships that comprise ORUs is the introduction of some form of internal or external "third." It can be argued that all the different ways of emerging from the paranoid-schizoid position – all the different ways of discovering external objects and the external world – involve some variant of the psychological third.

Chapter 10

This chapter focuses on the work of Thomas Ogden on projective identification. Ogden argues that, paradoxically, projective identification is both a hallmark of the paranoid-schizoid position and a vehicle out of that position. In this chapter I catalog a number of different ways in which projective identification leads to character changes in both the projector and the recipient of projective identification.

Chapter 11

This chapter is unique in this book in that it focuses on a single article – a highly controversial and misunderstood article by Winnicott – that seems to have as many different interpretations as readers of the article. I offer my own interpretation of what I think Winnicott is saying and I discuss some important clinical implications.

Chapter 12

"Interpretation," the bedrock of Freud's clinical approach, has become the subject of much controversy in both object relations theory and relational and intersubjective theories. In this chapter I attempt to cool the often overheated rhetoric on the subject and offer a view of this intervention that respects and acknowledges its dangers and shortcomings while recognizing its contribution to our therapeutic work.

Chapter 13

As with interpretation, "transference" – the other foundational Freudian concept – has come under much recent attack. In this chapter I examine the controversy and try to extract from the debate a working definition of transference that I consider to be reasonable while justifying the notion that working in the transference is an essential part of any psychodynamic work. As in Chapter 8, I try to differentiate between Freudian and object relational conceptualizations of transference both in theory and in clinical application.

Chapter 14

In this chapter I argue that while all psychodynamic theories have implicit or explicit focuses on loss and on dealing with loss, most treatises on clinical work tend to ignore or understate the role of grieving in psychotherapy. My position is that some form of grieving is an essential part or all clinical work, across all diagnostic categories.

Chapter 15

As Chapter 10 focuses on the work of Ogden and Chapter 11 focuses on Winnicott, Chapter 15 is derived primarily from the work of Jessica Benjamin. Benjamin argues (persuasively, to my mind) that we can help our clients only to the extent that we can "identify" with them. This represents a fairly radical departure from the traditional view in which a therapist's identification with the client was greeted with fear and innumerable cautionary notes.

Chapter 16

While previous chapters have focused on the process of getting from the paranoid-schizoid position to the depressive position, this chapter focuses on a pathology of the depressive position: what Winnicott called "False Self" pathology. I argue that, as with so many of Winnicott's concepts, the concepts of the True Self and the False Self are frequently misunderstood and misapplied. I also argue that these are extremely important concepts and that the recognition and abandonment of False Self functioning and the discovery/creation of the True Self is an inherent part of all psychotherapy.

Notes

1 This model is derived primarily from the writings of Thomas Ogden.
2 Although these two concepts are primarily associated with Melanie Klein, they owe as much to the influence of object relations theorist Ronald Fairbairn. Klein had originally proposed that external "objects" (people) get internalized as part of the psyche. It was Fairbairn who ultimately prevailed in postulating that it is "object relationships" that get internalized (see Grosskurth, 1986).

Part I

The psychological birth of the infant

1   The holding environment

Commencing a semi-developmental structuring of this book, Chapter 1 reexamines Winnicott's concept of the holding environment in terms of both the mother/infant and the therapist/client relationships. The holding environment is commonly thought of as a unidirectional communication: the mother/therapist communicating safety and caring to the infant/ client. I argue that Winnicott actually presented a two-way communication model wherein both the mother/therapist and the infant/client communicate to the other and, in doing so, learn about themselves. As such, the holding environment becomes not a precursor to therapy but a prototype of therapy.

Winnicott's term "holding environment" has become a buzzword in psychotherapy theory. Like all buzzwords, it has lost, through overuse, much of the power of its original meaning and it is well worth reexamining the concept. The term "holding" is both highly symbolic and fundamentally concrete. The original holding environment is the mother's (or mother-substitute's) arms. It is through the mother's arms that the infant first learns about itself and the world. The infant does not focus visually for the first week of life, nor does it appear to make much sense of sounds (with the exception of the startle response to sudden, loud noises). But infants appear to be exceptionally sensitive to the way they are held. By the way she holds her neonate an anxious mother will communicate to her baby that the world is a dangerous place. So too will a depressed mother convey to her infant the world's (her) indifference. And likewise will a secure, loving mother let her baby know that he or she is safe and cared for.

This is not simply a matter of holding a child firmly. It involves the mother's intuiting the baby's humanness, its sensitivities, and its needs, and responding appropriately. How does the baby *want* to be held? What feels good to the baby and what does not? What degree of firmness is too much and what degree is too little? It is the mother trying immediately to discover *who this baby is* (as opposed to all the other babies in the world) and to respond accordingly. Holding does not refer simply to the way the arms of the mother hold the infant. It refers to the way the arms of the mother probe the infant, seeking to discover who it is, so that they can respond to its idiosyncratic needs. Winnicott (1960a) says that this kind of mothering cannot be taught. It is intuitive and is based on the mother's cellular memories of her own infancy. Classroom-taught mothering is, at this stage, robotic and inadequate.

What does the infant learn in this early holding environment? It learns (hopefully) that it is safe (that its mother protects it) and that it is loved (that its mother loves it). But far more important, says Winnicott, the infant begins to learn who he or she is, what feels good and what feels bad, what satisfies and what frustrates, what frightens and what soothes. It is the beginning of the discovery of what Winnicott calls the True Self, of a sense of who I really am and what makes me similar to and different from every other person on the planet, of what makes me feel real and alive.

Winnicott (1960a) emphasizes the mother's intuition, her ability to access the cellular memory of her own infancy, her ability to project herself into her infant and discover what she would want (feel like, be afraid of) were she in her infant's skin. But it is also clear that Winnicott does not envision the holding environment as a one-directional system involving an active, observing subject-mother and a passive, observed object-infant. Winnicott emphasizes a nonverbal, dialectical dialog between mother and infant. It is the mother using her arms not just as a kind of "mouth" to inform her infant but as "ears" with which to hear her infant's preverbal communications.

The holding environment starts out concretely as the mother's arms but quickly expands into a whole range of factors that symbolically equate to the way the world "holds" the infant, the child. There are myriads of ways the environment can respond to, or fail to respond to, the infant's True Self. Is the infant fed when it cries (feels hunger) or by the clock? Does the infant learn about satiation by feeling full or is it told that it has eaten enough? Is it picked up when it needs comfort or allowed to cry for fear of being "spoiled?"

So what?

There is much current discussion over the appropriateness of hugging in the therapy session. Even therapists who are comfortable giving hugs to their clients tend to do so judiciously and infrequently. Yet the holding environment in the therapeutic setting, like the maternal holding environment, has its roots in the physical. Midway through my own therapy I began to notice how important it was to me to shake my therapist's hand at the end of each session. I brought this up to him with some hesitation, expecting, as he was a fairly orthodox Freudian, some interpretation in terms of "latent homosexual tendencies." Instead, he simply shrugged his shoulders and nonchalantly said, "Of course! Physical contact!"

The holding environment in the therapy session, like the maternal holding environment, tries to establish an aura of safety and caring. Early discussions about confidentiality, the adoption of a non-judgmental manner, nodding, smiling, (the warmth of a handshake), all contribute to a feeling in the client of being safe and cared for. Aspects of what is often referred to as "the frame" also contribute to feelings of safety and concern. Charging a client for a missed appointment is best explained as being done (in part) in the client's best interest: "That hour is reserved for you, whether you use it or not. It is yours and yours alone." The fairly strict policy of ending the sessions on time also contributes to the safety of the holding environment: "No," the message is, "you may have unconscious fantasies of devouring me with your unfathomable neediness, but I can take care of myself. In not allowing you to devour me I will remain present to meet your needs."

But again, as with Winnicott's original concept, the idea of the therapeutic holding environment goes far beyond safety and caring. It involves providing an environment in which each client can discover himself or herself. If I have at 9:00 a client, Sally, who was sexually abused for years by a stepfather and who feels for me a mixture of longing and loathing, attraction and disgust, a desire to crawl into my lap and an urge to rip my testicles off, and if I have at 10:00 a client, Tom, who was raised by a single mother and who sees me as being unreal, "like somebody from a television program," then it is incumbent on me not just to remember that these are two very different people but to remember also that each needs something very different from me: a different kind of holding. How much I smile, how much I introduce my own material into the session, how much eye contact I maintain, even how often I nod, all of this has to be determined by who the client is and what his or her needs are. As with Winnicott's mothering, this, I believe, cannot be taught. To try and teach a therapist how to act with certain types of clients is to teach a programmed response that is inevitably artificial and inhuman. It is teaching to treat the diagnosis instead of the client. Irvin Yalom (1997, 2002) virtually shouts out his credo, "Create a new therapy for each patient!" I believe this is part of what he is talking about.

Programmed, by-the-book holding is like being held by a robot. It does not facilitate true feelings of safety or trust, nor does it enhance self-awareness. It is *never* helpful and, at times, it is disastrous.

> A client came in for treatment following the breakup of a relationship. It was not, he hastened to explain, the breakup itself that was upsetting to him, but rather that it was the young woman who had left him. "It's not supposed to be that way. I am the one who is supposed to leave them." I struggled to find a way of being helpful to him in that first session. I was appalled by the callousness with which he used other people. But I felt compelled to offer him some modicum of "support." I tried to speak empathically, offering some sympathy and understanding for the injury he had sustained and the resulting "disintegration of self" (Kohut, 1971).
>
> The following week he returned to my office but, he said, for the sole purpose of telling me how enraged he was at me. He had left my office swearing to himself that he would never return, but had then decided to come back just so that he could tell me what a horrible therapist I was. I had made him feel "like a pathetic whiner," and he had been sputtering with rage towards me for the entire week.

Clearly, my attempt to "hold" this client had failed. In my desperation to provide some kind of empathic response (an empathy I did not feel), I reached for a textbook response and failed miserably.

Winnicott's holding environment is not just a model for the identification and recognition of infantile (inarticulate) needs. It is also the vehicle through which many of those needs are *met*. So what does it mean to "meet our clients' needs"? There is an ancient (and by now somewhat tedious) debate within the psychoanalytic dialog, dating back at the very least to the Freud-Ferenczi disagreements of the early 1920s, on the appropriateness of the therapist (psychoanalyst) meeting the client's (patient's) needs. Winnicott's (1960b) solution is to distinguish between different kinds of needs. Using the Freudian jargon that still dominated the field, Winnicott differentiated between what he called "id needs" from those he termed "ego needs." Id needs are those relating to drives or instincts. They are essentially *physical* needs such as the needs for food, liquid, (physical) warmth, and sex (in all its Freudian permutations). Ego needs are the needs of the ego for its full development. They include such needs as the need to be seen, recognized, and appreciated as well as the opposing needs for privacy and secrecy; the need for object relatedness and its opposite need for solitude and aloneness; the need for novelty or new experience as well as the contrary need for familiarity and security. Winnicott's rule of thumb is simple: id needs should never be gratified in psychotherapy; ego needs should always be.

What does this look like in therapy? Let me start with a very simple example.

> A client of mine had been working on the horribly inadequate mothering she had received from her severely alcoholic mother and on the paucity of nurturing figures in her present life. In the middle of a session she suddenly blurted out, "You know what I want? I just want somebody to *feed* me. I'm sick of cooking all my own meals." This client had a very strong maternal transference towards me and I, in return, was aware of a powerful complementary countertransference. So I was not surprised when, upon hearing her wish, I suddenly had a vivid fantasy of greeting her in our next session with a huge submarine sandwich.
>
> I, of course, thought better of this and did no such thing. Instead, however, I told her of my fantasy. To have actually brought her a sub would have been to have completely missed the point. Because it was not her body (id) that she wanted nourished, it was her ego. She had not been starved for food in her childhood. She had been starved for attention, love, and validation. And in sharing my fantasy with her I was nurturing her ego by giving her something from my own ego (imagination). I was not giving her milk from my breasts. She hadn't really been asking for that. Nor was I giving her my penis (the phallic shape of the submarine sandwich in my fantasy did not escape my notice). I was giving her a counter-fantasy to her fantasy. I was letting her know not only that I recognized, understood, and validated her needs, but that I responded to them with an emotional reaction of my own, one that was completely complementary to hers.

A second example was much more difficult, both for me and for my client.

> I had spent some time trying to work with a client with severe abandonment issues around my upcoming three-week vacation. "It's alright," she had said, "neither of my parents came back. I know that you are coming back." But when I came back it was not alright. It took weeks for her to work through her rage at me. At one point she reported a fantasy of stabbing me with a knife.

The "id" (physical) aspects of her reaction were clear. There was her murderous aggression (granted, it was reactive rage rather than instinctual aggression. Still, her fantasy was *very* physical). And the rage was in reaction to a very primitive equating of abandonment with destruction and annihilation. She had felt like a baby antelope on the savanna, abandoned by its mother to a world of lions and jackals.

I was aware of two brief impulses to respond directly to her id issues. To her rage and aggression, I had the impulse to become her whipping boy, to say, "Oh my god! I'm so sorry to have caused you so much pain." To her abandonment issues I was tempted to sooth and reassure her: "Don't worry! I rarely take vacations this long. It won't happen again for a long time." Both of these impulses would not only have been inappropriate, both would have been inaccurate: they would have missed the mark. I did not, after all, *cause* her pain. My actions *triggered* some pain that had been buried deep inside of her since her early childhood. I had not stabbed her. I had inadvertently lanced a long-festering boil. To have responded as though I had caused the pain (that the pain was about *me*) would have been to miss the essential nature of the pain.

Instead of saying either of these things, I listened. I listened as intensely and as empathically as I could. I tried to put myself inside her and to feel for myself (as much as I could) the terror and the pain that underlay her rage. I made no apologies and no promises. I did not allow myself to become defensive or to counterattack. I simply tried as hard as I could to find, appreciate, and feel the pain and the terror that had been triggered and to communicate that understanding to my client. In processing this, weeks later, my client was able to confirm that this was exactly what she had needed.

Another example:

Jasmine, a client in her early twenties, had been sexually abused when she was seven by a friend of her grandparents (who probably would have been the age I was when I was treating her). When she finally felt comfortable enough with me to give me details about the event, I was struck not by the vileness of the molestation itself (some inappropriate touching) but by the terror evoked by his subsequent threats in his attempt to silence her. I had an image of a small child terrorized by a creature twice her size. In a certain way, to young children all adults are giants. But this had been a rampaging, threatening, out-of-control giant.

By our second year of therapy her fondness for me had grown considerably, and her fear of me had diminished. But they were still pretty evenly counterbalanced. In one session she was talking wistfully about how much safer she felt around women than around men. "That includes me," I offered neutrally. "Yes," she replied with a rare direct (and somewhat defiant) glance, "You are a man."

Now this young woman wanted desperately to be able to trust me, as she wanted to be able to trust all men. And I, on my part, always find it gratifying to be trusted. But rather than attempt to directly satisfy an id need (the need for physical security), I chose to speak to an ego need, the need to be seen. "I'm not just a man," I said, "I'm a very big man" (I am six-feet-four and my client was nearly a foot shorter than I) and I proceeded to share with her the impression I had had when she first told me about the assault.

My client reacted to my intervention the way clients tend to when they feel seen. She smiled with gratitude and she physically relaxed. She also spontaneously produced the insight that she never dated men taller than herself. Ironically, my effort to make her feel seen allowed her to feel more secure.

Before moving on I would like to reiterate that "holding" is not just *informing* the client (or infant) that the environment (world) is safe, accepting, and loving. It is equally *learning from* the client (infant) what feels safe, what needs accepting, what feels loving. Holding involves finding out from the client whether love is a good thing or a bad. Holding is definitely not always desired. One client told me that for him receiving love felt like "being suffocated."

For Hester proper holding initially meant not being touched. It is difficult to imagine what kind of holding Hester received as an infant from her mother. When Hester was 18 she went to a psychiatrist and was placed on antidepressant medications. After some months of little improvement, she overdosed on her remaining pills and, in a desperate attempt to reach out, told her mother what she had just done. Her mother looked at her and said, "This therapy thing doesn't seem to be working. Maybe you should stop," and turned her back and walked away. This was not a warm, loving mother.

When Hester came into therapy with me in her late twenties she was severely depressed and severely withdrawn. A self-described misanthrope, she had no friends and professed not to like people. Whenever

I saw her the refrain from one of Kipling's *Just So Stories* came to my mind, "I am the cat that walks alone. All places are the same to me."

But Hester wasn't a cat. Cats like to be held when they choose to be held. Hester did not want to be touched. So the metaphor that I kept in mind working with Hester was not a cat but a chipmunk – the kind I had seen as a child while vacationing in the mountains. As a child I was taught that if you squatted down near a chipmunk with a peanut in your hand, arm extended, and if you were very patient and if you didn't move at all, you would eventually be rewarded by the feel of tiny paws removing the peanut from your fingertips. This, I learned from Hester, was how she needed to be held.

So our early sessions were marked by many long silences in which I had the impression that Hester would forget that I was in the room. Indeed, when I would make the mistake of breaking the silence myself, she would frequently react with a startled response as though I had awakened her from a deep reverie.

I never encouraged her to speak to me or to open up to me in any way. She would have experienced any such intervention as intrusive. Instead, I was content to sit and wait until, emerging from her reveries, she would notice that I was still there (metaphorical peanut still extended) and would allow herself to think that perhaps, just perhaps, I might have something to offer her.

The role of identification

What is the psychological process by which "holding" works? Winnicott (1960a) says that it is identification.

> The important thing in my view, is that the mother through identification of herself with her infant knows what the infant feels like and is so able to provide almost exactly what the infant needs in the way of holding and in the provision of an environment generally. Without such an identification I consider that she is not able to provide what the infant needs at the beginning which is *a live adaptation to the infant's needs*. The main thing is the physical holding, and this is the basis of all the more complex aspects of holding, and of the environmental provision in general.
>
> (p. 54, italics in original)

What, exactly, is meant by "identification"? In *Psychoanalytic Terms and Concepts* (Moore & Fine, 1990), the authors define identification as a term "often used in a generic sense to refer to all the mental processes by which an individual becomes like another in one or several aspects, and so its meaning overlaps with [those of internalization, incorporation, and introjection]" (p. 103). Winnicott (1956) uses the word "in more ordinary language" (p. 300) in a way that in some ways is almost the opposite of the classical definition. Rather than identification as a kind of incorporation of another (or parts of another) into the self, Winnicott sees it as a sort of projection of the self into another, in search of commonality. He describes this as a "heightened sensitivity" of the mother to the infant's needs, achieved when the mother can "feel herself into her infant's place, and so meet the infant's needs" (p. 304).

Winnicott (1956) says that this psychological state of heightened sensitivity, of being able to feel oneself into the place of one's infant "deserves a name." He calls it "Primary Maternal Preoccupation." He goes on to characterize this preoccupation as follows:

- "It gradually develops and becomes a state of heightened sensitivity during, and especially toward the end of, the pregnancy.
- It lasts a few weeks after the birth of the child.
- It is not easily remembered by mothers once they have recovered from it. I would go further and say that the memory mothers have of this state tends to become repressed" (p. 302).

He then adds: "I do not believe that it is possible to understand the functioning of the mother at the very beginning of the infant's life without seeing that she must be able to reach this state of heightened sensitivity, almost an illness, and then recover from it" (p. 302).

Identification then, in the Primary Maternal Preoccupation, is a state of heightened sensitivity, a state of "normal illness" (p. 302) in which the mother feels herself into her infant's place, thus to discover and meet his or her needs. It should be emphasized here, however, that this does *not* mean that the mother substitutes her psyche (her needs) for the psyche (needs) of her infant. That would be a disaster of the kind described by Alice Miller in *The Drama of the Gifted Child* (1981). Miller describes the trauma to the child produced by a narcissistic parent substituting his or her own needs for the needs of the child. What Winnicott is describing is very different. It is a kind of *dialectical dance* happening between the needs of the infant as perceived by the mother through her identification with him/her and the needs of the infant as experienced by the infant.

The infant lacks the verbal language to express its needs, hence the need for the mother to act as interpreter as well as responder. But the infant, through its body language, is sufficiently articulate to let the mother know whether or not her interpretations are correct, if she has sufficiently heightened sensitivity to be able to "hear." Thus, our earlier description of the mother's arms as providing a medium for communicating the state of the world to the infant is only half of the story. The infant communicates back to the mother/world by its responses to the way it is being held. We might go so far as to say that the term "holding environment" is inadequate. A more comprehensive term would be the "holding/being-held environment."

So what?

The literature on therapists' identification with their clients is primarily cautionary and focuses on what is termed, "over-identification." The "over" in over-identification refers to an excessive focus on the similarities that are perceived to exist between the therapist and the client at the expense of the neglect of the important differences. Identification (over- or otherwise) with the client certainly has its dangers. One danger is that the therapist will begin treating himself or herself vicariously instead of treating the client. There is an inherently huge problem when the therapist says, "I understand completely what you are saying," based on his or her own identification with the client. Such a statement completely shuts down the work of the client ("Why," says the client, "should I continue to work on this issue when my therapist has already said that he/she completely understands?"). The other potential problem is that the therapist will think that he or she understands (based on identification) when, in fact, there may be a serious misunderstanding.

> A client of mine presented her anger at her father for having stolen money from the family trust in order to support the failing family business. The family business went under anyway, and the stolen money was lost. This meant that my client had lost the financial support for her starting a career that she had expected. I empathically supported her rage for weeks before it became clear that her rage and my rage were over completely different issues. My rage at her father had to with what he had done to my client (stealing her money, disrupting her financial future). My client, it turned out, had easily forgiven him for this. Her continuing rage had to do with his effect on the extended family. The family trust he had stolen from had stolen from also belonged to her cousins and this had created a family schism – cousins not speaking to

cousins – and it was for this that she could not forgive him. My client and I had been on the same page but in entirely different books.

The essence of therapy

In this chapter I have tried to emphasize that the learning that happens in the holding environment is a two-way street. The mother (therapist) not only attempts to *inform* the infant (client) that the world (environment) is a safe place, that the infant/client is valued and appreciated, that the infant/client is not alone in the world; the mother (and therapist) is *informed by* the infant (and client) of who he or she is, of what feels good and what does not, of what feels true and what feels false.

And – and this is the crux of what I am trying to say – in communicating to its mother who it is, the infant begins the lifelong process of creating/discovering itself. When the infant is held in a way that does not feel good and responds by arching its back and trying to pull away from the embrace, it is not only informing its mother that she is doing it wrong, it is discovering for itself what feels good and what does not. It is discovering/creating a self.

This said, we can see that, when applied to a theory of therapy, the complex concept of the holding environment represents the essence of the therapeutic process. Without doubt there are identifiable stages of therapy. A satisfactory therapeutic holding environment needs to be established before "deep" symbolic (verbal) interpretations can be made. But it is incorrect and misleading to see the symbolic interpretive interventions as the *real* therapy and the holding environment as merely a *precursor* to actual therapy. Rather, I suggest that the therapeutic holding environment and the symbolic (verbal) dialog that most people think of as "psychotherapy" are simply two different forms of the same process: *a process of creation and discovery of a self through interaction with another human being.*

Thus "therapy" does not begin with the establishment of a "therapeutic alliance," nor even with the signing of an "informed consent" contract in the first session. *Therapy* (a process of creation and discovery of a self through interaction with another human being) begins when the therapist first opens the waiting room door and says, "Hello, I'm . . ." and takes note of the client's comfort with eye contact, length and firmness of handshake, smile or non-smile, where the client sits on the couch, whether or not the client begins to speak first, and on and on. And again, this is not just the therapist beginning to discover who the client is. It is also the client discovering (rediscovering), creating (recreating), establishing (re-establishing) who he or she is, what feels comfortable and what does not, what feels safe and what does not, what feels warm and supportive, and what feels artificial and threatening.

I also believe that it is an error to see the holding environment in psychotherapy as being relevant only in the early stages of therapy. The holding environment is *always* an essential component of therapy. And, as the client changes and grows during the course of therapy, so too will the holding environment change and adapt as appropriate. Infants change in the type of physical holding they require. The kind of swaddling that is comforting to a neonate would be enraging to the same infant a few months later. So too does the nature of the holding environment in therapy change as the client grows and develops. I believe that this is part of what Bion (1967) meant by his famous dictum that therapy sessions should be approached "without memory or desire." If we rely too much on our memories, we tend to approach each therapy session addressing the client who we saw the previous week (or the previous month, or the previous year). But clients grow and change during the course of therapy and it is important to see the client for who he or she is in the moment . . . and, to adjust our holding accordingly.

> Jasmine, the client presented earlier in this chapter who had been molested by a friend of her grandparents, approached me about two years into her therapy with the statement that she needed me to "be more challenging" in therapy. After some discussion, I refrained from making the obvious interpretation that this was a transference of her two passive and woefully inadequate parents onto me. Instead, I simply took her at her word.
>
> Initially, given her history, I had bent over backwards to provide an atmosphere of safety. Since challenge and safety tend to be antithetical, I was deliberately non-challenging. I tried to be warm, empathic, supportive, and understanding, but I scrupulously avoided any appearance of being pushy or intrusive. Now she was telling me that I was violating Bion's dictum. She was no longer the fragile, frightened child who had come into my office. She no longer felt like she was made of porcelain, and she no longer wanted to be held as if she were. My holding had become too safe and, therefore, sterile.
>
> So I changed my holding style: I was no longer holding a fragile infant, rather I was holding a rambunctious toddler, eager to explore the world and herself. I held here in a way that was less protective and

more encouraging of her exploration. And Jasmine's work deepened, and she blossomed.

Then, a couple of years after that, she did it again. The holding environment I had been providing was no longer serving her needs. Once again, I was treating the client I remembered (a rambunctious toddler) rather than the client in the room with me (a vibrant and vital young woman).

Again, given her history, even when I was being more "challenging," I had bent over backwards to keep myself, especially my sexuality, as far out of the room as possible. Now she seemed to be telling me that my disengagement was becoming more problematic than the threat of my sexuality had once been. In Winnicott's terms (see Chapter 11), she had left the infantile world of omnipotence and projection and entered the real world of external subjects. And, as happens with that transformation, she was seeking real, external subjects to keep her company in that world.

It is difficult to say exactly how I changed in response to her request. Though I censored myself less, I continued to monitor myself, and my sexuality, closely. And I did not see myself becoming more flirtatious or seductive. But in monitoring myself, neither did I notice any particular *impulses* to be flirtatious or seductive. What I really felt about her emerging adulthood and adult sexuality was *celebratory*.

Along with the overt trauma of the sexual assault, Jasmine had grown up with the cumulative trauma of a misogynistic family where the men were quite blatant in expressing their hatred of and contempt for women, often referring to them in crude sexual epithets. Jasmine had grown up hating and ashamed of her sexuality and terrified of its implications. As she had matured, she had separated physically and emotionally from her family and had encountered others who, unlike her family, appreciated and celebrated her gender and her sexuality. Jasmine was beginning to allow herself to be glad that she was a woman, and I was perfectly willing to celebrate with her.

There is something particularly powerful about symbolic thought and symbolic (linguistic) communication. It is an evolutionary achievement of which humans are justifiably proud. But that pride sometimes overstates the issue. Psychoanalyst Owen Renik (1993, 1999) has written persuasively on the interdependence of "thought" and "action." He argues that thoughts are *always* symbolic representations of actions. The thought,

"I am afraid" is a symbolic representation of certain (perhaps not consciously noticed) "actions" such as increased heart rate, increased perspiration, a shift to faster and shallower breathing. The thought, "I like this person" is similarly a symbolic representation of certain actions: leaning the body towards the person, spontaneous smiling, a flushing in the skin. As therapists we recognize that there is something particularly satisfying, something that gives a sense of completion, in being able to find or put the right words to our experiences. But we are wrong to value, or to think we should value, the word over the experience. They are two complementary and equally critical manifestations of our lives. The symbolic language with which we speak to our clients and the nonverbal holding environment we attempt to provide are two manifestations of the same therapeutic process.

> A young therapist, who had been in treatment with me for several years, began one session by telling me that she had suddenly realized that she was angry at me. She had realized that she gives her own clients a lot of verbal feedback about how hard they are working and how much progress they are making, and that I give her very little of that. She said that she needed to be "mirrored."
>
> My reaction to her complaint was mixed. It has never been my style to *cheerlead* my clients and there is something about that role that makes me uncomfortable. On the other hand, her use of Winnicott's concept caught my attention and made me think. I started to explain to her that I believe that things such as a sense of personal change or growth have to come from an internal experience rather than from an external judgment or evaluation, but as I was speaking these words I could see her begin to shake her head in disagreement. So I spoke to her head shaking: "I know," I said," "that what I am saying is bullshit. But it's only part bullshit. The part that's bullshit is that an 'internal experience' is never completely internal. It comes, in part, from the outside, from a relationship." Before I had a chance to present the other side, she did it for me. "Yes," she said, "but I see your point. I don't want to sit here feeling judged or evaluated."
>
> I need to point out that I have always considered myself to be very giving in my expressions of support, empathy, caring, even love. But these expressions have been predominately nonverbal: smiles, winces, nods, laughter, etc. I had forgotten (repressed?) how much we need verbal feedback.

So I told my client that she was one of the hardest working clients I have ever had and I found the progress she had made inspiring. She smiled at me but her smile did not look like the smile of a small girl who had just been patted on the head. She already knew the truth of what I had just told her. Her smile was that of someone whose inner knowledge had just been mirrored, validated, witnessed, by someone important to her.

2   The mirroring role of the mother

Although quite similar, the holding function and the mirroring function of the mother are different in terms of the experience of both the infant and the mother. The holding function begins before the infant has learned to differentiate between self and non-self (environment or object). The mirroring function begins when the infant is beginning to be able to identify the mother as a separate object. It is the infant's first intersubjective experience.

Overlapping with the period of the maternal holding environment, developing after the first few days of birth, when the infant has begun to focus visually, particularly on the mother's face, is what Winnicott (1971a) calls "the mirroring role of the mother." Nature has provided us with an array of senses with which to learn about our world. But we are remarkably handicapped when it comes to learning about ourselves. We can see and scrutinize every face we encounter except our own. In order to discover what we ourselves look like we need something called a mirror. Winnicott (1971a) goes further than this, saying that we need some kind of mirror to discover not just what we look like but who we are as people. That mirror, he says, is the mother and, in particular, the eyes of the mother. "What does the baby see when he or she looks at the mother's face? I am suggesting that, ordinarily, what the baby sees is himself or herself. In other words, the mother is looking at the baby and *what she looks like is related to what she sees there*" (1971a, p. 112, italics in original).

The logic of small children is simple and concrete and we may assume that whatever the preverbal logic of the infant looks like, it must also be simple and concrete. Thus, when the infant looks into its mother's eyes and sees adoration it recognizes itself as being adorable. When it sees fear or anxiety it recognizes itself as being vulnerable and endangered. When it sees sadness or exhaustion it perceives itself to be a burden. When it sees joy and excitement it sees itself as being alive and vital. And when the baby looks into its mother's eyes and sees indifference, when it sees its mother not returning its gaze but instead looking right through it, then the baby logically concludes that it does not exist (at least in terms of this crucial relationship).

The Case of the Dirty Dishcloth

There was a time many years ago when my marriage was in trouble. I had lost both parents to cancer within two years of each other. And my wife was an aspiring academic trying to find a regular faculty appointment while the entire country was in deep recession. We were both depressed, both needy, and neither had much to offer the other.

One night, when my wife was working late, I decided to make a grand gesture. As was typical of me then it was as much the kind of gesture a little boy makes to please his mommy as one a man makes to comfort his despairing wife: I decided to clean the kitchen.

And I really cleaned it. Every counter was polished; every cupboard knob gleamed. When my wife got home I proudly showed it off. She looked around appraising my work and finally gave her verdict. "It looks good," she said, "but why did you leave the dirty dishcloth in the middle of the sink?" I was devastated. Everything was perfect except for that. Why did she have to single that out? It was a severe narcissistic injury.

It was a narcissistic injury that I duly reported to my therapist at our next session. My therapist listened patiently to my story, and when I had finished he said only, "So why *did* you leave the dishcloth in the sink?" I was doubly devastated. *Et tu Brute!* Not only my wife, but my therapist!

It was months later in my therapy that I realized that this was indeed a crucial question, perhaps the central question in my therapy. Why did I work so hard only to seemingly sabotage myself? As soon as I took the question seriously, an answer appeared: the dirty washcloth in the sink was my *signature*. It was my way of guarding against the possibility that my wife would simply come home to *a clean kitchen* rather than to a *kitchen that had just been cleaned*. I needed to put some kind of signature on my work of art so that my wife would have no doubt that it was mine. Over the years I came to see that this was a recurrent (and highly destructive) theme in my life. I would make frequent unnecessary screwups in my work, always the source of much shame and embarrassment, always sure to get me noticed, always sure to reaffirm my existence.

About the same time as the dishcloth incident I was in a process group comprised of psychotherapists. One of my colleagues made the passing observation that, "of course mothers know everything about you." Nonplussed, I asked her what she meant. "Well," she said, "they know that you shit in your diapers!" I cognitively understood her meaning, but on an emotional level it still made no sense to me. Reading Winnicott's article on the "Mirroring Function of the Mother," many years later, helped me understand better. My mother had been a highly self-focused, obsessively driven, writer. When she had been changing my dirty diaper she would have been only barely aware that I had soiled it. Her mind, her gaze, would have been a thousand miles away, working out the intricacies of her current book. I, and my shit, were almost invisible to her.

For years the metaphor of unconsciously believing myself to be invisible was extremely useful to me. On a conscious level it is a ludicrous metaphor, as I am 6'4", bearded, and have been told by more than one that my presence can be intimidating. But on an emotional level I believe it to be true. When I walk into a room, I do not expect to be seen or noticed. In making this metaphor conscious I was able to consciously combat it. I made a concerted effort to make myself *visible*, to make my *presence felt*. And, over the years, I was able to recognize that I was better able to do this by my good works than by my screwups.

Not many years ago I had another epiphany regarding this issue. I was working with an obese client who was a successful attorney. At the onset of my work with him I had been struck by what Winnicott would have called his False Self presentation. Everything this man said sounded stilted and artificial. He seemed not to know a true feeling from a hole in the ground. I wondered, in the words of Gertrude Stein, if there was "any there, there?" The absence of True Self functioning was understandable. He was the child of a cold, withdrawn, rejecting father and a narcissistic mother who demanded that her son be a clone of herself. In Winnicott's "mother-infant unit" (see Chapter 3) she would not have been the auxiliary ego that Winnicott said was necessary for the child to develop an awareness of his own internal states. Instead, she would have completely dominated the Unit, leaving no room for his own nascent ego.

During one session about a year into therapy he reported, with a kind of embarrassed smile, that he had forgotten a deadline for filing an important brief and had had to rush down to court to beg the court for an after-the-fact extension. An exploration of the mistake led to a kind of semi-apologetic discussion of his need to "play with fire," a term which he said characterized his interpersonal relationships as well as his work.

This work appeared true and useful, but I was unable to get out of the back of my mind the nagging question/judgment: "How could anybody that intelligent do anything that dumb?" My question was answered when I quite suddenly realized how much I identified with this client. The type of screwups he was prone to were essentially the same as my own, and they existed for the same reason: he needed to be noticed. He was able to confirm my hypothesis. The word in his office was, "Keep an eye on the fat guy! He is a smart lawyer but if you don't watch him he will mess up."

But by this time I knew my client pretty well. His fear was not of being invisible, his unconscious fear was of not existing. He had not existed as a separate, autonomous person for either of his parents. And, while he had made much progress in therapy, his sense of self was, at best, still budding. With this awareness I went back to reconsider both Winnicott's thesis . . . and myself.

My original formulation, that because my mother must have looked right through me I would perceive myself to be invisible, was an adult misconception of infantile logic. "Invisibility" is far too complex a concept for an infant to comprehend. Infants and young children are simply not capable of the intellectual complexity to come up with a concept that says: "I exist but I can't be seen." Infants and young children are much more literal. For an infant and young child the logic is simply, "If I am not seen then I do not exist."

Of course this cannot be taken completely literally. Infants obviously know that they exist. If nothing else, every hunger pang, every loud noise, every wet diaper reminds them of their existence. But there remains a profound truth in Winnicott's observations. How might this apply to me?

Back in the difficult days of our marriage mentioned earlier, my wife and I got ourselves into couples therapy with an excellent therapist. In the course of one of our sessions our therapist queried me about my experience of a recent trip my wife had just taken. Did I, she asked, believe that my wife thought about me when she was away?

"No," I responded matter-of-factly, "of course not." My wife looked at me and with a sincerity that penetrated my defenses, said, "I thought of you all the time!" I was flabbergasted! I was flabbergasted, but I believed her.

I had not really believed, on an emotional level, that I really existed for my wife any more than I had existed for my mother. And this does not mean that I felt that I did not exist *for them* (as opposed to for someone else). No, if I did not exist for the two most important people in my life then, logically (in infantile logic), I simply did not exist. In Winnicott's terms, I was not *alive*. I was a wraith, passing unseen, unfelt, unfeeling, dead, through my allotted time on this earth.

I want to emphasize here, once again, that Winnicott does not propose a direct, linear relationship between the mirror and the resulting self-concept. This is a dialectical relationship. Ogden (1994) points out the odd phrasing in Winnicott's statement: "*and what she looks like is related to what she sees there*" [in the infant]: not "is" but rather, "is related to." Infants cannot simply accept at face value that what they see reflected in their mothers' eyes is a perfect depiction of who they are. Mothers, Winnicott points out in discussing the "good-enough mother," frequently get it wrong (and, for the sake of the infant, often need to get it wrong). If the infant were to accept at face value that what he sees reflected in his mother's eyes is a perfect depiction of himself then his self-concept would be entirely an introject, an internalization of the view of an external other. It would be a self-concept divorced from self-awareness.

No, if the eyes of the mother are a mirror for the infant then we need to remember that all mirrors distort, some more than others. And the infant must know this too – or learn this very early. When an infant looks into its mother's eyes and sees adoration, it momentarily feels itself to be adorable. But very early on the infant knows (as soon as some sense of what Winnicott (1956) calls "going-on-being" is achieved) that it does not always *feel* adorable. It may not have the words or the preverbal concept of how it does feel, but somehow it knows that "adorable" isn't quite right. When a toddler is having a temper tantrum (when it is full of rage and hate) and looks into its mother's eyes and sees adoration and looks at its mother's lips and sees a loving smile, it is likely to become even more enraged. "No," it will want to shout, "I'm serious!" The child will project its own rage and hatred onto its mother and her adoring expression will be interpreted as a mockery.

So what?

It is drilled into every intern and neophyte therapist that one must "maintain eye contact" with one's clients. After I tried as gently as possible to tell one of my interns that he had failed to respond to almost anything his client had said, he responded defensively that he judged it an excellent session because, "We maintained eye contact the entire hour!" Mirroring is not simple eye contact; it is not a staring contest. It is a form of communication (a form of interpretation, if you will) in which one person learns about himself or herself by seeing himself or herself reflected in the eyes of another.

> In our first session together, Carla was clearly uncomfortable. A 16-year-old, inner-city Latina in the room with an older, white, male doctor was not her idea of an easy match. Carla decided that the best tactic was to entertain me, and (under the apparent assumption that all older, white, male doctors are basically "dirty old men") she chose to entertain me with the story of how she lost her virginity. Carla reported that she had been walking down the street when a boy she knew stopped her. They talked for a while, he told her that she was pretty, and he asked her if she wanted to go with him. Ghetto-raised girls of this age frequently pair up with boys both out of a need for protection, and out of a desire for social status. But it appeared that Carla agreed to this boy's proposal more because she couldn't think of a reason to say no. "Okay," said the boy, "if we are going to be going together then sooner or later we are going to have sex, so we might as well do it now." So they did. "And that's how I lost my virginity," said Carla with a bright smile as though she were telling the punch line to a funny joke. I stared at her for a while trying to come up with a few words about the utter absence of love in her first "lovemaking." But before I could say anything she looked at me and exclaimed, "Dr. Brodie! You look so sad!" It was the sadness in my eyes (as opposed to what she expected to see there, which was a look of prurience) that enabled her to drop her mask-smile and begin to weep gently at the tragedy of her own story.

On the other hand, mirroring can sometimes be unwelcome. Over the years I have lost more than a couple of clients who, in the first session, remarked uncomfortably on the "intensity" of my gaze. Freud is said to have come up with the practice of using the couch partly because he found the constant eye contact so draining. Winnicott (1960b) has said that there are parts of all of us that, even in our most intimate moments, need to stay hidden. Thus, feeling "seen" (being mirrored) is a mixed bag. It is inherently threatening, as it exposes the individual to the risk of "impingement" or rejection. But when the relationship is sufficiently safe and intimate, feeling seen can be the most exhilarating of experiences.

> In all the years of my own therapy I only asked my therapist a single question about himself and that one was blurted out impulsively. My wife and children were away on a trip and I had been talking to him about how much I missed them. At the end of the session I found myself asking a classic "doorknob" question. "Do you have children?" He simply smiled at me and said, "You really *do* miss them!" He had chosen not to answer my question itself, but rather to answer the question behind my question: "Can you truly understand how I feel?" His answer left me feeling seen as I had rarely felt seen in my life, and I floated out of his office.

Proper mirroring not only feels wonderful and exhilarating, it allows us to learn and accept who we are and everything we are comprised of. To do so, mirroring not only has to be accurate, it has to be *complete*. In Kleinian or object relations terms (see Chapters 4 and 5), this means that we have to be mirrored as "whole objects" rather than as "part objects." The damage done when only the negative qualities of a child are mirrored ("You are such a whiner!" "You are oversensitive!" "You are too needy!" "You are so annoying!") is obvious. When the negative mirroring becomes too harsh and too overwhelming, it becomes child abuse. But excessive positive mirroring can also damage a child. Parents (or therapists) frequently believe that they are boosting a child's (or client's) self-esteem by saying things like, "You are so smart" or "You are so beautiful" or "You are so brave," while in fact they are creating a deep sense of fraudulence and shame. Children who have been told that they have a "natural aptitude" for math will often feel humiliated when they find themselves struggling through calculus or analytic geometry. The woman who is receiving her umpteenth complement on her beauty will smile while she thinks to herself, "Yes, but you have never seen me when I first get out of bed in the morning." The "brave" child will learn to work extra hard to suppress or hide the shameful feelings of fear and anxiety that naturally come up in dangerous situations.

There are two important lessons that therapists need to remember from Winnicott's work on mirroring. First, we need to mirror our clients as whole objects rather than as part-objects (even as *good* part-objects). Second, mirroring needs to be accurate, but perfect mirroring is neither possible nor even desirable.

We need to be mirrored as whole, complex human beings, not as unidimensional part objects or cartoon characters (even if the cartoon characters are superheroes). As I said earlier, a child throwing a murderous temper tantrum does not want to be mirrored with adoring eyes. Such mirroring will only make it angrier. A raging child wants its rage seen, acknowledged, and validated. "Yes," the child needs to be told, "I see and respect your anger. I even see and respect that at this moment in time you may hate me. And I am working to understand the feelings underneath your anger and hatred, whether they be disappointment, frustration, or a sense of injustice and betrayal. I may not agree with what you are feeling, but I acknowledge and respect it."

As to the second lesson, what I wrote earlier about the mirroring of the mother is equally true about the mirroring of the therapist. Both the child and the client need to discover/create a *self*, an identity. Neither a self nor an identity can be externally imposed. If one were to ask someone who he or she is, and receive an answer along the lines of, "Well people tell me I am . . ." or "Well, people see me as being . . ." then I would say that that person has little or no experience of self. No matter how "accurate" such an externally imposed self or identity might be, it can only remain just that: an introjection (an internalization) of an externally defined perception – of someone else's perception – of who one is.

Of course, a sense of self cannot be purely internally generated either. Such a self would be an autistic creation, devoid of any "reality check." It would be a make-believe self which would be as useless as an introjected self. A real *self* is neither purely internally nor purely externally generated. It is generated in the dialectic between the internal and the external, between the self and the other, between the mirror and the mirrored.

It is narcissistically gratifying to any therapist to have an interpretation (an act of mirroring) met by the response, "Yes, that's exactly it! You really nailed that one, Doc!" but such a response is not necessarily best for the client. Any interpretation – any act of mirroring – needs to be taken in by the client, chewed on, partly spit out and partly swallowed, digested, and *metabolized*. A response from a client that would reflect this process would be more like, "Yes, Doc, that's right. Except not quite! Its more like . . ."

Thomas Ogden writes,

> A principal goal of clinical psychoanalysis is the progressive recapturing of self-alienated personal experience, isolated from the intrapersonal and interpersonal discourse, a process that allows the analysand [client] to more fully recognize and understand who he is, and who he is becoming. In the retrieval of the alienated, the analysand [client] becomes more fully alive as a subjective, historical human being. He becomes more capable of engaging in a fuller (less self-alienated) intrapersonal as well as interpersonal dialogue. He becomes less fearful of that which he formerly isolated from himself and, to that extent, he becomes more free.
>
> (1990, pp. 3–4)

What Ogden refers to as the "self-alienated" are all those thoughts, feelings, impulses, and other aspects of the self that are denied, repressed, split off, left unformulated, or projected onto others because they are frightening, shameful, or otherwise unacceptable. We cannot help our clients retrieve these self-alienated parts and, in the process, become more whole and more "free," unless we, ourselves, as clinicians, are willing to see, acknowledge, validate, and respect those parts. We do not treat cartoon characters. We do not treat diagnostic categories. We treat whole, complex, conflicted human beings. We do them no good by joining them in their flight from the Shadow.

3   The mother-infant unit

Winnicott's "mother-infant unit" may be seen as another kind of proto-type for therapy, but a different kind from the holding environment. In the mother-infant unit, the infant learns about itself and others by the use of the mother as a surrogate ego or, more specifically, through the fantasy that its own ego and its mother's ego are fused. The fantasy of fused egos also becomes a part of the psychotherapy relationship and allows for the repair of early ego damage.

We all thought that Terry was slightly dull ("we" being both the treatment team and his peers). He seemed unable to respond to the simplest of questions. Even that iconic therapeutic question, "So how did that make you feel?" would elicit a deer-in-the-headlights, panicked stare. Terry was 16 and in a locked residential treatment facility where he had been sent after assaulting his younger siblings. But Terry was not a bully. He was not even mean-spirited. He was simply profoundly inarticulate, especially in the area of affective vocabulary. When he was upset he would, Billy Budd-like, use his fists because the words could not be found.

In one therapy group Terry presented his fantasy career: brick laying. Yes, we all nodded, that sounded right for Terry. One brick after another after another. The dullness of the task seemed a perfect match for the dullness of the subject. But Terry did not become a bricklayer. He became a mechanic, and a successful one, rising to shop foreman the last time we heard from him. He was so successful that we invited him back to the facility to speak to the current residents. "People used to ask me how I felt," he said, "and I wouldn't know. I knew if I felt okay or not-okay, but that was about it. It wasn't that I got in touch with my feelings. I learned that I had feelings."

How does this happen? How can a child grow into adolescence and not know he has feelings? How can a child not learn to differentiate beyond okay and not-okay?

Chapter 1 presented Winnicott's concept of the "holding environment." Winnicott asserts that the holding environment is the infant's first inter-subjective experience; it is where the infant first encounters an Other. It is where the infant first learns that mother and itself are not one and the same. They are different, separate objects and therefore, in need of com-municating with each other. And each must learn to communicate in a lan-guage with which it has no familiarity and no confidence that the other will understand. The mother, of course, has some advantage over the infant in that she once spoke that language herself, but has long since abandoned it (forgotten it?) in favor of symbolic (spoken) language. The mother must learn (re-learn) to communicate with her arms and her eyes, and with the tone, rather than with the meaning, of her words. And she must learn (re-learn) to understand her infant's language in response to her language: to read his muscle tone, the arching of his back away from her or his surren-der into her arms, his cries and coos and whimpers. And the infant must learn how to read his mother – how she communicates safety, love, alarm, indifference, or anger. And Winnicott says that in discovering the Other, the infant simultaneously discovers its self, since self and other define each other dialectically.

But there is a problem – for the infant – with this discovery of sepa-rateness, with this differentiation into self and other. Axiomatic to object relations theory is the notion that infants are born with an essentially instinctual awareness of their own utter helplessness, vulnerability, and dependency.[1] Winnicott's (1960a) famous dictum, "There's no such thing as an infant (without the maternal provision)" has – as with everything in Winnicott – multiple layers of meaning. But the most superficial level of meaning is far from the least important. An infant (human, antelope, lion – any infant) left alone on the African Savanna would not survive for more than a few moments. The infant is completely dependent on its mother – or mothering figure – for nurturance and protection. Without either, the infant is dead. And, says object relations theory, the infant, on some level, knows this.

The infant's sense of its total dependency on its mother or mother-substitute makes its growing awareness of separateness, its nascent dif-ferentiation into self and other, something that is profoundly threatening. It exacerbates the infant's sense of vulnerability and reinforces a sense of dependency.

So Winnicott proposes that, coincident with this progressive development into differentiation, this shift from oneness to twoness, is a regressive movement back into a fantasy of oneness, of something he calls the "mother-infant unit": a fantasy of an undifferentiated, unified, "mother-infant." It should be emphasized here that the progression into differentiation and twoness and the regressive fantasy of oneness and unity is *not* an either/or choice. The infant does both. It moves progressively and regressively at the same time. Indeed, the progressive development into differentiation and twoness is not impeded by, *it is made possible by*, the protective illusion of unity and oneness. This is one of the many phenomena that Winnicott delights in calling a "paradox." Ogden refers to this kind of functioning as a "dialectic," in this case the beginning of a lifelong dialectic of aloneness and connection, of unity and differentiation, of oneness and twoness.

The mother-infant unit is a *fantasy* based on the defense mechanism of *denial*. The infant simply denies that he/she and mother are completely separate, that the birth process was ever completed. In doing so, the infant enters into an (unconscious) fantasy that it and the mother are one. Winnicott (1951) speaks of this as "the fantasy of creating the breast." The infant enters into the unconscious fantasy that the breast, and the mother attached to it, are really extensions of itself, that it is its hunger that calls forth the breast and his subsequent full stomach, just as it is its uncomfortably full bowel and the relaxation of his anal sphincter that results in the subsequent full diaper. There is no separate mother who responds to its needs; there is a part of itself, and extension of itself, that is created by his needs for the purpose of fulfilling its needs.

It is not quite accurate to say that the infant does not "know" that it and its mother are separate. The infant never enters into what in adult terms would be a psychotic delusion. If the infant were in the equivalent of psychotic then there would be no panic at the disappearance of the mother since the infant would have no way of being aware of such an event (it would simply hallucinate her presence). Instead, there is a dialectical tension between knowledge and denial. The infant knows but does not know. Or, more accurately, the infant knows but cannot let itself know.

As presented so far, Winnicott's theory is not radically different from other psychoanalytic theories of his day. Mahler (1972), for example, writes of an early stage of "Symbiosis" with a notion of the infant fusing its identity with that of its mother. But Winnicott does not stop with this. He goes on to postulate that at this point the infant is *joined* in this fantasy by the mother. The mother joins the infant in the fantasy that the birth process has not been completed or, at least, that the umbilical cord has not been completely severed and that she and her infant are somehow still connected.

Winnicott (1951) refers to the mother's contribution to this now mutually supported, jointly held fantasy, as "the illusion of the needless infant." The mother believes (convinces herself) that she is so attuned with her baby that she can feel herself inside its body and feel and anticipate its needs even before the baby feels them itself.

It is common for young mothers to claim that they are able to understand their infants' languages, that they can differentiate between a hungry cry, a tired cry, a wet diaper cry, and a "pick me up" cry. I (as a male of the species) am unconvinced. To be sure, such an illusion cannot be called a psychotic delusion any more than can the infant's. The mother has much external data upon which to base her interpretations of her infant's cries. If she knows that her baby has not eaten for several hours, she is reasonable in interpreting its cries as cries of hunger. If her baby is not yet crying but her breasts are uncomfortably full and perhaps leaking milk, then she may well anticipate its needs before it experiences them as needs, or even as wants.

But what Winnicott is saying here is much more radical than just that the mother can interpret or even anticipate her infant's needs. He is saying also that the element of fantasy, the illusion that she can feel what her baby feels, that she can know and read its preverbal mind, is essential for the formation of a mother-infant bond. The correct interpretation, based on the available data – the awareness of clocks and feeding schedules and nap times, of dirty diapers and full breasts – is not enough. If only these are present, caretaking becomes mechanical and never becomes mothering. The infant remains "the infant" instead of "my baby." And the woman who gave birth remains a woman but never becomes a "mother." The reframing of "My breasts are full" to "My baby is hungry" is an essential (if occasionally incorrect) transmuting process.

Winnicott (1956) calls this successful joining of the mother and infant into a shared fantasy of partial fusion or incomplete separation the formation of the "mother-infant unit." The successful formation of a strong mother-infant unit is essential for the well-being and the development of the child. First of all, as we have seen, it relieves the infant of unbearable anxiety relating to its survivability. Equally important, however, it provides the infant with a second ego: a mature, adult ego to supplement and complement its own infantile ego.

If infant and mother have joined together in a fantasy of oneness, if in this shared illusion of the "mother-infant unit," it is jointly believed that the mother can enter into the psyche of the infant, can feel her feelings, know her needs, read and understand her preverbal language, then the mother (or the mother's ego) can serve the infant as a guide in ways that the infant's own infantile ego is completely unable to do.

The most important guidance that the mother's surrogate ego provides is early charting of the infant's own internal world. As discussed in the first two chapters, children are able to learn a great deal about the external world on their own. By falling they learn that the ground is hard. By touching fire they learn that it burns. The success parents have in teaching their children to say "Mama" and "Dada" is dwarfed by the enormity of the achievement of language acquisition, which children seem to do almost entirely on their own.

But, ironically, what children do not seem able to learn on their own are the intricacies of their own inner worlds. We have already discussed how the infant uses its mother – Winnicott (1971a) says the eyes of the mother in particular – as a mirror to learn about him or herself. But the metaphor of the mirror is inadequate to describe the role of the mother's supplementary ego in the mother-infant unit (and the therapist's supplementary ego in the therapist-client relationship). In the mother-infant unit the mother acts not just as a mirror but as an *interpreter* as well.

In the case of the infant, the mother does this nonverbally. The infant (it seems clear) understands discomfort but seems unable to differentiate different forms of discomfort. All that the infant appears to know is that things are not right in the world, and it has only one response which (in our adult translation) is rage. What the mother does is teach the infant that there are different kinds of discomfort. She does this not with words but by her actions. When she presents the infant with her breast (or the bottle) she is saying (nonverbally) to the infant, "Your discomfort is of a particular kind: it is called hunger. And I teach you this not just with words, but by the remedy I provide." Similarly, when she changes its diaper, she is teaching it about the particular discomfort called "wetness." And when she picks it up and cuddles it, she is teaching it about a particular need it has which is called the need for "physical comfort." As the child matures, the self-learning – the differentiation of feelings – takes on more and more of a symbolic form and the child learns such words as "scared," "mad," and "sad," but much of this learning still comes from the use of the mother (or mother-substitute) as auxiliary ego.

Later on, through its "love affair with the world" (Mahler, 1972) the toddler will continue to look to its mother to be a surrogate ego (an interpreter of her inner world, of the external world, and of the relationship between the two). When, suffused with pride and self-delight, the young toddler's first unbalanced steps are interrupted by the experience of its bottom suddenly hitting the floor, the intrepid adventurer will frequently look up at her mother to see how to interpret this unexpected event and consequently how to react. If the mother, out of her own anxiety, shrieks out, "Oh my goodness! Are you alright?" the child is likely to burst into tears. If, on the other hand, the mother is able to smile and say, "Baby go boom!" then the child is likely to laugh with delight at its own cleverness.

So what?

What then is the significance of all of this to the therapist? Obviously, if we hypothesize that the therapy experience recapitulates to a certain extent the developmental experience, then we can expect that, to a certain extent, the therapist will come to be used as a surrogate ego to the client. Of course, the therapist-client relationship never achieves the power or intensity of the original mother-infant unit, but this is just as well.

It seems to me that a great deal of the work we do as therapists has to do with fulfilling our role as surrogate egos.

> A male client in his early thirties discussed near the end of his first session his feelings of "abandonment" by his wife in certain social situations. His young wife sounded socially insecure and would apparently go overboard with solicitude when talking to others, particularly to other men, in social gatherings. This behavior produced such an experience of abandonment in him that, "out of hurt," he would withdraw from her for days.
>
> As non-judgmentally as I could (I was feeling quite shocked by his cruelty towards her) I said, "Along with feeling hurt by her you may also have been feeling a need to punish her." He was surprised by my comment.

The intervention just described seems to me to be a good example of a therapist acting as a surrogate ego. I did nothing in this intervention more or less than a mother is supposed to do in the mother-infant unit. I interpreted to him (verbally in my case) what might be going on inside him. I offered my own ego as a supplement/complement to his and *interpreted* to him what I guessed of his inner workings (based on my own internal process). It was a verbal equivalent of the kind of interpretation a mother gives (nonverbally) to her baby when changing its diaper: "The particular discomfort you are experiencing is called a VERY poopy diaper. And boy does it stink and boy is it a mess! But we all have sides to ourselves that are ugly, and I love you so much that I am happy to clean it up anyway and not even mind that much" (nonverbal communications can be extremely complex!).

Without the good interpretive function of the mother-infant unit, highly verbal children grow up without an *affective vocabulary* and highly intelligent children grow up without an *affective intelligence*. It is amazing to me how many apparently "high-functioning clients" (clients with academic or financial success who are able to hold down jobs and relationships) have such limited awareness of their own internal states.

> One client, a college educated designer, spent months complaining about his chronic depression. When I finally said to him that what he called depression sounded to me more like anxiety, he inquired simply, "What's the difference?"
>
> Another client, a young woman with a doctorate in the social sciences, spent hours talking about her grief, her outrage, her pain, her anger, all with tears flowing and chest beaten, all of which left me completely unmoved (this is uncharacteristic of me as I am usually easily moved by a person's tears). What I finally interpreted to her was that these did not appear to be her feelings, but rather the feelings she thought she should have and then convinced herself that she did have. The real work then began: helping her shake off the assumed feelings and begin to discover her own, true feelings. This was extremely difficult work, as this young woman had as little sense of self as any non-psychotic person I have known.
>
> This same client would frequently complain (with apparently genuine angst) that neither I nor anyone else "saw" her. When I would ask her what it was about her that I failed to see, she was unable to answer. What I ended up interpreting to her was that her need to be "seen" was in fact a need to have her existence recognized and validated. Otherwise she felt like a cartoon ghost without a sheet: invisible to the point of nonexistence. Again, this interpretation rang true for her and we turned to the difficult work of discovering who she was, not just that she existed.

The parents of both of the clients just discussed were "good" parents in the sense that they provided for their children, did not physically abuse them, and provided a better-than-average education for them. But the parents were narcissistically self-involved and simply did not take the time or make the effort to ponder their children's inner states. Other parents either lack enough of their own affective intelligence to be able to be useful in this way to their young children or are simply not present enough. The delinquent teenagers I worked with for nearly 20 years were almost all completely unaware of their own feelings. They seemed aware of one – and only one – feeling: anger. When a close friend was killed in a gang shootout, they would feel only anger (no sadness). When a situation arose that I would have associated with shame or humiliation, they felt anger. Somehow, they even managed to transform fear into anger. Granted, gangs are a kind of warrior society in which anger is valued and other emotions (especially fear) are not. But these kids did not seem defiant when asked about other feelings; they seemed lost and confused. Among themselves they would mock their therapists by repeating the iconic question, "So how does that make you feel?" and they would laugh or snicker. The question seemed like gibberish to them.

Winnicott, learning, and intersubjectivity

There is a fundamental difference between therapists who describe themselves as psychodynamic and those who call themselves behaviorists or learning theorists in the way they think about learning. When a client cannot provide an adequate answer to a simple question about him or herself, the behaviorist/learning theorist will assume that the client either failed to learn something through inadequate teaching or was dissuaded from learning through punishment. The classic psychodynamic therapist is more likely to assume that the learning actually happened but is, for some reason, repressed or otherwise inhibited in its expression. This would seem to categorize Winnicott as a behaviorist. But he is not. Rather, Winnicott is one of the early intersubjectivists.

Winnicott is very focused on learning (and on learning deficits) but he is exclusively focused on a kind of crucial learning that can only happen in relationships: that can only happen intersubjectively. Basic, crucial learning about the self, says Winnicott – answers to questions such as, "Who am I?" "What feels good; what doesn't?" "What makes me happy?" "When do I feel alive?" "When do I feel dead?" even questions like, "Do I exist; am I capable of existing (as a meaningful part of a relationship)?" – are all learned intersubjectively, in our earliest relationships. Without the maternal provision of the holding environment, without the mirroring function of the mother, without the maternal provision of the mother-infant unit, a sense of *Self* does not emerge. To again use Winnicott's (1951) famous phrase, without the maternal provision, "There is no such thing as an infant."

Filling in these crucial learning deficits, therefore, cannot be done by didactic teaching, by "*correcting* cognitive distortions," or by any manualized therapy. Filling in deficits from inadequate holding, faulty mirroring, or an inadequate mother-infant unit can only be done through a substitute relationship: through an intersubjective experience. Cognitive therapists pay lip service to the importance of the therapeutic relationship but they see it as a kind of *platform* upon which therapy can happen. Winnicott, object relations theorists, and intersubjectivists see the therapeutic relationship as the *vehicle* in which therapy happens. To facilitate the discovery/creation of a Self that is more whole, more alive, more adequate to meeting life's challenges, the therapist must be willing and able to provide adequate holding, accurate mirroring, and a willingness to suspend rigid boundaries (in a partial and controlled way) between himself/herself and another human being.

Providing the "maternal component" (the adult ego component) in the mother-infant unit – or in the therapist-client relationship – ranges from the relatively simple to the very complex. But it always involves the same process. The therapist (mother) projects herself into the psyche of the client (infant) and sees how well she fits in there. By "projecting herself into" I mean that the mother/therapist imagines herself as inhabiting the psyche of the infant/client. This is a very simple process. It is what Winnicott calls the mother "identifying" with her child or "feeling herself into" her child's psyche. It is as simple as, "If I were in your shoes, this is how I might be feeling." By seeing "how well she fits in there," I am referring to an active dialog between mother and infant or therapist and client to see how accurate the projections (the identification with) really are. With the mother and infant, this will be a nonverbal dialog. The mother will pick up the crying child, intuiting that he must want to be held. And then, when the holding produces no positive effect, she will decide that her baby might just be exhausted after all and put him down in his crib. With a therapist and client, the dialog will, of course, be verbal.

> The simplest of examples is my work with delinquent teenagers, whom I have already described as having only one feeling: anger. Regularly, one of these young gangsters would come into my office and tell me that they had just learned of the death of one of their "homeboys." "I am so, so sorry," I would say. "How are you feeling?" "Mad," they

would answer (mad at the shooter and mad at me for asking such an imbecilic question).

And, indeed, they would look rageful. Anger was not the only feeling these kids knew; it was the only feeling accepted in the gang culture. And, in the gang culture, there was a proscribed way of dealing with anger: "payback!" Someone in our gang was killed; someone in their gang has to die. And it didn't matter if it was the shooter or not. Someone – someone-of-theirs – had to die to even the score. And when the score was even, the loss could be forgotten.

I had no trouble empathizing with (identifying with) his rage. His friend was a young man who, in the prime of his life had been shot down like a dog. And this was a loss of a friendship such as I could hardly imagine (gang friends will literally "take a bullet" for each other). But along with my anger I could feel overwhelming sadness: not just for his friend, not just for his loss, but for the whole insane, pernicious system in which one payback leads to another, leads to another, on and on forever.

So, in keeping with the mother and her infant, out of my own projection of myself into their psyches, I said to my clients, "I understand your anger. It makes perfect sense to me. But, if I were in your shoes, along with the anger, I would feel a huge amount of sadness."

I did not follow up with any verbal inquiry as to the "fit" of my projection. I did not ask, "Am I correct? Do you feel sad?" because to do so would have felt challenging and disrespectful. Instead, I allowed the subsequent work to go on in their minds alone. I had offered myself as a role model. I had acknowledged my identification with them. If they were willing to return the compliment and identify with me in my sadness, that was up to them.

A more complex version of this process is offered in the following vignette.

A client worked as the principal of a therapeutic nursery school that reminded me in many ways of the adolescent treatment program I had worked in for many years. She came to one session complaining bitterly about the staff she worked with. They were "so stupid," she complained. She was very annoyed with them. She appeared very upset with herself for being annoyed, but she couldn't help herself: they were just "so stupid!"

I purposefully projected myself directly into her psyche and did so overtly in the session. "Yes," I said, "I can so understand. When

I worked in residential I would get angry at the incompetence of the staff. I cared so much about the kids, I couldn't forgive the staff for being lazy, incompetent, or uncaring."

We continued our dialog for a while until it became clear to me that while we seemed to be in basic agreement, we seemed at the same time to be insistent on using different words. I kept talking about my staff as having been "incompetent," while she persisted in describing her staff as being "stupid." She even seemed to be pushing me to adopt her favored word. So our discussion shifted: from our empathic agreement to a focus on the differences in our word choices. Why did I insist on "incompetent," while she insisted on "stupid?"

It turned out that "incompetent" and "stupid" had radically different implications. "Incompetent" was a blameworthy epithet. If someone was incompetent it was their fault. They needed to do whatever it took – read, study, take courses, get supervision – to become competent. If someone was stupid, it was just who they were. One could insist that an incompetent person gain competency, but one could not reasonably demand that a stupid person become smart. So, I was completely sanguine in my anger at my staff: they were incompetent and it was their job to make themselves competent. My client, however, was guilt ridden over her anger. "These people couldn't help being stupid. It wasn't their fault. It was just who they were. How dare she be angry at them for who they were and what they couldn't help."

The second issue that emerged around the stupid vs. incompetent issue was helplessness. My "incompetent" staff were not helpless. Courses were available to them which they ignored. Supervision was available which they shunned. Their incompetence was a kind of *choice*. To my client's mind, her "stupid" staff had no choice. They were what they were. This meant not only that one shouldn't get angry at them, but that one couldn't expect more from them. Their incompetence was not willful, not a result of laziness or choice, it was inevitable. And the logical consequence of this was that she, my client, had to take care of her staff, because they were incapable of taking care of themselves. And, "taking care of them" meant doing their work for them because they were incapable of doing it themselves.

My client had been raised by a single mother who was severely mentally ill. Her mother seems actually to have been a good mother to her very young daughter. I say this because my client had an impressive affective vocabulary and an extraordinary affect intelligence. But there seem to have been two issues which her mother could not, herself, deal with, and which she was therefore not able to help her daughter deal with. These were: to what extent could she be *blamed* (was her daughter justified in raging against her) for her own incompetent mothering (her own mental illness) and, to what extent could she be blamed (was her daughter justified in raging against her) for forcing her young child into the "parentified child" role in which the young girl had to constantly feel responsible for taking care of her incompetent mother?

Once again, these two examples represent very different levels of reenactment of the mother-infant relationship. But both involve the same processes. In both cases I projected myself into the psyche of the client (identified with the client, "felt myself into" the mind of my client). After that came an analysis of the "fit" of my projection. With the delinquent adolescents, I left that analysis entirely up to them. To do more would have felt intrusive, controlling, and violating. With my other client, with whom I had a much stronger bond (therapeutic alliance), the mutual analysis of the fit of my projection became the body of our work.

Note

1 For a philosopher's discussion of the infant's awareness of its own helplessness, see Martha C. Nussbaum (2001). *Upheavals of thought: The intelligence of emotion.* Cambridge: Cambridge University Press.

4   Potential space and transitional objects

Potential space is one of the least understood and most ignored of Winnicott's concepts. But I argue that it is crucial for understanding the goals of psychotherapy. Potential space is the space "in which we live." If potential space is empty our lives are empty. If potential space is full, our lives are full. The task of the therapist is not to try and fill the client's potential space. Rather, it is to discover and repair potential space damage that stems from disruption of the early separation/individuation stage of development.

When we left off in the last chapter the infant was feeling happily protected by the fantasy of "oneness" with the mother, a fantasy joined in and reinforced (in a gradually diminishing way) by the mother. The fantasy of oneness with the mother – the fantasy of the "mother-infant unit" – provides a number of critical benefits to the infant. It protects him/her from unbearable anxiety of being alone and completely vulnerable. And it provides an auxiliary ego – the mother's adult ego – with which the infant can interpret the world and him/herself.

But there is a huge price to be paid for the fantasy of the mother-infant unit. This price is reflected in a deeper interpretation of Winnicott's (1951) famous dictum, "There is no such thing as an infant (outside of the maternal provision)." What he meant by this was that the psyche of the infant cannot be considered independent of the psyche of the mother. The psyche of the infant is merely a component of the more complex psyche of the mother-infant unit. If there is no such thing as an infant (outside of the maternal provision), then there is no such thing as an infant's identity (outside of the combined identity of the mother-infant unit). In "fusing" (in fantasy) with the mother, the infant loses any possibility of an independent identity.

In the infant's utterly dependent neonatal state, aloneness is equated with annihilation and the supplementary ego provided by the mother is essential for making sense of the world. So the price of identity is well worth paying. But as the infant grows, matures, and becomes increasingly autonomous, this price becomes increasingly onerous, and the infant will begin to work towards some escape from the gilded cage of the mother-infant unit.

Observers of this period describe it as a kind of seesaw between terror and exhilaration and joy. The terror is the terror of the small child who, toddling blithely down the supermarket aisle, suddenly realizes his mother is not where he thought she was. The joy and exhilaration is the baby who, crawling into the kitchen, pulls open a cabinet and discovers the wonders of pots and pans and the fabulous noises they make when banged together. What these joys and terrors entail is the infant's discovery of – acceptance of – the potential for space to exist between itself and its mother. This is, of course, ultimately physical space. "Mother and I are not one. There is space between us. We are separate beings." But, as the infant emerges out of the fantasy of the mother-infant unit, the space in question also becomes emotional space and cognitive space.

Winnicott takes this simple developmental process – the infant's discovery of and acceptance of the potential for space to exist between itself and mother – and, in his typical way, turns this into a concept of enormous richness and complexity. Winnicott postulates what he calls a paradox (Winnicott loves paradoxes).[1] The space between infant and mother has all the potential for joy and excitement. It is the potential space in which all the world's pots and pans are waiting to be found. It is the space of fantasies of knights and dragons, of alien worlds and alternate families. It is the space of finger painting and block towers. On the other hand, it is the space of terror. It is the space of suddenly finding oneself alone in a strange place, of feeling overwhelmed by one's helplessness and powerlessness. It is space that cannot be lived without and cannot be lived with. Winnicott's solution to this paradox? The space can be tolerated and used, *lived in*, only if it is kept *potential*. What this means is that it can be kept open only if it is filled with something, only if it is not allowed to be experienced as a void. Winnicott calls this concept, the concept of an area of experiencing that has to exist but cannot be allowed to exist, a space that can exist only if it is filled, "potential space."

And what is potential space filled with? Play! By *play*, Winnicott clearly refers to creative play. The bored child spending endless hours playing solitaire, even the superb athlete who makes the perfect kick or the longest pass, may not be actually playing as Winnicott uses the word. Play, for Winnicott, is creative. It is an exercise of the mind, of the imagination, of the creation and attribution of meaning, as least as much as it is of the body.

Winnicott (1971a, 1971b, 1971c,) says that play is the first thing with which the infant fills potential space. Later, potential space will be filled with such things as transitional objects, artistic creation, cultural experiences, and interpersonal relatedness, but none of these later phenomena will ever completely lose their connection with play, and this play will never completely lose its function as filler of a potential void between infant and mother. Indeed, if we extrapolate in the other direction, we may even say that the creation of the fantasy of the mother-infant unit is the infant's first act of play, in that it "fills" the potential for space between infant and mother with a fantasy (an act of play) that ironically denies even the potential for potential space.

Potential space is one of those wonderful Winnicottian concepts that exists with multiple layers of meaning. At times Winnicott (1971c) presents it in almost mystical terms. Potential space is "not *inside* by any use of the word. . . . Nor is it *outside*, that is to say it is not part of the repudiated world, the not-me, that which the individual has decided to recognize (with whatever difficulty and even pain) as truly external, which is outside magical control" (p. 41). It is "an intermediate zone of experiencing," (1971d, p. 104) between the internal and the external.

But at other times Winnicott (1971d) presents it as a very simple, experience-near idea. Potential space, he says, is "the place where we live" (p. 104). When we describe someone as having a "full life" (someone who loves work and finds it rewarding; someone who has numerous, deep, intimate relationships; someone who appreciates and is invested in art and culture) it is Potential space that is full. When we describe someone as having an "empty life" (the teenager who spends his life playing video games, the man who spends hours each day watching porn), it is Potential space that is empty.

It is interesting that Winnicott (1971d) describes Potential space not as a "what" but as a "where." This makes sense if we remember that it is presented in contrast to two other "wheres": the internal (autistic, hallucinatory) and the external (concrete, reality-focused). Potential space is the psychic space in which *experience* is generated. It is neither a pure feeling, nor an external thing or event (a painting in a museum or a concert). It is an intermediate place. It is our *experience* of the painting or of the concert, including our feelings about it, but also much more, such as the personal meaning we attribute to those external phenomena. And, Winnicott emphasizes, this Space originates in, and never completely loses its connection with, the space between infant and mother.

Potential space filled with play

Winnicott strongly associates Potential Space with play, and play with creativity. There is no disputing the developmental value of organized sports. Sports contribute to a sense of mastery and accomplishment that are vital to a child's growth. And they teach crucial life lessons: they teach that victory is better than defeat, but that defeat is bearable; defeat does not mean annihilation. However, although a superb athlete may dazzle us with his or her creativity, organized sports are not inherently *creative*, and thus not what Winnicott specifically refers to by the concept of *play*. Winnicott would probably have been more interested in the *fantasies* about sports than sports themselves: the last-second basket that wins the game, the come-from-behind dive into the end zone, the being carried off the field on the shoulders of one's teammates.

Play is first and foremost about the acquisition (in fantasy) of power. The child playing with dolls or action figures has the power to script and direct social relationships, from the familial to the heroic. That child, in its play (through its play), becomes Shakespeare's Prospero, or even Shakespeare himself. That child is the master of his or her (play) universe. The child has the power in play – in fantasy – that it knows it lacks in real life. And the child will process everything in its world, from desire to threat, via play.

> Some years ago, we received a disturbing phone call from our son and daughter-in-law. Their neighbor's home had been burgled and, tracing the burglar's footprints the next morning, they discovered that the stone that had been used to break the window had been taken from their yard. They had decided not to tell our then two-year-old grandson about this for fear of needlessly alarming him.
>
> But their son found out (probably by overhearing our phone conversation). And they discovered that he had found out because the crime had entered into his play. For days after, his fantasy play involved "bad men stealing things." But in his play he was in control. He was writing the script. He was determining the outcome. He was controlling the action. He was in charge. He had the power.

As the child develops and matures, other things can fill Potential space besides creative play. Some of these are functional, some are not. But all retain their connection to play. What follows is a discussion of *some* of the things that can fill Potential space.

Potential space filled with clutter

Winnicott writes extensively about filling potential space with play, with creativity, with cultural experiences and other such positive phenomena. But in our clinical practices we frequently see potential space filled with various forms of clutter. We need always to remember that if potential space is to be kept open at all, it needs to be filled with something. Often that "something" is silly, uncomfortable, even, at times, noxious. But a noxious fill is still better than a void.

> Tom was a middle-aged, professional male in a long-term therapy group. Intelligent and charming, his character was, nevertheless, essentially schizoid. He had few friends and adamantly maintained that he would never allow himself to get close to people. To do so, he said, would be "too painful." His only social contacts, outside of the small business he ran, were the group and a weekly bridge club he seemed to enjoy. Tom would periodically come to the group in severe distress, pleading for help, only to ultimately reject the utility of the group and any support or advice it might give.
>
> In one such session he sobbed with sadness, anxiety, and frustration. He was absolutely swamped with work, he said. He was working on reorganizing his company, rewriting its policy and procedures statements, revamping the way the business functioned down to the most minute detail. In a word, he felt completely "overwhelmed." He appeared lost, defeated, and dejected.
>
> His individual therapist had lectured him sternly on his need to learn to delegate, to pass on some of his workload to his subordinates. The members of the group quickly echoed this notion. "You have intelligent, competent employees," they urged, "let them do some of the work." Tom listened impassively and unmoved. The expression on his face seemed sour and pouting, as though saying, "How come nobody ever understands me?"
>
> I encouraged the group to try and find a different way of "supporting" Tom: a support that might challenge his assumptions rather than

acquiesce to them. Finally, a woman who had been quiet until that point, someone who had known Tom for years, spoke up. "Tom," she said gently, "I don't think you have too much in your life; I think you have too little. You have no friends, no interests, nothing that brings you happiness or satisfaction. I've been to your house. It's appalling! It's nice enough from the outside but inside it looks like a home for transients. There is nothing on the walls. You have lived there for years but you appear to be living out of boxes. The backyard is brown dirt. Tom, your life is empty so you try and fill it with busy work and then you get overwhelmed by the amount of busy work you create for yourself. You don't need to delegate more; you need to get a life!"

Tom said nothing, but he stared at her with his eyes wide. It was as if he had been seen for the first time.

To the casual observer, Tom would have seemed to have a relatively good life. He had a successful business, was reasonably affluent, did not drink or abuse substances. Some people would assume he was lonely, and he was moderately obese. But his essential emptiness he kept well hidden, hidden even to himself, by clutter.

So too would the casual observer see Sandra.

Sandra, a graduate of a prestigious law school, was a reasonably successful attorney, and was intelligent, personable, and attractive. In her mid-thirties, she was still single, but until very recently that was not problematic to her. She had many friends, some she considered close but, to my ear, none that sounded particular intimate. Her friends considered her to be fun, easygoing, though somewhat eccentric.

What was "eccentric" about Sandra was her anxiety and her obsessive-compulsive functioning. Anxiety was Sandra's baseline. Her generalized (unfocused) anxiety diminished dramatically shortly after she began therapy, though the reason for this was unclear. But her obsessive-compulsive features appeared intractable. Her obsessional thoughts were of the "normal" sort: "I've left the stove on. I've left my iron on. I've forgotten to lock my apartment door. I'm too fat." Her compulsive behavior consisted primarily of checking and re-checking and re-re-checking her work for errors. She was torn between recognition of the problems these behaviors posed ("I am always behind in my work because I spend too much time on each project") and justifying these same behaviors ("But I do make mistakes that need to be caught." "But I have gone out leaving my iron on."). Sandra was rational and intelligent enough that, in some way, all of her obsessions and compulsions "made sense."

Sandra rejected all my suggestions about medication, saying that she preferred to "work this through in therapy." But the work in therapy seemed frustrating (to both of us) and unproductive. At one point I began to be aware that, rather than helping Sandra, I had been coopted into her defensive system. Therapy had become a place where she could obsess about her obsessions.

About this time I had a sudden thought: "What would Sandra think about if she didn't have her obsessive thoughts?" My thought appeared to come out of the blue but it must instead have come out of what Ogden (1994) calls the "analytic third" – a subjectivity that arises out of the therapeutic relationship – because shortly thereafter Sandra came up with an interesting insight on her own. She reported that she had recently had a cold for which she had taken an over-the-counter cold remedy and that under the influence of this cold remedy she had been "unable to feel anxious."

Sandra was willing to explore her choice of words. She had felt "unable" to feel her anxiety rather than feeling "freed" or "liberated" from her anxiety. She went on to say that she had "missed" her anxiety and that she had felt somewhat "lost" without it. This was a clear, though not definitive, turning point in the therapy. Sandra frequently tried to use the sessions as a forum for further obsessing, but was progressively more willing to do real work on what the obsessions *meant* to her.

A few weeks after the just discussed session Sandra spontaneously provided a stunning insight: "I think," she said, "that I feel less anxious when I feel loved." I call this insight "stunning" for two reasons. First, the insight itself is profound and important. Second, the insight came entirely from Sandra and was entirely spontaneous. Before this moment, Sandra had seemed almost determined to have me do all her thinking for her. "Tell me what is wrong with me," was almost a mantra. Sandra's insight was an act of creativity. She was beginning to fill her potential space with something besides clutter.

On the surface Sandra's life was much richer than Tom's. But we are not talking here about the external facts of one's life. Winnicott (1971e) defines potential space as an "intermediate level of experiencing," between the internal and the external. And in this place, this intermediate place, Sandra's life was, if anything, even more barren than Tom's.

A third case was presented to me by a young psychologist who consults with me.

> Jane, a woman in her mid-fifties, had once been a successful busi-nesswoman, but was now entirely reclusive and isolated. She had no friends and spoke of her acquaintances with contempt. Her husband had decided that the only way he could stay married to her was to move abroad and maintain a safe, seven-thousand-mile distance between them. Their daily phone calls – during which she appeared to do nothing but berate him – were not only her only social contact but also appeared to be her only activity each day.
>
> Jane's potential space was filled literally with clutter: Jane was a hoarder. Had her husband ever returned home he would have found his side of their bed piled with boxes. But for Jane, nothing she hoarded was junk. To the contrary, each thing was a "treasure" of one sort or another. She told her therapist that the only way she could bear to part with anything would be if that item were given, in safekeeping, to someone who also recognized it as a treasure, and would keep and value it accordingly.
>
> I wrote earlier of potential space as referring to whatever it is that we mean when we say that someone's life is "full" instead of "empty." To both Jane's therapist and to me, Jane's life, her potential space, was bleak and barren. But Jane had convinced herself that her life was full – to the point of overflowing – with treasures.
>
> There were, of course, times when this fantasy could not be main-tained, when she would break down and be consumed by loneliness, to the point of suicidality. However awful and terrifying these moments were for Jane, these were the moments when Jane was "workable," when therapy could happen.

I wish at this point to take issue with a common and "common sense" treatment of depression: the advice (or some variant on the advice) to, "Get busy!" Of course, to a certain extent this advice can be effective. Activity, including physical activity, does tend to ameliorate depression. So, at times even the most experienced of therapists will find themselves telling their clients (or being tempted to tell their clients), "You need more friends in your life (or different friends). You need to get out more. You need to be more active. Start going to the gym. Take up a hobby."

Now in calling these interventions mistakes I am in no way disparag-ing exercise or the importance of a passionately held avocational interest.

Indeed, hobbies, when they represent a passion, are exactly what Winnicott would call a healthy way of filling potential space. But in advising someone to "take up a hobby," we are not necessarily helping them discover a passion. To the contrary, we may be telling them to "fill up your potential space (with clutter) so you don't notice or are distracted from how empty your life is."

Potential space filled with self

Interestingly, Winnicott locates the discovery of the *self* in potential space. Winnicott (1971c) writes, "It is in playing, and only in playing, that the individual child or adult is able to be creative and to use the whole personality, and it is only in being creative that the individual discovers the self" (p. 54). Winnicott immediately goes on to say that the discovery of the self is not to be found in the products of creativity. Rather, the self is discovered in the *experience* of creativity or in the *"creative gesture"* itself. To these two concepts – self and creativity – Winnicott adds a third – relaxation (based on trust) – which, in the therapeutic setting, is essential for the emergence of the first two. Hence, Winnicott offers the following therapeutic sequence: "(a) relaxation based on conditions of trust based on experience; (b) creative, physical and mental activity manifested in play; (c) the summation of these experiences *forming the basis of a sense of self*" (p. 56, italics added).

I would like to call attention to the differences in the ways Winnicott speaks of the self: in the first quote the self is *discovered*; in the second, a sense of self is *formed* or *created*. I believe that Winnicott's concept of self, particularly of the "True Self'" is widely misunderstood (this will be discussed more in Chapter 16). Focusing exclusively on Winnicott's discussion of the discovery of the self often leads to a notion of the self that is concrete and reified. The self is seen as what one truly likes and truly dislikes, what one genuinely believes and genuinely disbelieves, what one really feels and what one really does not feel. By my reading Winnicott is saying the exact opposite. The moment something becomes concrete or reified it *stops* being part of the self (or at least of the True Self). The self, says Winnicott, is discovered in the experience of creativity, in the creative gesture. As such, it is always changing, always in flux. "I am myself," Winnicott seems to be saying, "when I am being creative, when I am not reading a script – even if I, myself, wrote the script." I believe we are wrong to see the discovery of the self as a simple, linear process – a process of uncovering much like Freud's formulation of the uncovering (discovery) of the unconscious. I believe that (in Winnicott's model) the self is better conceptualized as a dialectical concept that is both discovered and created, much like Winnicott's concept of the transitional object (discussed later in this chapter) which, he insists, must be both discovered and created: a process in which the paradox can never be resolved.

I believe that my interpretation of Winnicott's *self* as a dialectic of discovery and creation is supported by the clinical example with which he ends his important 1971 article. At the end of an extended session one of his clients asked a question about a dream she had presented (which had involved a search).

> I said that the answer to the question could take us to a long and interesting discussion, but it was the *question* that interested me. I said: "You had the idea to ask that question."
>
> After this she said the very words I need in order to express my meaning. She said, slowly, with deep feeling: "Yes, I see. One could postulate the existence of a ME from the question, as from the searching [a reference to the dream]."
>
> She had now made the essential interpretation in that the question arose out of what can only be called her creativity, creativity that was coming together after relaxation, which is the opposite of integration.
>
> (1971c, p. 64)

While I believe that the theoretical issues discussed in the earlier paragraphs are extremely important, I return, at this point, to the basic issue of this chapter: the implications of a particular construct's being located in "potential space." And, that implication is always the same: the issue in question always relates back to how the infant deals with (or fails to deal with) the perception of a potential for space to exist between itself and its mother.

> Sonya was referred to therapy by her best friend, Kim, who was a graduate student in psychology, and who was concerned about her friend's "failure to launch" and her "fused" relationship with her mother. Sonya, a Latina in her late twenties, still lived at home and seemed to be a perpetual undergraduate, drifting from major to major, never finding any subject that "reached out and grabbed" her. She seemed to have few interests in life beyond her relationships with her mother and with her friend Kim. She was, indeed, very close to her mother, such that when she was at school she would phone her mother two or three times a day, "just to talk."

Sonya was a dutiful client, who took her friend's concerns about her very seriously, but she did not seem to share them. She seemed also to expect me to share her friend's concerns (which I did). In one session she talked about being out shopping with her mother and having had her mother pick out a dress for her and buy it for her. She described this incident in detail, looking at me carefully the whole time, checking to see my reaction. When we discussed this, she said that she expected me to be critical, as her friend Kim had been, telling her that she needed to be more independent, more autonomous. Instead, I simply asked her if she liked the dress, to which she answered, "Yes, of course," as though it were a given.

Several months into therapy, I thought that a significant change had occurred when she announced that she had a "crush" on a young man who was a friend of Kim's. This might have been a very positive movement for her: a step towards adulthood and differentiation. But I could discover very little passion behind her "crush." She described this young man as "good-looking" and "nice," but seemed unwilling (and strangely uninterested) in describing him in any greater detail. Finally, I asked her what it was about this man that made her have a crush on him? Instantly she blurted out, "Well, because Kim has a crush on him." I could not hide my shock. Here was a woman who had so little sense of self, so little *potential space*, that she could not even come up with her own erotic fantasies: they had to be borrowed from her best friend.

Sonya had been born in Latin America and when she was about six months old, her mother had left her with relatives and come to the United States looking for work. When she was about three her mother sent for her and they reunited. The forced separation had apparently been traumatic for each of them, and each seemed to have responded by not only trying to re-establish the mother-infant unit but by attempting to retie the unbiblical cord. The "space" between mother and child had not remained potential; it had been brutally and traumatically real. And when they reunited, the idea of that space reopening was so threatening that it could not be considered, even as potential. *Potential space* was replaced by (or in Ogden's terms, had "collapsed into") the mutual fantasy of fusion, of *oneness*.

The artificial prolonging of the mother-infant unit by means of a shared fantasy of fusion between mother and child causes the parameters of potential space (mother and infant as separate units) to slam together. There is no room for space, so even its potential is denied. But the foreclosure of potential space can also be caused from the opposite direction: the premature breakdown of the mother-infant unit. Nowhere in my experience has this been more prevalent than among the delinquent teenagers I worked with. These teens, mostly gang affiliated, had almost to the one suffered from severe, early maternal abandonment. The reasons were varied – maternal substance abuse, maternal focus on men, or simply pure, physical abandonment – but the results were the same: no mother. I am fond of comparing potential space to the space bounded by the open wings of a hinge. If, in contrast to the case of Sonya whose wings slammed shut after having been prematurely forced open, with these adolescents it was like the hinges had been explosively blown apart. There was no circumscribed space between self and mother; there was endless space, a boundless void. And these young kids went through life shell-shocked, as though they had been in an actual explosion. There was no room for creative gestures because they were in a "survival mode," completely focused on external reality. There was no room for the discovery/creation of self because the best they could hope for was a script to follow.

By the end of latency that script was provided for them in the form of gangs. Gangs provided a collective identity that substituted for a sense of self. And that collective identity was powerful. It included a strict dress code including prescribed and proscribed colors, hairstyle (shaved head), and limits on how high one's pants could be worn. It provided its own language, including verbal and signing forms of communication. It began with a strict, and ruthlessly enforced, oath of loyalty, an oath that provided in return a band of "brothers" who promised to "have your back" when the bullets begin to fly. It provided an extended family for those whose biological families were broken. It provides a sense of belonging, a feeling of pride, and an insistence on "respect." It provided everything a sense of self provides, except for a sense of self, since it is itself is a substitute for a "Self."

> One of my favorite clients during my years with this population was a Mexican-American gang member named Francisco. Except that whenever you called him by that name he would smile and deny the name. "Yes," he would say, "that's my name. But that's not who I am. I am Frank from F-13" (*Florencia Trese* is a notorious Los Angeles area street gang). And behind his smile was a determined will. "No," he was clearly saying, "don't try to make me something other than how I have defined myself. If you make me other than a pure gangster, you are taking something away from me that I cannot do without."

Francisco had been born in Mexico City. When he was three his mother had abruptly left him and his sister with some less-than-friendly neighbors and had gone north to seek work [this being a tragically common story]. Francisco was told, when he was old enough to remember, that as a toddler he had taken to wandering the streets of his neighborhood looking for his mother. "No," he had been told, "your mother is a long, long way away." In his toddler's mind he interpreted this to mean that each day he would have to wander farther and farther away from his home. And each day he would push the perimeter of his wanderings a bit more, searching for that yearned-for reunion.

Francisco was finally brought to the United States not by his mother but by his father, who had established himself modestly in the Los Angeles area. Frank's father was, in many respects, a traditional Mexican male, good and well-meaning but without maternal impulses or skills. Again, Frank was left essentially to raise himself, to wander aimlessly in quest of his mother, until *Florencia Trese* reached out and plucked him from his wanderings.

Frank's mother finally reappeared when he was in the residential program. In a large, multifamily group she tearfully told about how hard she had tried to reach her children, how she had sent money for them to the caretaking family only to learn later that none of the money, nor the accompanying letters, had ever reached her children. She had once returned to Mexico City and taken her daughter back to the United States, leaving Frank behind. This, she now explained, was not because she valued her daughter more than her son, but because she feared her daughter was being sexually abused.

The mother told this story in Spanish with another mother translating. Tears poured down her cheeks and there was barely a dry eye in the group. Except for Frank. Frank stared at her coldly, listening with neither acceptance nor rejection. "So Frank," his peers shouted, "what do you think now?" But Frank was unpersuaded and I intervened to urge patience. "This is very new to Frank," I said. "Give him time to digest it." But Frank's caution turned out to be justified. A few months after suddenly returning to his life his mother as suddenly left it again. It turned out that one of her brothers had gotten ill back in Mexico and she felt compelled to go and take care of him.

Theoretically, a child should have a fairly well-developed sense of potential space by the age of three. And it seems likely that Frank did. His determination to not have his gang identity challenged was not so much a failure to have potential space opened in the first place as it was a refusal to have it reopened (and re-exploded). Frank made remarkable progress in treatment and several years after terminating the program he came back to visit. He told me that he had never quite left his gang, but that he had joined a group that worked to reduce gang violence, especially gang warfare. Whenever rival gangs would go to war, Frank was there trying to negotiate a truce. He was proud of himself and proud of his work, and I was proud of him. But then he turned to me and said with a sad smile of self-awareness, "But I'm never as happy as when I'm in the middle of things and bullets are flying around me." Frank was tragically aware of his own continuing death wish which, I believe, came from the continuing void in his potential space. His passion for his work was genuine, but not enough to completely fill the void where his mother had been. The adrenaline-rush that came with the flirtation with death did not fill the void either, but it allowed him, for the moment, to forget about it.

Potential space filled with transitional objects and transitional phenomena

The *mother-infant unit* is based on what is frequently called "as-if thinking." In as-if thinking a person *knows* at a certain level that A is true but decides (unconsciously) to act *as if* B were true. Modern infant research has demonstrated fairly conclusively that the neonate very quickly knows that it has left the womb, that the umbilical cord has been cut, and that he or she is a separate object from mother. But, says object relations theory, the infant seems also to know that it is utterly dependent on its mother for its very survival and that it could not survive for more than a few moments without the mother's (or other caretaker's) vigilant protection. Thus, the infant is faced very early in its existence with the prospect that the object upon whom its very existence depends is free to leave, to come and go, at her own whim. This awareness, posits our theory, leads to the potential for unbearable anxiety, and this potential anxiety is avoided by the creation of an infantile fantasy: "Mother and I are not really separate; Mother and I are one." This is as-if thinking. The infant knows that he/she and Mother are separate but chooses to act *as if* they are not.

The mother-infant unit thus provides an essential avoidance mechanism for unbearable anxiety. It also, as we have seen, provides the infant with an essential "auxiliary ego" without which knowledge of and development of a sense of self is impossible. But very early on the fantasy of the mother-infant unit becomes problematic. To use Mahler's (1972) terms, the infant must separate and individuate if it is to grow and mature and not remain forever a psychological infant. If the fantasy of fusion with the mother is necessary to avoid intolerable anxiety and if the auxiliary ego provided by the mother has become an essential tool for attributing meaning to the environment, then how is this separation and individuation achieved?

Winnicott (1951) offers a solution, and it is based on a new variation of *as-if thinking*, a new variation he calls "transitional object relatedness." "Between four to six to eight to twelve months"[2] the toddler will (though not always) form a strong attachment to a previously undistinguished blanket or to some particular stuffed animal. Winnicott calls this object a "transitional object." This seemingly commonplace and innocuous event is, according to Winnicott, a milestone in the child's movement towards autonomy.

The transitional object has elements of mother (the ability to sooth, the ability to comfort) but it is not mother. It has elements of self (it is the product of the child's imagination), but it is not self (a thumb, though capable of soothing when sucked, is by definition not a transitional object since it is not an external object. Winnicott refers to thumbs as "soothing objects" rather than "transitional objects").

The transitional object facilitates the transition from dependence on (fantasized fusion with) the mother to autonomy (the capacity to be alone). Winnicott states that the ability to utilize a transitional object is dependent upon the ability to maintain (without resolving) a paradox. That paradox is that the object was created by the infant while at the same time the object was there waiting to be discovered by the infant. These are mutually incompatible beliefs. Something is either already there (old), waiting to be discovered, or it is new, something one creates. Logically, it cannot be both. But Winnicott (1951) asserts that the infant must be able to simultaneously hold both as true. If, he says, we were to force the infant to choose between these incompatible realities, the power of the transitional object would immediately be lost.

It is not hard to see how this is true. If we were to force the infant to say, "Yes, the power of this object [the power to sooth, to comfort, to nurture: the mother-like qualities] is purely the result of my imagination, is purely my creation. In reality it is but a scrap of cloth. All of its magical qualities are products of my fantasy life," then obviously the object would lose its power. Anything that is acknowledged to be purely a product of my imagination cannot be attributed to have any real power. If, on the other hand, we were to force the child into the claim that the object was "there waiting to be discovered" (along with all the magical/maternal powers attributed to it), then all of its mother-like qualities would be seen as being inherent in the object itself. The object would simply represent a mother-replacement (a non-mother mother-substitute) and it would lose all its value as a "transitional" object. It would simply represent the substitution of a cloth mother-surrogate for the real, flesh-and-blood mother, and thus a continued dependency on some kind of mother figure.

The infant must be able to hold onto both (incompatible) truths simultaneously for the transitional object to serve its function. This amounts, says Winnicott, to a new and important level of play on the part of the infant. The "play" represents a new dialectic of knowing and not knowing. To play in this way, the infant must be able to juggle knowing and not knowing together with such skill that neither is allowed to hit the ground.

In a sense, this is merely an important refinement of an old play skill. The infant's contribution to the mother-infant unit is a similar kind of paradoxical thinking: "I know that mother is separate, but I will function as if we were still one." When the infant, in the paranoid-schizoid position, splits, he is playing in a similar way. Splitting involves the same kind of "as if" thinking. When we split, we are saying to ourselves (unconsciously), "I know that this object is one (I am not psychotic), but I will act *as if*, and relate emotionally *as if*, it were two." Transitional object relatedness involves a quantum jump in "as if" thinking. The new play stage is about maintaining the incompatible paradox of creation and discovery. The infant or toddler says (unconsciously), "I know (and *must* know) that this [the mother-like quality of the transitional object] is the creation of my imagination, but I will act *as if* it were objective fact (discovered)."

As with splitting, the implications of transitional object relatedness are far-reaching and underappreciated. The capacity for transitional object relatedness does not simply allow the child to add a comforting "binkie" or teddy bear to an arsenal of aids in getting through the difficult "separation-individuation" period. It forms the foundation for future interpersonal relatedness that will serve him for the rest of his life. The ability to say (unconsciously), "I have found you and I have created you," and to preserve and maintain this paradox allows the child to ultimately do the exact same thing with another human being rather than simply with a selected inanimate object. Without this ability, the child would be stuck forever in its love for and attachment to its first love object: his mother.

When a teenage boy meets and falls in love with a teenage girl, it is the capacity for transitional object relatedness that makes this love possible. It is this capacity that enables the boy to say (unconsciously) to the girl,

I have found you and you are perfect. And I will create you so that you will be perfect. You are everything I need, and I will imbue you with the power to meet my every need. You will be you, and I will invest in you all the power to nurture and to comfort that I once found in my mother. I will love you for you, and I will love you as I once loved my mother. I have found you and I have created you and I will never resolve that paradox.

Thus, wonderfully, transitional object relatedness seems to offer us a way of having our cake and eating it too. We can achieve intersubjectivity. That is to say, we can discover, respect, and appreciate the otherness, the alterity of another human being. We can learn and grow from that relationship in a way that Ogden demonstrates can happen *only* with an Other. And, at the same time we can legitimately receive from that Other the kinds of comfort, nurturance, love, and support that otherwise would be the exclusive domain of the mother-infant relationship.

So what?

The power of transitional object relatedness to free us from bondage to the original love object choice and allow for a range of subsequent object choices has a particular relevance to the practice of psychodynamic psychotherapy. This power, the power to say, "I have discovered you and I have created you," is the quality that enables the formation of transference (transference will be discussed at greater length in Chapter 13).

Transference in psychotherapy is, in this sense, only a special manifestation of post-mother object choice. In the transference the client says (unconsciously) to the therapist, "I know that you are really my therapist, another person, out there that I have discovered. But I will create in you a replica of my mother (or father, sister, brother, etc.) and I will act towards you, and feel about you, *as if* you were really that person, all the while knowing that you are not."

If the client cannot maintain the paradox, if either side is ultimately held to be "true," then the transference also cannot be maintained. If the client says, "You are just a doctor: a nice one, a smart one, a good one, but ultimately nothing more than that to me," then there is no transference and psychodynamic psychotherapy cannot proceed. If, on the other hand, the client becomes convinced that his therapist *is* (or *should be*) his parent, then he has lapsed into a psychotic transference (or borderline transference) and again the therapy cannot proceed (or can proceed only with great difficulty).

Transitional object relatedness is a specific form of play, and as such it serves to fill potential space. The potential space between mother and infant, the yawning, frigid void, can be kept potential (and therefore bearable) if it is filled with things like blankets and stuffed animals and, ultimately, other love objects. Thus, *transference is a form of play* also. Winnicott (1971c) is quite clear on this.

> Therapy is something that takes place at the overlap between the play space of the therapist and the play space of the patient. If the therapist cannot play, then he is not suited to the work. If the patient cannot play, then something needs to be done to enable the patient to become able to play, after which psychotherapy may begin.
>
> (p. 54)

Lupe, a Latina in her thirties, presented in therapy as very bright and extraordinarily insightful. Lupe had excellent "eyes." She saw people clearly and accurately, admiring their virtues and forgiving them their shortcomings. Her ability to see and "read" me was frequently unnerving.

Lupe quickly formed a powerful Oedipal transference towards me. Early in the therapy, when our work together had taken on a kind of tug-o-war quality, I asked her (out of frustration as much as anything else) what she wanted from me. Her response was instantaneous and characteristically insightful: "I want to be five-years-old and for you to be my father."

The choice of the age of five has two significances. First, it is the height of the Oedipus complex, when a little girl's attachment to her father takes on a distinctly flirtatious and sexual quality. Second, it was when she was this age that a younger brother was born. Until then her father had doted on her. But at that point he dropped all interest in his former favorite and focused all of his attention and affection (even more than is typical within his culture) on this new and cherished male-child.

My response to Lupe's answer, then, was a tacit, "I can work with that!" This, after all, was transference. This is what psychodynamic psychotherapy is all about. Lupe would transfer onto me her unresolved feelings and issues with her father and together, with patience and courage and perseverance, these issues would be resolved.

But it did not happen that way. The process continued to feel more like a fight than like work. Lupe accused me of seducing her into a relationship and betraying her. I interpreted this as transference: her father had indeed seduced and abandoned her. But she adamantly rejected the transference interpretation, insisting that it was I, not her father that she was dealing with. And gradually I came to agree with her. There was something amiss in the "real relationship" rather than simply in the transference relationship.

Finally, I understood. Lupe, for all her intelligence, insight, and sensitivity, was unable to play. When I had tacitly agreed to accept the role as (transference) father, she had heard me as agreeing to become her (real) father. Everything I did or failed to do after that was, in her experience, a lie, a betrayal of my original promise.

The use of transference as a vehicle for change in psychodynamic psychotherapy is dependent on the client's having achieved the developmental stage of the capacity for transitional object relatedness.

Potential space filled with symbol

One of the many important things about transitional objects and transitional phenomena is that they are the child's first symbols. Winnicott (1971f) says that it is as important that these things are *not* the mother as it is that they stand for the mother. If we return to our discussion of transitional objects we are reminded of Winnicott's injunction that the paradox – I created the object/I discovered the object – not be resolved in favor of either of these two mutually exclusive possibilities. If the child were forced to admit to having created the object ("It is all make-believe") then the transitional object loses its power. If the child were forced to admit to having discovered the object ("It really does have magical, maternal powers"), then it would simply be a substitute for the mother and would serve no transitional functions. In order to serve a transitional function, the transitional object has to be mother-but-not-mother. It has to be a symbol for mother. Thus, says Winnicott (1971f), in the creation of transitional objects and transitional phenomena, potential space becomes the "*place where symbols are born.*"

The capacity for symbolic thinking has always been considered one of the higher cortical functions and (incorrectly) a cognitive capacity that separates humans from their animal cousins. So Winnicott's assertion, that symbolic thought arises in potential space – which is to say in the handling of certain aspects of the mother-infant relationship – is a radical statement indeed.

> A female intern presented a case to me in which the client's presenting complaint caused her much distress. The client, Mr. H., an educated, middle aged, single male, sat down in his initial session and immediately asked, "You are a young woman. You know what women want. Tell me how I can get laid?" Needless to say, the young intern was less than pleased with this opening gambit. She had not spent years in graduate school, written a dissertation, accrued thousands of hours of unpaid training and tens of thousands of dollars of student loan debt, to deal with questions like that one.
>
> "Okay," she said coolly, "and are there other issues you want to work on in therapy?" "No," said the client, "that's it. Just tell me how I can get laid." The intern struggled in vain, for some time, to find a topic, any topic, that might provide the basis of a mutually acceptable treatment contract, and finally returned to the question she should have asked immediately. "So, what does getting laid mean to you?"
>
> "Oh," responded the client, "getting laid means everything. It means my manhood, it means human contact, it means I'm acceptable." Quite relieved, the intern then proceeded: "Okay, so let's talk about some of those things." The client almost shouted back at her: "No! I'm not here to talk about any of those things. I'm here to find out how I can get laid." Fortunately, the intern was skilled, and by the end of the session and in subsequent sessions those topics were successfully worked on.

In Ogden's conceptualization, this client's potential space had *collapsed* into itself. There was no potential space. The client came in looking for a mother substitute (a person with whom he could physically join) rather than a transitional (symbolic) experience. He was unable to play and therefore he was unable to symbolize. He was unready for therapy. When the intern asked the right question, potential space momentarily opened up. He was able to recognize sex as a complex symbol rather than simply a concrete act. But when pressed, at least in the beginning, potential space slammed shut again, and symbolic thought had no room.

Although this vignette seems almost farcical, it nevertheless provides what I believe is an excellent example of the ingeniousness and importance of Winnicott's postulation. Symbolic thinking, says Winnicott, is not simply a "higher cognitive function" that one has or does not have, depending on one's IQ or the intactness of one's frontal cortex. The capacity for symbolic thinking waxes and wanes depending on one's willingness to enter into an "intermediate area of experiencing" that Winnicott calls potential space. That willingness in turn is dependent on one's ability to feel safe (Winnicott (1960a) says "relaxed" but I submit that these are the same thing, both facets of a proper holding environment) and on the specific variable in a current relationship that defines the dialectic of separateness and connectedness.

When Mr. H presented with his somewhat offensive initial demand, his therapist restrained her impulse to tell him to "Get out of my office." Instead, she attempted to engage him, and to engage him both around an attempt to understand him and a desire to meet his needs – not his needs as presented, but his deeper, underlying needs (Winnicott (1968a) describes this as meeting a client's ego needs rather than his id needs). And this attempt to understand and to nurture took place in the context of a relationship that itself represented a laboratory for the exploration of the self/other dialectic. In Summers' (2005) terms, the therapist helped turn the "void" into productive potential space.

But this example goes even deeper. It demonstrates, I believe, Winnicott's remarkable assertion that symbolic thought, arising as it does within potential space, can ultimately be traced back to permutations of the early mother-infant relationship, specifically around separation/individuation issues. The demand, "I want to get laid," presented in its original concrete, pre-symbolic form, means, literally, "I want to physically unite with another [in this case, female] human being." This is exactly the position of someone who has not escaped from – or longs to return to – the mother-infant unit, in which mother and infant are one and in which there is not even considered to be the potential for potential space. Separation from the mother is inconceivable. And if separation from the mother is inconceivable, Potential space is inconceivable. And if potential space is inconceivable, there is no space for symbolic thought.

A proper holding environment provides the conditions under which potential space can open and symbolic thought arise. In this particular case, the proper holding environment included safety (including the therapist's willingness to move beyond her own initial annoyance), a persistent desire to understand, and a willingness to put the client's needs before her own. It also included a modicum of properly dosed failures. Thus, ironically, the therapist's initial stumbling efforts to redirect the client may have ultimately facilitated the establishment of a "therapeutic alliance." Had the therapist been too competent in her work to understand the client, the client may well have opted to try and fuse with her instead of keeping his fusional fantasies directed on some external sexual partner.

The opening of potential space and its filling with symbol marks not just a shift in the kind of thought processes employed, from "lower" order (concrete) thinking to "higher" order (symbolic) thinking; it represents a shift in the *meaning* of the thoughts. "I want to get laid" as a concrete thought and "I want to get laid" as a symbolic expression *mean* very different things. Concretely, "I want to get laid" means, "I want to physically join with another human being." As a symbolic expression, "I want to get laid" means (as the client himself explained),

> I want to feel better about myself. And by "myself" I mean not some unboundaried component of a larger fused object, but an autonomous subject separate from, but relating to, other objects. And by feeling "better" I refer not to physical satisfaction but rather to enhanced self-esteem, self-worth, and a more satisfying sense of balance in my sense of relatedness, my dialectical struggle between self and other.

Once again, what Winnicott postulated is that the development of symbol represents not just the development of a new *kind* (a "higher" kind) of thinking. It marks a crucial shift in our psychological and emotional development, specifically around the issue of the emergence of a sense of self in relation to other, of an active dialectic of separateness and connectedness.

Potential space filled with psychotherapy

> [P]sychotherapy is done at the overlap of the two play areas, that of the patient and that of the therapist. If the therapist cannot play, then he is not suitable for the work. If the patient cannot play, then something needs to be done to enable the patient to become able to play, after which psychotherapy may begin. The reason why playing is essential is that it is in playing that the patient is being creative.
> . . . It is in playing and only in playing that the child or adult is able to be creative and to use the whole personality, and it is only in being creative that the individual discovers the self.
> – (Winnicott, 1971c, p. 54, italics in original)

This enormously rich statement begs our attention in so many details. Note the return of the dialectic between creativity and discovery. "[I]t is only in being creative that the individual discovers the self." This is a reincarnation of the paradox that defined the transitional object: the object must be created; the object must be discovered. Both must be held true at the same time (dialectically). If the child is forced to choose one or the other of these logically incompatible statements, the transitional object loses its power. In therapy, the client must be able to relate to the therapist exactly as the child relates to a transitional object: "I know that you are not my mother, but I will relate to you as if you were." This is what we call *transference*.

Some clients cannot, and others will not, play in this way. "Have feelings towards you? Hell no! You are only a professional I consult with. You give me your professional services and I give you my money. That is the entirety of our relationship." Ironically, some clients have difficulty playing because they are too cognizant of transference. Psychotherapists themselves make notoriously difficult psychotherapy clients. "Well, I know that this is just transference, but . . ." reflects a cognition that essentially destroys the paradox: one needs to be able to know and not know at the same time.

The "play" in psychotherapy goes well beyond the issues of transference and countertransference. Psychotherapy is, in essence, a game of imaginative play.

> How would I have been different if I had had a more loving mother? How would I have been different if I had had a less punitive father? How did it affect me that my father looked at me with such intensity when I was naked? How did my dyslexia affect my self-esteem? Did my mother really know that my father was abusing me? How might I be different if you had been my mother? My father?

These questions are all manifestations of play. They are creative in that they relate to fantasies of "what might have been," or of "how things might have been different."

One of the frustrating aspects of Winnicott's statement is his sentence "If the patient cannot play, then something needs to be done to enable the patient to become able to play, after which psychotherapy may begin." How do we "enable" a person to be able to play? What is the "something" that "needs to be done?" Whatever it is, it is certainly not teaching. One cannot *teach* a child to play – to be creative. Indeed, teaching and creativity seem, in Winnicott's view, to be inimical to each other. One can teach a child to play the piano. One can teach here about tone, rhythm, melody, and harmony. One can even teach "composition." But one cannot teach anyone to be creative. Creativity, according to Winnicott, is found in the "spontaneous gesture." Indeed, in my own experience, every time I have had a non-playful client suddenly show a moment of creativity it has come like a clap of thunder, completely unexpected, jarring me to my senses.

I think that the answer Winnicott provides to my questions, to the dilemma of the unable-to-play client, is to be found in his concept of the holding environment (Chapter 1). If play (creativity) is spontaneous rather than taught, then the best we can do as therapists (and as parents) is to provide an environment that is safe but not confining, understanding, and encouraging. A case from Thomas Ogden illustrates this well.

> Ogden (1990) presents the case of a young child being placed in a bath by his mother, shortly after some trauma had made him afraid of the water. The mother places her son in four inches of water, holding him gently but firmly, talking to him in a reassuring way: "I have you. I will not let go of you." The child not is assuaged. Then the mother reaches for some toys: a tea set. "May I have some tea?" The child joins in the play: "Tea not too hot, it's okay now. My blow on it for you. Tea yummy." All went well until the mother reached for the washcloth and all of the initial anxiety returned. "After the mother reassured him that she would hold him so would not slip, she asked him if he had any more tea. He did, and playing was resumed" (pp. 206–207).

Ogden presents this story as an example of the power of play. Through play, a threatening medium – water – was transformed into something that was now no longer threatening, but was nurturing, as well as a basis for interpersonal relatedness.

This story illustrates the power of play, but it is also an example of an exquisite holding environment. Had the mother held the child too loosely the he might have been overwhelmed with terror, and play would have been impossible. Had the mother held her son too tightly, the potential space between mother and child would have collapsed into an illusion of fusion, and play would have been irrelevant. It is not just that the mother communicated safety. She also communicated an understanding of, and a response to, the child's nonverbal communications: "I see when you are tense, and I will respond accordingly [by holding you more firmly], and I see when you are more relaxed, and I will respond accordingly [by relaxing my grip and by encouraging play]." In such a "holding environment," the child (client) is able to spontaneously embrace play.

I presented Hester in Chapter 2 on the holding environment. Hester was the client about whom I decided that a proper holding environment would be one modeled on holding out a peanut to a wary chipmunk, with infinite patience and infinite stillness. A watershed moment in our treatment was when Hester started a session reporting to me, with eyes wide and a tentative smile, about an extremely bizarre incident she had just witnessed in the waiting room before our session. When this quirky and humorous incident had been reported Hester and I looked at each other for a moment, and then both burst into laughter.

Laughter was Hester's nascent play. In Ogden's example, play allowed the child to transform a threatening substance (water) into something that was simultaneously nurturing and a vehicle for re-establishing relatedness with its mother. Humor had the same function for Hester. A strange and inappropriate social interaction in near proximity was transformed from a threatening intrusion into a source of amusement and a (safe) way of connecting to me. Humor is clearly a sophisticated form of play. Hester had accepted the long-proffered, metaphoric peanut out of my hand and was not only beginning to be assured of my good will, but also of my ability to bond empathically with her. We were, in Winnicott's terms, ready to begin therapy.

The fundamental role of play (creative and spontaneous) in therapy is one of the several reasons why Winnicott, at the end of his career, advocated extreme restraint on the part of the therapist in the providing of interpretations. Winnicott (1968a) wrote of his regrets for having, earlier in his career, interpreted so much, and stated that, by the end, he offered interpretations "mainly to let the patient know the limits of my understanding" (pp. 86–87). The client, as with the child, must be allowed the space (the potential space) within which to play creatively in order to discover/create his or her self.

Summers (2005) differentiates between a "void" (a term he uses positively) and out of which develops Winnicott's potential space, which Summers refers to as "transitional space." Summers writes:

> The void is precisely the formlessness needed for the establishment of transitional space. If recognized as the opportunity for the emergence of previously dormant capacities, the void becomes the transitional space in which the creation of the self can take place. At this point, repeated efforts to understand are counterproductive because they intrude on the formlessness required for self creation. Therefore, the

analyst's first job in helping to create a new structure is what we might call "maintaining the void."

By presenting the space as a shapelessness that can be given form by the patient, the analyst offers the space as a potential for the creation of new ways of being and relating (Summers, 2005). When the patient responds to the void by saying, "I don't know what to do!" the most productive attitude the analyst can adopt is to applaud the position of the analytic couple. The patient believes the process is stalemated and must be moved ahead but does not see that the movement she seeks is an avoidance of the potential space. Confusion born of understanding, rather than being avoided, should be embraced as a space in which creation can take place. The analyst's response to the patient's confusion is some form of "That's the point." This attitude not only maintains the void but also suggests its creative potential, and, in doing, it shapes a bounded formlessness. In this way, the analyst transforms the void into transitional space (p. 136).

Summers here essentially presents an object relations rational for the ancient Freudian "rule of abstinence." Freud stressed the need for *abstinence* (verbal and emotional withholding on the part of the analyst) as a way of increasing the regression of the patient so that more primitive unconscious material could be brought to consciousness. Summers offers essentially the same prescription for very different reasons. The "void," exacerbated by therapists' abstinence, allows for a potential space in which the self can be created/discovered.

It should be noted that the "play" which fills the kind of potential space described by Summers is far from anything that could be described as "fun." I believe the following vignette describes something of the kind of interaction Summers is describing.

We tell our students, our interns, our clients, and ourselves that clients frequently feel "worse" in therapy before they feel "better." But this reassurance is seldom of much comfort.

> Joan came into therapy voicing common but vague complaints about her spouse, her children, her job. Of course, none of the above were perfect, but none was the true source of her discontent. And "discontent" accurately describes Joan's affect during the sessions. Joan expressed no anger, very little sadness, no joy, no enthusiasm: merely a kind of vague but pervasive *discontent*. She knew that she was married to a good and loving husband; her children could be annoying

but were doing well; and her job was potentially rewarding. But Joan could not find it in herself to be happy.

Our sessions together were neither unpleasant nor boring (to me). Joan was intelligent, poised, and a good storyteller. They were merely . . . *empty*.

Gradually, the emptiness of our sessions began to permeate the *content* as well as the *feel* or the work. Joan became increasingly aware of an internal emptiness that nothing external seemed able to fill. She seemed to lack the capacity to live creatively, to live joyfully, to feel alive at all. And the increasing awareness of these "lacks" filled her with despair. And the despair turned into self-loathing. And for the first time in her memory, Joan began to have thoughts of suicide.

And as her feelings "worsened," Joan increasingly turned to me with a mixture of rage and terror. Both her eyes and her words asked the same questions. "What is happening to me? What are *you* doing to me? I came into therapy to feel better, not worse. What is wrong here? Do something! Get me out of this!"

What I want to emphasize here is how difficult it is, even for a seasoned therapist, to stick to the *frame* described by Summers. The accusations were unspoken but clear: "You/therapy are making me worse! Get me out of this!" The pain and the terror were enormously difficult to sit with and the demands for relief were insistent. There was enormous pressure/temptation to rescue, to placate, to say, "It's okay! This is just some temporary thing you are going through. You will be alright again." How could one possibly follow Summers' lead and say, in the face of this pain and terror, "Yes, that's the point!"

But, of course, that was the point. Along with all the projected guilt, terror, pain, and responsibility that I was carrying with her/for her, was also a sense of relief: "At last! Here is something that is *real*. Here is some work to be done." So that was the intervention that I went with:

> There is a sad, terrified, abandoned little girl in you whom we are finally hearing from. Let her speak! Tell me about your terror. Describe to me how empty and frightening the world looks to you. Tell me how alone you feel. Tell me how abandoned you feel, abandoned especially by me.

The mutual agony that comes to both client and therapist with the uncovering of this kind of True Self is fraught with dangers for the therapy. It is hard to imagine a client who would want to do anything but flee instantly from such pain and despair. The problem for the therapist is that it requires every ounce, first of consciousness, and second of self-control, not to immediately join the client in that flight. Most of us become therapists because we want to help people. We want them to love themselves, to love life, to be and feel successful and deserving, we want them, in short, to *feel better*. Confronted with a client in a crisis such as Joan's, even the most strong-hearted therapist will be sorely tempted to try and make the client "feel better." "No, there really are people who care for you. You are not alone. You are a good person! The fact that you were abandoned as an infant doesn't make you worthless."

What's wrong with these reassurances? The basic issue is that they all feed the False Self (Winnicott's concepts of the True Self and the False Self will be discussed in greater detail in Chapter 16). What they are saying is that, "You shouldn't be feeling what you are feeling. You should be feeing something different – something more positive, something more acceptable – something less painful – to the both of us." The True Self is screaming out, "I am alone. I am abandoned. I am terrified. And I despair." And the client and the therapist are in danger of conspiring to say, "Oh no! Don't feel that way. Your feelings are not valid – not acceptable. Your feelings are wrong. You should feel something else." This would be a complete reenactment of what created the False Self in the first place.

Neophyte therapists are taught a mantra: "Don't do the clients' work for them." There is a myriad of rationales for this proscription. But the most profound, in my view, is that the True Self, found in and defined by the spontaneous gesture, can only be impinged on by a script provided by the therapist. It doesn't matter whether or not the script is "brilliant," "correct," "empathic," or "insightful." *Any* script, provided by any external object, is, by definition, False Self functioning. To the extent that we, as therapists, provide scripts for our clients – however perceptive, however accurate – we are contributing to, and reinforcing, False Self functioning. True Self functioning resides in the "spontaneous gesture" and we, as therapists, can only sit back and wait for that to happen, and to pounce on it, protect it, nurture it, when it happens. Our clients may willingly embrace the scripts we provide them. The scripts may be much more sympathetic, more flattering, sometimes even more "accurate" than were the scripts under which they had labored before. But ultimately the client will be replacing one False Self script with another. This new False Self may be "better," more "functional" than the old False Self, but it will still be a False Self and, implies Winnicott, the inner experience of deadness will be unabated.

In ending this chapter, I think it is important to return to Winnicott's (1971c) opening gambit: "psychotherapy is done at the overlap of the two play areas, that of the patient and that of the therapist." It is here that I completely agree with Benjamin (1990, 1998) in seeing Winnicott as being a crucial figure on the cusp between object relations theory and intersubjectivity. Winnicott's therapist is never a dispassionate observer. Winnicott (1971c) asks himself what clients need from their therapists and his answer is decidedly non-dispassionate: "Devotion!"

So, what is meant by this "overlap" space in which both client and therapist play? I think that one example is when Hester and I laughed together. We were both "playing" in this moment. We were both trans-forming, through play, through humor, something threatening into some-thing benign, something alienating into something bonding. My ability to share the play space with her (to overlap her play space) enabled rather than interfered with her ability to play. I was not directing her play. I was not teaching her how to play or what the rules of play were. I was there playing next to her (with her), validating her play by sharing it, bonding with her through our shared play experience.

Another example can be found in a session with Caitlin.

Caitlin was a very bright, insightful, and hard-working young woman in her early thirties. The only child of a bipolar mother and an aban-doning father, Caitlin was working in one session on a number of dif-ferent issues that appeared to have a common relatedness to having been a parentified child and thus not having really been allowed to *be* a child.

Near the end of the session a chain of associations led her to the movie *Men in Black* which she explained as a quest by the protago-nists for a lost universe. At the end of the movie the lost universe was discovered. It had been present all along, inside a small glass ball worn around the neck of a cat.

At this point Caitlin began to weep quietly and to repeat over and over the phrase, "An entire universe inside a tiny ball!" After a while she looked at me and asked me if I knew what she was talking about. To my surprise, I said that I thought that I did, not in any way I could articulate, but on some kind of intuitive level. Then, after some reflec-tion, I decided to share with her my own association. I said that it reminded me of the awe I sometimes feel when I look at a small child, especially a preverbal child. There is an entire universe of thoughts inside their little minds which is unable to be expressed and therefore frequently unappreciated. Caitlin responded to my association with a radiant, child-like smile. "Yes," she said, "That's it! The small little ball is the child's tiny little head."

As with Hester, I did not play *for* Caitlin, nor did I structure or determine her play. Our play intersubjectively influenced each other's. We played separately and together, in play spaces that overlapped.

Potential space and drugs

I have often been asked by students and by interns whether or not drugs and alcohol fill potential space. It is an interesting question and after much reflection I now answer with an unequivocal "No!" In the first place, substances are neither objects (like transitional objects) nor activities (like play). Drugs are not representational; they are not symbolic. Their importance is in the direct, mind-altering effect they have on the brain. More to the point, they do not meet Winnicott's basic criterion for something that fills potential space: that that thing or activity must be something creatively generated that in some way has elements of – forms a connection to – the absent mother. It might be argued that drugs and alcohol fulfill the maternal function of soothing, much like rocking, singing to oneself, cutting, or even head-banging have soothing effects on very disturbed children. But I take issue even with this. It seems to me that the essence of maternal soothing is in conveying the message (verbally or nonverbally), "You are okay. You are safe. Mommy is here. Everything will be alright." Drugs do not convey safety; they mask the need for it. Drugs numb rather than soothe. Drugs and alcohol do not fill potential space; they obliterate the awareness of it. To again use Ogden's terms, drugs don't fill potential space, they *collapse* it.

Notes

1 Winnicott's respect for paradoxical thinking has historical antecedents. It is not unlike the poet John Keats' concept of "Negative Capability."
2 Winnicott is wonderfully and purposefully vague about such things. His aim is to provoke thought rather than to establish timelines or provide data.

Part II

The paranoid-schizoid position and internal objects

5   The paranoid-schizoid position

Splitting and "as if" thinking

The paranoid-schizoid position, along with the depressive position, is one of Melanie Klein's two modes of emotive-cognitive functioning. The paranoid-schizoid position is defined by the use of splitting. Splitting happens for emotional reasons, but it leads to certain cognitive consequences. I argue in this chapter that splitting leads to a complex, interwoven, and consistent logical system: what I call, "the logic of splitting."

Let us move forward developmentally, always remembering as we do that development itself is not necessarily linear. The infant enters the world with some primitive awareness of its own separateness (which it quickly denies) and finally (more or less) achieves the *capacity to be alone*, also by using some denial. What happens in between (and forever after) is a kind of dialectical progress that results from successive shifts in the relative power of the opposing forces of acceptance and denial, aloneness and fusion.

As the infant gradually shifts towards an increased ability to tolerate separateness (based, ironically of course, on an increase in its ability to feel connected and protected), it encounters a new and profoundly disturbing conundrum. If the infant is to trust itself into the caretaking of an "other," (as opposed to maintaining the illusion of complete control over its own caretaking by subsuming the "otherness" of the caretaker into itself), then the "other" to whom it is entrusting itself must be pretty dammed trustworthy. In short, the caretaking other must be perfect.

But, disturbingly, this is not, and never has been, the infant's experience. There are times when the breast is full and available; the milk sweet and warm and freely flowing; the arms strong and reassuring; the skin soft, fragrant, and comforting; and life is bliss. There are other times when the breast is empty, when the milk refuses to flow, when the maternal voice is sharp rather than cooing, and when survival appears at best questionable. The infant's solution: split!

Splitting, as I have said earlier, is defined as the fantasized division of a single whole object into two-part objects, one of which is good and the other bad. The good caretaker, the "good breast,"[1] eternally and perfectly loving, bounteous, and protective, easily deserves our trust, but it offers more than the assurance of our continued survival, it offers joy, happiness and contentment. The price, however, that one pays for the creation of the good breast is the existence of the "bad breast."

The bad breast is not bad in a way that is simply the reverse of the good breast; it is not everything that is awful and undesirable. To the contrary, the bad breast remains a breast, and therefore the potential source of all happiness and contentment. The bad breast is bad not because it is undesirable, but because it is unavailable. And, when (according to Klein) the infant projects his own aggression onto the bad (unavailable) breast, the (passively) bad breast becomes actively, maddeningly, maliciously, teasingly unavailable. The bad breast remains just out of reach, tantalizingly offering everything that the good breast offers, but sadistically refusing to give any of it.

> I remember, as a young therapist first working with adolescent gangsters, my bewilderment and frustration at their complete absence of guilt when it came to their "enemies." "These other kids that you call your enemies . . ." I would point out, "are kids like yourselves. They have mothers and fathers and girlfriends and maybe even babies of their own. They have their own hopes and fears. They are human beings no different from you." Invariably, I would be met with a bewildered look. "You don't understand," they would respond, "They are enemies." That was all there was to it. That was the beginning and the end of it. They were "enemies" and nothing more.

As the bad breast must be kept purely bad, so too must the good breast be held inviolate.

Among this same group of delinquent adolescents, the "good breast" was typically projected onto the person of the mother. I say "projected onto" with particular emphasis because the actual women who had given birth to these children rarely had done much to actually earn such a sobriquet. These teens were, by and large, the victims of horrendous maternal physical and verbal abuse, neglect and abandonment. Yet an unspoken rule among the teens during group therapy was, "Never speak ill of a mother!" When one of the group members would begin to get too close to feelings of bitterness and resentment pertaining to his childhood history, the group would be quick to respond, "Remember, your mother loves you!" The way in which this was said always had the quality of a warning or rebuke ("Don't go there! Take your anger elsewhere"), as much as of an effort to sooth or comfort.

Occasionally, one group member would have had such a horrific maternal relationship that he would not be able to turn his biological mother into a good breast. "*My* mother did not love me!" he would say defiantly to the group and would proceed to chronicle such a nightmarish litany of abuse that his statement would be indisputable. Interestingly, the group would usually listen to this passively and unchallengingly, seemingly undisturbed by such apparent blasphemy. What their sanguine acquiescence seemed to suggest was that they felt that their peer was talking about an entirely different kind of mother than the one they had otherwise felt such a strong need to defend. This was a bad-breast mother, and while they had some familiarity with it, it was completely different from, and unrelated to, the good-breast mothers that they had so fervently championed.

Melanie Klein saw splitting as originally resulting from a failure of integration. The infant, she thought, initially relates exclusively with its mother's breast. As it begins to be able to focus, it begins to relate to its mother's face. But Klein believed that at first the infant made no connection between the breast and the face. The recognition of the mother as a "whole object" was, she believed, at least in part an integrative developmental achievement. Only later, she believed, did splitting shift from a developmental stage to a defensive maneuver.

Ogden (1990) rejects the notion of an early failure of integration, citing modern infant research that strongly suggests that infants recognize the "wholeness" of external objects at a very early age. But like Klein, he does see a normal, biological precursor to the defensive aspects of splitting. The original (non-defensive) essence of splitting refers to our innate (neurologically determined) tendency to bifurcate: to see things in terms of good and bad, tall and short, fast and slow, fat and skinny, etc. Clinical splitting is a defense arising out of this innate tendency.

Ogden (1990) says that splitting – the defensive paradigm of the paranoid-schizoid position – is essential for the well-being of the child.

> The infant must be able to split in order to feed safely without the intrusion of anxiety that he is harming his mother, and without the

anxiety that she will harm him. It is necessary for the infant to feel that the mother who is taking care of him is fully loving and has no connection with the mother who "hurts" him by making him wait. The anxiety arising from the thought that the nurturing mother and the frustrating mother are one and the same would rob the infant of the security that he needs in order to feed safely. Similarly, the ability to desire safely would be lost if the infant, while feeding, experienced himself as the same infant who angrily wished to control and to subjugate the breast/mother in her absence. While feeding, the infant must experience himself as loving in an uncomplicated, uncontaminated way in order to feel that he can want without damaging.

Splitting not only safeguards the infant's need to give and receive love; it also safeguards his need to hate. If the object of the infant's hate is contaminated by facets of the loved object, the infant will not be able to hate it safely.

(p. 54)

Thus, the bad breast is not just the emotional price we pay for the existence of the good breast. The bad breast also serves the useful function of giving the infant a vehicle for unleashing its anger, rage, frustration, and aggression. Whether one believes that aggression is instinctual (as did Freud and Klein) or the result of frustration (as did Winnicott), anger, rage, and the desire to destroy are part of the infant's existence. With the good breast the infant can love purely and unambivalently, secure in the knowledge that what one loves is eternally loving, nurturing, and protecting. With the bad breast the infant can hate purely and unambivalently, secure in the knowledge that what it attempts to destroy has no redeeming virtues, no compensatory qualities, nothing for which the child's unmitigated hatred should produce *guilt*.

Ogden's assertions about what an infant "must" do in order to "feed safely" might seem a bit far-fetched. But I have seen that very scenario enacted in my office.

> Sharon was an adolescent girl with whom I had worked during two lengthy stays in residential treatment. After her first stay she was disastrously released to the custody of her severely disturbed mother. During her second stay she made her mother into the bad object and her grandparents into the good objects. There was enough objective

reality in this split that we went along with it and she was released the second time to the custody of these well-meaning but old caretakers. I continued to see Sharon both individually and with her grandparents on an outpatient basis.

Sharon's split quickly flipped. Her grandfather, who was showing signs of mild dementia, quickly began to drive her crazy with his forgetfulness and his repetitions. Her grandmother, who was genuinely loving, could nevertheless be mean and sarcastic when she was annoyed, and Sharon was frequently annoying. The grandparents became the bad objects and her mother was resurrected as the good object.

In one family session she initially sat fuming: arms crossed, head down, the classic picture of defiance and intransigence. Then, suddenly, with clear anxiety and moist eyes she turned to her grandmother. "The other day you brought home those cookies with sprinkles on them that I used to love when I was little and I thought 'Oh my god she does still love me,' and then I remembered all the mean things you said to me and I got so confused."

I believe that with some reflection most of us can conjure up memories of the pleasure of pure love and, for that matter, of pure hate. The former of the two, the pure love, is what I refer to as "being in love" with someone (as opposed to "loving" someone which a depressive position process). When we are "in love" with someone (a paranoid-schizoid position process) we see nothing but wonderfulness in them. Romantic songs are full of lyrics like this. "Loving" a person (as opposed to being in love with a person) means maintaining a similar passion, positive regard, and affection while at the same time being cognizant of the love-object's flaws, blemishes, and defects. Discussions of a therapist's "love" for his or her clients need to keep this distinction clearly in focus. I believe that it is perfectly appropriate (perhaps even necessary) for a therapist to feel some kind of depressive position love for his or her clients. But being "in love" with a client is a sure recipe for disaster.

I (briefly) saw a client who had emerged out of an horrendous childhood with a schizophrenic mother; a cold, aloof, distant father; and a bipolar brother, into a seemingly healthy adulthood marked by a successful career in poverty law. I was dazzled by this young woman. People with childhoods like that are not supposed to be so healthy, so successful, so put-together. How had she done it? I was in awe.

The client terminated after our second session and as soon as she did, I realized that she was right to have done so. I was in danger of being "in love" with this client rather than simply loving her – I was in danger of being *dazzled* by her and being "dazzled" means being blinded. And I suspect that at some level she sensed this. And on some level she knew that she did not need to be looked at by eyes that "can never see"; she needed to be *seen*. And she needed to be seen not as a *good object* but rather as a *whole object*. She was correct to terminate with me and to find another therapist who could see her more *objectively* – more as a whole person.

Splitting is the *sine qua non* of Melanie Klein's "paranoid-schizoid position." When one splits, one is in the paranoid-schizoid position. When one does not split, one is in the depressive position. This is an either/or situation. One either splits or one does not; there is no in between position (although there is a dialectic tension between the positions: a relentless shifting back and forth between them, sometimes quite rapidly). The fact that Klein gave splitting such a pivotal role in her conceptual schema speaks to its clinical importance as well.

Splitting is often misunderstood as an interpersonal event rather than an intrapsychic one. Splitting can end up being interpersonal: when one facet of a split object, one part object, gets projected onto an external object, then that external object is seen as, and related to as, an all good or an all bad part object. If one external object gets seen as the good breast, then another external object has the misfortune of becoming the bad.

But as destructive as splitting can be for interpersonal relationships, splitting *per se* is an intrapsychic process. Splitting is driven by what might be called an emotional deficit: the inability to tolerate ambivalence and the resulting need to love purely and to hate purely. But the act of splitting creates in its wake a complex network of cognitive distortions that nevertheless fit together into an organized and systematic pattern of thought, a *logic* of splitting. Cognitive Behavioral therapists who attempt to "correct" cognitive distortions miss, to my mind, the extent to which these distortions are interrelated and interdependent. To give up one cognitive distortion may require giving up an entire logical system.

The logic of splitting I: the undoing of history

The first[2] thing that we can see happening with splitting is that history is undone. This, in fact, is the whole purpose of splitting. Let me present a "mythological" scene – an archetypal scene – a scene of "The First Split."

The infant is at the breast nursing happily. All is right with the world. He is in the presence of the Breast, for whom he has nothing but love and from whom he can expect nothing but bounty. When, however, in his passion, he inadvertently bites down too hard on the nipple, the Breast is likely to be suddenly removed, the lullaby that was being sung softly in his ear is likely to be replaced by a startling yelp of pain, and, in some cultures, the withdrawal of the breast may be followed by an instructive knuckle on the top of his skull.

What is the infant to make of all of this? It cannot be that the breast has suddenly become withholding; that is not in the nature of breasts. Nor can it be that the breast has decided to suddenly frighten him with a loud yelp. That is not in the nature of breasts either. And it cannot possibly be that he, even inadvertently, has hurt the beloved breast thus causing this aberrant behavior. To hurt a breast is unthinkable. Breasts exist to be adored, not hurt. The "logical" explanation is that there must be two breasts, one good and one bad. What must have happened is that the Good Breast suddenly disappeared and in its stead the Bad Breast suddenly appeared. This allows the infant to go on adoring and trusting the (good) breast while, at the same time, allows for the creation of an object (the bad breast) upon which all frustrations can be blamed and towards which all rage and aggression may safely be directed.

Thus the infant *undoes history*; cause and effect are abrogated. The historical perspective (happy infant accidentally bites breast which causes it to be withdrawn in pain) is replaced by an ahistorical perspective (good breast suddenly and randomly disappears; bad breast suddenly and randomly appears in its place). If the paranoid-schizoid position can be said to be defined by splitting, it might well be renamed as the "Ahistorical Position."

This is not to say that dwellers in the paranoid-schizoid position cannot provide an accurate chronology of their lives. But a chronology is different from a history. A chronology is a listing of events, perhaps random, unrelated events, each of which happened at a certain time, and thus happened in a certain order. A chronology is discontinuous. It is a list rather than a paragraph. A history is continuous. It is a seamless flowing together of events, each connected to the others by some kind of web of cause and effect. A history is a narrative; it is above all, a construction.

I was co-leading a therapy group of delinquent girls when my co-leader introduced a "group task" to one of the sessions. The task was simple: "Take a piece of paper and write down three events in your lives that changed who you are."

What amazed me was not their inability to follow the instruction, but their seeming inability even to *comprehend* them. "Wait a minute, Ms. W." they would protest, "Three things that did what?" Finally, one of the more psychologically astute of the girl said, "I think I know what she means. I was raped and so now I am afraid to walk by dark alleys."

Now these were high school aged girls and they were far from stupid. Furthermore, *all* of them had had numerous "life-changing" events: rapes, abuse, abandonments, etc. The reason they could not comprehend the task is that the task involved the creation of a history and these girls were all locked essentially in the paranoid-schizoid position. If the task had been "Write down three traumatic events that happened in your lives and the order in which they occurred," then none of the girls would have had a problem. But the task involved an attribution of *cause and effect*: "Tell me events that caused you to be different from who you were before or from whom you might other- wise have become." This was beyond their comprehension as long as their comprehension was structured in a paranoid-schizoid framework.

This is not to say that people in the paranoid-schizoid position do not *understand* cause and effect. We are not speaking here of a "developmen- tal delay" or of a "cognitive impairment." It is rather that they have no use for it (or, more accurately, are motivated not to use it). It is like a carpenter who has a certain tool which he knows to be useful but which for some reason he dislikes. If you ask him about it he can accurately describe it and its uses. But otherwise he keeps it high up on some back shelf, out of sight and out of mind.

People in the paranoid-schizoid position will also often speak using lan- guage that gives the *appearance* of depressive position thinking. When asked to justify an act of aggression, a young gangster might easily say something like. "I hit him because he made me mad." Does this sentence necessarily imply the use of cause and effect? Not necessarily.

The sentence, "He made me mad" may imply an awareness of cause and effect and it may not. If the specific incident being referred to as the "cause" is being taken out of its context of a long series of mutual provo- cations, then *history* is certainly being undone even as it is being verbally referred to. But it is the *experience* rather than the *words* that is important.

I was leading a group of delinquent girls early in my career, before I had much sensitivity to gang culture. One girl was working on why she had been cross and irritable for several days. I had naively asked her what she knew about her "crabbiness" when I was shocked and bewildered to see her suddenly go rigid, begin to turn red, and stare straight ahead in silence, while her best friend exclaimed anxiously, "Ooooh my god! Ooooh my god!" I quickly realized my blunder. The girl was from a Crip gang and I had inadvertently used the ritual term to disrespect ("diss") Crips, which is "crab."

More annoyed with the group than upset with myself, I told the group briskly to get itself together and then addressed the young girl. "You know," I said to her, "that I had no intention of disrespecting you. You know that I like and respect you. You know that I am still unfamiliar with the gang culture. To your thinking, I am almost from a different world as you. So, let's forget that that word was used and go on with your work." The group calmed down, the girl relaxed, and the work was resumed.

Everything I said was true. The girl had known all of the above, yet it had been irrelevant to her. She had never had the idea that I was purposefully "disrespecting" her. Rather, her *experience* was that an evil, magical word had been uttered and that that word had magically transported her to a place of murderous rage. My explanation to her was not to tell her anything she did not already know. It was to remind her that words have an historical context and that that historical context matters. It was spoken out of the depressive (historical) position, to someone locked in the paranoid-schizoid (ahistorical) position.

The delinquent teens I worked with at the Center were often accused of being disingenuous when they would deny knowing the "whys" of things: why were they kicked out of class, why did they receive a certain punishment, why were they singled out for a certain honor? Some even denied knowing why they got locked up. But they were not lying, or even covering up. If they were asked for a chronology of events that happened before the event in question, they could provide a full and accurate list, usually including the crucial variables being asked for. It is more that the question of "why" itself does not make sense in the paranoid-schizoid position. The question "why" demands a response framed in terms of causality that is simply not part of the paranoid-schizoid way of thinking.

Listening from a depressive position (historical) perspective to someone speaking out of a paranoid-schizoid position can often be disconcerting. A teen from the Center would come to my office enraged at having been kicked out of school. "Why were you kicked out?" I would ask. "No reason at all!" was the shouted reply. Again I would reframe my question in terms of chronology instead of a causality, and the "reason" would immediately be apparent: he had been disruptive, he had been asleep, he had refused to do his work. The "obviousness" of the answer to my question distracted me from cognizance that my question itself made little sense from the paranoid-schizoid position of most of my clients.

This is not to say that we should never confront our paranoid-schizoid clients with issues of causality. Winnicott (1949) says that every time we make an interpretation, we are speaking to our clients out of the depressive position in a way that provides a connection (a causality) that the client, in the paranoid-schizoid position, cannot (chooses not to) provide. But it should be remembered that our clients will move from the paranoid-schizoid position into the depressive position when (with our help) they are ready to. Until that point, we need to be prepared to make the constant linguistic translations that are required for communication between the positions.

Ogden (1990) writes about how he is always "stunned" (p. 62) to experience an apparent historical flow crumble in front of him into a disjointed chronology. I can attest to this.

Bill, a paranoid psychotic, was in therapy with me for nearly two years. Bill had an encapsulated delusional system in which he believed he was being bugged and his words and movements monitored by a nebulous group with unclear motives. Bill had terminated with his former therapist when he began to believe that the therapist's office had been bugged.

For some reason my office, and our work together, were never contaminated by Bill's delusional system and for many months we worked well together. Bill was extremely concrete in his thinking, but very intelligent and over the months we both noted steady improvement.

Then, one day, I made a mistake. From my (depressive position) perspective, it was a minor mistake. From Bill's (paranoid-schizoid position) perspective, it was cataclysmic. In the middle of a session Bill remarked that he had been thinking about something I had said several weeks ago. When I asked him what it was I was struck that I had no memory of saying such a thing and, more importantly, that it was something I was unlikely to have said since it was not something I actually believed. The mistake I made was to tell Bill that I suspected that he had heard me wrong.

From my depressive (historical) position perspective, such things are commonplace. History is a construction, and memory is an infirm foundation upon which to construct anything. Furthermore, as a construction, history is subject to different attributions of meaning. Bill may indeed have heard and remembered my words accurately, but he may have ascribed an entirely different meaning to them than I had intended.

But from Bill's paranoid-schizoid (ahistorical) perspective the past is a series of immutable facts, each of which inherently means what it means. If Bill had a memory of something, then his memory was factual. For me to deny having said what he remembered me saying was tantamount to me lying. Then to make matters even worse, by implying that *he* may have remembered it incorrectly, I was covering up my own lie by accusing him of lying. Not only (from his perspective) did I tell a lie, I then accused him of being the liar.

For me, in the historical depressive position, the only "logical" thing to do was to talk about the misunderstanding and try and clear it up.

But Bill, in the ahistorical paranoid-schizoid position operated under an entirely different system of "logic." From Bill's perspective, he had just been lied to by his previously trusted therapist who then made matters even worse by accusing Bill of being the one doing the lying. From *any* system of logic if one suddenly realizes that one has a lying and manipulative therapist there is only one logical course of action: to get the hell out.

And that's what Bill did. I spent a few weeks desperately trying to backpedal, and Bill had just enough sense of history to spend those weeks valiantly trying to come to terms with what had happened, but in the end he was unable to make any sense of it beyond the framework of his logical system, and I was forced to refer him to another therapist. But I still cannot think back on this case without shouting in my mind, "Bill, it's me! Don't you know me by now? Don't you remember all the work we've done together? Don't you remember all the struggles we've gone through together?" But for Bill there was no "me" or, at least, no single me. There were two me's. There was me the good therapist that he worked productively with for nearly two years. And then there was the me who was suddenly revealed to be a liar and a fraud and from whom he (logically) had to escape.

I am tempted to say that the renunciation of history is a logical consequence of splitting, but this misses the point. A loss of history is a facet of (part of) splitting more than it is a consequence of (follows from) splitting. To split is to renounce history as much as it is to renounce ambivalence.

History and memory

A sense of history is necessary for any kind of meaningful and useful self-understanding. A sense of history enables one to say, "This is who I have become" as opposed to simply, "This is who I am." "This is who I am" is experienced as being carved in stone, immutable. "This is who I have become" implies I have changed and evolved over time and therefore I can continue to change and evolve (in whatever direction I choose) in the future.

But the experience of history is crucial in another way as well: the experience of history, in a way, makes *memory* possible. History, as I have said, is the experience of a continuous flow of events, made continuous by the web-like interaction of cause and effect. The awareness of cause and effect creates a sense of *agency*, of empowerment. "If I can alter the network of causes affecting my life, I can alter the outcome." But the fact that history is a *continuous flow* is also crucial. History not only allows us to hope for change in the future, it allows for a crucial recognition of change from the past. "I am not the same person I was when I was abused, abandoned, shamed, shunned. I am different now. I am bigger, stronger, smarter, more autonomous, less alone. I can *remember* what it was like to be that earlier version of myself, and that memory may well contain a powerful residue of the original affect. But as long as I am remembering (as opposed to reliving), I know, at a fundamental level, that I am not back there, I am not that helpless, frightened, humiliated child."

If, as in the paranoid-schizoid position, the past is experienced as discontinuous, as a chronology instead of as history, then one has no such experience of ever having grown, developed, or evolved in a way that allows one to feel *related to, but distant from*, the person that one used to be.

> When I first began working with delinquent teens at the Center over 20 years ago I was struck by their use of the term "flashback." They would emerge from their rooms, upset, and announce, "I was in my room having flashbacks." Why this word, I wondered, instead of "thinking back" or "remembering." I was aware of the term being used in severe drug withdrawal or in severe PTSD. But these kids were experiencing neither. Maybe, I thought, it was just a gangster term borrowed from drug users.
>
> What I finally decided was that "flashback" was an accurate description of their experiences. Alone in their rooms they did not have the experience of "remembering"; their experience was of "reliving." It was as though no time had elapsed since the event they had been

reliving. Or, more accurately, time had elapsed but "history" had not. Time, being experienced as disjointed, provided no distance, no perspective, no comfort.

I believe that this has profound implications on how we do therapy. The teens at the Center used to plead not to be made to talk about their pasts. "Please," they would beg, "don't make me go there." I spent a lot if time thinking of ways to persuade them. "The past is like a pit bull," I responded. "You may think it's leaving you alone then all of a sudden it will sneak up from behind and bite you in the ass. And when it sinks its teeth in it won't let go." My young clients listened dubiously: intrigued but far from convinced. I now believe that they were right, that I may have done them a serious disservice by pushing them to deal with past traumas before they were ready, risking even re-traumatizing them.

We do our clients a disservice by asking them to explore a past that they experience as a chronology rather than a history. We do them a disservice by asking them to remember when all they can do is relive. We can only be helpful to our clients if our efforts are focused on easing them out of the paranoid-schizoid position and into the depressive position where history and self-reflection have meaning.

The logic of splitting II: the denial of responsibility

If history is rejected as part of splitting, then so too is responsibility. If we go back to our archetypal myth of the "First Split," we remember that the infant cannot or will not accept the interpretation (attribution of meaning) that "I have just bitten the nipple I love and as a result it has withdrawn from me and turned against me." Instead, to the infant, the "good breast" has randomly disappeared and the "bad breast" (unrelated to the good breast) has randomly taken its place. History has been undone and, in the process, so has responsibility. Or, as seems more likely from the myth, responsibility has been undone and along with it went history. Both, in any case, go together.

The staff at the Center frequently ranted against the residents' "refusal to accept responsibility." But I believe it is more accurate to say that it wasn't that they "refused" to accept responsibility but rather that they did not *experience* responsibility. Often this was hard for even me to accept.

Mindy, a girl at the Center, of whom I was particularly fond, was a "cutter." She cut herself only when she was upset, but cutting followed her being upset as night follows day – and this was her experience.

I was called to her unit one day when she had found a sharp object and used it to try to turn her forearm into hamburger meat. As I was walking her to the nurse's station, I made some remarks to her that were not entirely "therapeutic." "Why the Hell did you do this to yourself?" I shouted. By this time, cool as a cucumber, she replied, "Dr. Brodie, shit happens!" "No," I countered, "this didn't just happen. You did this to yourself!"

But that was not her experience. Her experience was of something quite mechanical, something almost unrelated to *her* (certainly to her as an agent: someone who would *do* the cutting). Her experience was something like: disappointing things happen . . . followed by upset happens . . . followed by cutting happens. She experienced a chronology of events rather than a history of events. And without history (causality) responsibility does not exist.

The logic of splitting III: the experience of self as object

As the example at the end of the preceding section demonstrates, if one experiences no sense of *responsibility*, then one experiences no sense of *agency*. Mindy's *behavior* was to cut herself. But her *experience* was that cutting was something that simply happened to her: it was part of the inevitable cycle of life in which she was caught. In modern intersubjectivity theory, this is referred to as the *experience of self as object* as opposed to the *experience of self as subject*. The emphasis here is on the word "experience." People in the paranoid-schizoid position are in fact as much agents as anyone in the depressive position, but they do not experience themselves that way. I have taken to seeing Mindy's statement to me as a kind of credo for the entire paranoid-schizoid position: "Shit Happens!"

If we return to our increasingly overburdened myth of the infant biting the breast, we see that once the infant has split, it cannot experience itself as an agent, as one who does things that have consequences. The infant cannot have the experience of, "Dang! I just bit the breast that I love and that was feeding me and in doing so I caused it pain. I am so sorry!" Rather, the infant's post-splitting experience would be, "Wow! I was just blissed-out in the presence of my beloved Good Breast and suddenly Good Breast disappeared and horrible Bad Breast appeared in its place. Shit happens!"

Thus, in the paranoid-schizoid position one does not have the experience of agency. You can go through life, take care of business, do your job, raise a family, do everything expected in life, but not have the sense that you are in charge of your life. Instead, you feel that, somehow, life is happening to you. Ogden (1990) calls this "being lived by your experience."

In the psychotherapy office clients like this often present as storytellers, storytellers who have a range of skillsets. Some are quite entertaining dramatists who have all the affects down pat. Others drone on monotonously, sounding vaguely as though they are telling a story about someone else. And in a way, from their ahistorical perspective, they are. But in both cases the therapist will, after a while, need to interrupt the seamless stream of stories and say, "But where are *you* in all of this?" To this question the client will respond with a mixture of confusion and annoyance. "What are you talking about?" they will ask, "I've been talking about myself the whole time. Are you saying I'm doing it wrong?" The "myself" in this statement refers to the *object* to whom all of these events happened. In the paranoid-schizoid position the answer to the question, "Who am I?" is, "I am the sum total of everything that has ever happened to me. And nothing more."

The delinquent teenagers I worked with called these "war stories" and they were usually about harrowing gang experiences. The staff would strongly discourage such stories as they were seen as glorifying the gang culture. But to the kids being told they couldn't tell war stories was like being told that they couldn't talk about themselves. In contrast, I remember being incredibly struck by an older girl in the Center, very smart and one who had grown tremendously in the program, saying to a new girl, "You've got to stop telling war stories and get in touch with your feelings!" What she was saying, translated into object relations terms, was, "You've got to stop defining yourself by what happened to you and find out who you really are!"

But it is not just teenage gang members who experience themselves as objects.

> Sandra was an in-house attorney working for a large business. She was a good lawyer primarily because she was intelligent and she was terrified of making mistakes. Otherwise, she had no interest in her work nor in the law. She had become a lawyer, she said, because she knew she "didn't want to be a doctor." It would be incorrect to say that she then *chose* the lesser of two evils. In Sandra's (paranoid-schizoid) experience, rather, it was that she "didn't have a choice."
>
> As I worked with Sandra it became increasingly clear that this sense of not having a choice was paradigmatic in her life. She had worked hard in school, gotten into a prestigious law school where

she continued to work hard because, "That's what you do!" She had worked as a trial lawyer until the tension became unbearable and she made a career shift. Again, she did not experience this as a choice but rather as something she "had to do." Extremely unhappy in her current position, she was waiting until that too became unbearable. At that point she would again leave, and would again do so without the experience of having made a choice. The same was true of her relationships. She would start to date a man she didn't really like but then find herself unable to leave him, waiting instead for him to leave her.

Subjectivity and the attribution of meaning

Throughout his body of work Thomas Ogden makes a crucial observation about the achievement of subjectivity. Ogden writes that one of the most important aspects of subjectivity, of the awareness of one's agency, is the awareness of oneself as creator of meaning. Prior to the achievement of this awareness, in the paranoid-schizoid position, one experiences oneself as an object without the power or agency to create (attribute) meaning. Instead, meaning is experienced as residing in, being inherent in, the external object or action itself. Something is beautiful because it is inherently beautiful, not because of idiosyncratic taste or standards of beauty. If someone else fails to recognize the beauty of said object it is because of some inadequacy in that person, not because of differences in standards. If a thing frightens us it is because the thing is "frightening," not because one happens to be "afraid of it." If I am attracted to something it is because that thing is "attractive," not because I have a particular personal valence towards it. If someone else is not attracted to it, it is because he or she is "blind" to its attractions. In the current slang, "It is what it is."

In the depressive position one recognizes the subjectivity of value, attraction, taste, and meaning. One recognizes that a tarantula or a snake, to use an extreme example, may be an object of beauty and fascination to one person and an object of fear and loathing to another and, more importantly, that none of those qualities is inherent in the animal itself. The pursuit of money will be to one person the only sensible thing to do and, to another, the "root of all evil." To be sure, one will always be tempted to pronounce one wine "superior" to another, or one movie "good" and another "bad." But in the depressive position (or, perhaps it is more accurate to say, *returning to* the depressive position) one will quickly acknowledge that these are not inherent qualities but rather subjective valuations or meanings.

Why is this important? On a superficial level, the depressive position allows for tolerance while the paranoid-schizoid position is inherently intolerant. In the paranoid-schizoid position if I attribute a certain meaning to something then my experience will be that I have recognized something's intrinsic meaning, I have recognized it for what it is. If someone else attributes a different meaning to that thing, they are simply wrong. If someone else has a different religion than I, a different experience of right or wrong, a different opinion of a political issue, then they are simply *wrong*. They are not judged either stupid, ignorant, or demonically possessed, but they are simply wrong. And the reader will recognize that that is the experience of a great many people.

On a deeper level the recognition of self as the attributer of meaning allows for recognition of the distinction between self and other. This, to my mind, is the crux of what Ogden is saying. The statement, "I am the creator of my own meaning" is only an incomplete part of a more complex statement: "I am the creator of my own meaning as opposed to all the other meanings created by other people." I believe that the implications of this are huge. What Ogden seems to be implying is that the discovery of the self (of one's own subjectivity) and the discovery of the other (as subject) happen simultaneously. One discovers the other as one discovers oneself and one discovers oneself as one discovers the other. The implications of this for group therapy, and for intersubjective or relational forms of individual psychotherapy, are manifold.

Ever since Freud invented psychoanalysis it has been recognized that a successful outcome is marked by the *resolution of the transference*. But for Freud the resolution of the transference and the discovery of the "real" analyst or therapist are only incidentally related. For Freud, the resolution of the transference meant the resolution of the neurosis and therefore the end of the treatment. The discovery of the real therapist is essentially irrelevant.

But for Ogden, based on the foundation of Winnicott, the discovery of the self cannot happen independently of the discovery of the other. They are one-and-the-same discovery. Thus, in individual therapy, one cannot discover who one is without in some way discovering who one's therapist is. In group therapy, when one sees a fellow group member for who he or she is rather than as a container of one's projections, when one recognizes that he or she is a subject rather than an object, then one simultaneously is freed from one's own script in one's internal object relationships and one discovers one's own subjectivity.

And it doesn't really matter from which direction one approaches the same conclusion. If I finally recognize that a female group member is not my critical, abandoning mother but instead is simply a frightened, depressed woman, then I am in that moment liberated from my own role as a helpless, dependent child. If, from the other direction, I learn that I am powerful, intelligent, and competent in relation to this woman, then she is freed from the burden of carrying my maternal projections. In either case the result is the same, and in either case the two learnings happen simultaneously. This does not mean, of course, that individual therapy should be about the client learning who his or her therapist really is. But as will be discussed later on in the section on intersubjectivity (see Chapter 9), the client always has all the relevant information about the therapist. It is just a matter of recognizing it.

The logic of splitting IV: concrete thinking

If I experience myself as an object, if I fail to recognize myself as the creator of meaning, if I assume that meaning is intrinsic to the object or action itself, then I will show a kind of thinking that is remarkably concrete. Again, the phrase, "It is what it is!" is prototypical. If *meaning* is defined externally, then there is really no need for introspection. Why waste time pondering why a certain event, a certain person, or an incident has particular meaning for you when meaning is completely external to you?

This makes for an odd kind of psychotherapy. Psychodynamic psychotherapy has always revolved around the analysis of meaning. What is the meaning of a dream, of a symptom, of a slip of the tongue, or, for that matter, of the therapeutic relationship itself? Different branches of psychodynamic theory attribute meaning in different ways. For Freud, meaning was understood in terms of sexuality. Jung understood things in terms of archetypes. Meaning for Klein was understood in terms of the conflict between the life instinct and the death instinct and Adler attributed meaning around the issue of power. The common denominator is the focus on meaning in whatever parameters it is looked at. When a client has no concept of internally constructed meaning, psychodynamic psychotherapy becomes problematic.

> My client Bill was presented earlier in this chapter as the client who terminated therapy when a mistake I made transformed me from the Good Therapist into the Bad Therapist. When Bill first came in to therapy, he decided, on his own, that I should have all the information about him that I would need and for the first six sessions I said almost nothing as he gave me a very complete history. By the second month

our work became more interactive, but it never really became *work* in the psychodynamic sense of the word.

Bill would talk and I would mostly listen, until he happened to say something that caught my attention, usually something that raised questions (in my mind) about meaning. "I wonder . . ." I would say, in reference to whatever had caught my attention. But "wondering" was not in Bill's nature. Bill would react very patiently to my questions. He would digress from what otherwise seemed like a prepared speech and go to great lengths to *explain* to me whatever it was that I had not understood. At the end of each long and detailed explanation he would ask, "Do you understand now?" Utterly defeated, I would nod meekly, "Yes, Bill, thank you!"

Bill's DSM diagnosis would most likely have been paranoid schizophrenia. But this kind of concrete thinking can easily be seen in much higher functioning people.

Dan was a clinical psychologist in a process group I belonged to many years ago. Dan was known as being very schizoid and in one session the group was encouraging him to do some work on this. Dan responded much as Bill had, with an eagerly given explanation that attempted to provide answers while raising no questions. "You have to understand my mother," he explained. "After she and my dad divorced, I remember driving away from home with her and she turned to me and said, 'You are my kid now!'"

I asked Dan what he understood her to have meant by that statement. I, myself, could think of a number of different messages she may have been trying to convey: "You are my responsibility now." "I own you now." Or, "It's you and me now, kid." But Dan looked at me blankly, as though he didn't understand my question. Hadn't I heard him? The meaning, to him, was inherent in the words themselves. There was no question of interpretation.

At some times the concreteness of the thinking can approach a "thought disorder."

Max, a young professional, reported to me a conversation he had had with his older sister, Rachael, who was visiting from out of town. Rachael was somewhat infamous in his family, for her tendency to split. Near the end of an evening marked by some tension, the following words were exchanged:

RACHAEL: "Max, I want to know why you hate me."
MAX: "Rachael, I simply don't hate you."
RACHAEL: "Are you calling me a liar?"

Max was so flummoxed by this second question that he was speechless, completely unaware of how to respond. Indeed, from depressive position logic the conversation makes no sense. But from the paranoid-schizoid position, in the logic of splitting, Rachael's reasoning makes perfect sense.

In the logic of splitting there is no multiplicity of meanings. There is only a single meaning, inherent in the thing itself, and that meaning must therefore be the "true" meaning. Since Rachael perceived Max as hating her, that perception must therefore be true. And again, since there is only one truth (one meaning), Max's disputing Rachael's truth (*the* truth) could only mean that he was calling her a liar.

The frustrations with concrete thinking in the paranoid-schizoid are another of the reasons why Winnicott (1968a) says that, by the end of his career, he had essentially stopped making interpretations to clients when they were still in the paranoid-schizoid position.

Another facet of the paranoid-schizoid position, another facet of splitting, is that people in the paranoid-schizoid position display no curiosity. Indeed, there is no place for curiosity in the paranoid-schizoid position. Under the logic of splitting things are what they are. The meaning of things or events is inherent in the things or events themselves and, therefore, self-evident ("It is what it is!"). Splitting has undone cause and effect and, therefore, part-objects come and go randomly; events happen randomly. History has been undone, so an historical analysis of anything makes no sense. The past has no relationship to the present and the future is unknowable. So what is there to be curious about? And, if one isn't curious, one doesn't think.

This lack of curiosity can often be hugely frustrating for the "insight oriented" therapist. A therapist's line of questioning or attempt to make connections will frequently be met with by, "So, why are we talking about this?" or, "So, what is your point?"

One of my first clients was an impoverished woman who came into treatment because of "depression." "Okay," I said to her, "So what is going on in your life?" "Well," she answered, "my husband has been unemployed for months and he just sits in front of the TV drinking beer. My teenage son is in a gang. My daughter dresses like a slut, is promiscuous, and uses a lot of drugs." Then she stopped herself. "Wait a minute! Why are we talking about all of this stuff? We are here to talk about my depression."

People who live predominantly in the paranoid-schizoid position often seem (annoyingly) to have all the answers. But it's not that they have all the answers, it's that they have no questions. And if one has no questions, there is really no reason to think (or anything to think about). There are of course "facts" in the paranoid-schizoid position, and facts and data can be noticed or ignored, valued or not, but data will remain always and forever just data until we get curious about it and therefore start to think about it. "What does this data mean?" "What is this data telling us?"

Lucy, a severely depressed, relentlessly self-hating woman in her mid-thirties, presented with an almost complete absence of curiosity and, although she was highly educated, seemingly without much thinking. In moments of stress in our early sessions Lucy would retreat into a trance-like dissociative state. When she recovered, I would ask her what had been going on in her mind during those episodes. "Nothing!" she would respond matter-of-factly.

When I would "wonder" out loud about something Lucy had said that puzzled me, Lucy would say, in the small voice of a schoolgirl who had been caught unprepared for a quiz, "I am afraid I don't have an answer for that." At first I thought that this was some kind of hostile projection on Lucy's part, that I was being made into a critical parent. But I eventually came to see it as simply the concreteness of her thinking.

During the first months of therapy she talked about her highly critical, verbally abusive adoptive mother. This mother had given the clear message that she could love Lucy "if only Lucy could be perfect." This would have been an impossible enough task for any child, but Lucy had been born with some physical deformities that made her feel doubly inadequate, doubly hopeless.

After a few months of therapy Lucy trusted me enough to share another aspect of her story with me, something she had never told anyone before. Lucy remembered looking to her adoptive father for support during her mother's verbal assaults, only to see the man looking at her apologetically and then look away. Then, one evening when

Lucy was ten or eleven, he came to her, not to support her, but to rape her. Between then and when Lucy left home for college at 18 her father would sexually assault her every time her mother was out of the house. I remember asking Lucy what her memory was of that first assault and she answered with a single word: "Pain!"

This second revelation helped me further understand Lucy's relentless self-hatred. A verbally abusive mother and a sexually abusive father: yes, this would explain self-hatred. But somehow, for me, it didn't. There was something so untouchable in Lucy's self-hatred, so relentlessly determined, that I was left still feeling puzzled.

Then, about a year into therapy, Lucy suddenly retrieved a repressed memory. The incestuous relationship with her father had been a secret but never repressed memory. But this one was suddenly, though clearly, remembered in a therapy session. The memory was of herself at age three, being picked up by her older adoptive brother, who would then have been in his early twenties, and taken away in his camper for a weekend getaway. During these weekend getaways Lucy would be subjected to unspeakable perverted and sadistic sexual abuse. Suddenly Lucy made sense to me. Of course her self-loathing was intractable! For her entire childhood she had been treated as a kind of human toilet, into which the most important men in her life would discharge their most vile impulses.

Then, a few sessions after this revelation, Lucy spontaneously asked the following question: "I wonder if my father knew what my brother was doing?" I nearly fell out of my chair. For a year all of my "wonderings" had been met by the same incurious wall. Now here was Lucy wondering for herself! Lucy had discovered curiosity and with that discovery, she began to think.

I believe that what had happened was that the same thing that had helped me emotionally understand Lucy had helped her understand herself. Lucy's splitting had been undone. She had developed a sense of *history*. No longer did she see herself as a horrible, nasty little girl but instead as a little girl to whom horrible, nasty things had been done. No longer was her vileness a quality that was intrinsic to herself. Instead it was a *meaning* that she had *attributed* to herself that had previously helped her make sense out of her life.

The logic of splitting V: belief in a just world

If the purpose of splitting is to deny any connectedness between Good and Bad, then the two must be kept in entirely separate realms. This means that good must be protected from all bad, and bad must be kept separate from all good. Bad things cannot happen to good objects and good things cannot happen to bad objects. If bad things happen to an object then the object must be bad, and if good things happen to an object then the object must be good. The paranoid-schizoid world is, ironically, a completely just world.

In 1981 a rabbi named Harold Kushner wrote a book called *When Bad Things Happen to Good People* about his crisis in faith following the death of his son from Tay Sachs disease. This book could only have been written out of the depressive position. Bad things do not happen to good people in the paranoid-schizoid position. If something bad happens to you it means that you are bad. The paranoid-schizoid world is a just world. Everyone gets what they deserve and, therefore, if you get something you must deserve it.

> One of the most chilling things about working with delinquent (gangster) teens was that peculiar sense of justice: if something happened to somebody it was because it was deserved. I would challenge them about "drive-by" shootings. "What if you accidentally kill an innocent person instead of one of your enemies?" "Well," they would respond coldly, "then they were in the wrong place at the wrong time." This did not appear to be a simple indifference to the fate of others. Nor did it seem to be an expression of paranoid-schizoid fatalism (Shit Happens!). Rather, it was fairly clearly a moral judgment. If something happens to you, you must deserve it. Being in the wrong place at the wrong time means you are bad. Being bad means you deserve to die.
>
> The flip side of such cold moral absolutism was the rage and protest we would hear when some of these same kids were told they had misbehaved. The kids who were in open rebellion to the program and who were self-described as "bad" would accept our negative judgments with equanimity. It was the ones who were doing well who would flip out at any negative feedback. It was the kids who had "turned themselves around," who were following the rules, advancing up the merit ladder, who, at the slightest misstep, fly into a destructive rage that would momentarily undo all the progress they had made. From a depressive position perspective it was incomprehensible that an insignificant consequence given for a minor rule infraction should have produced such a powerful reaction. But from a paranoid-schizoid perspective (in the logic of splitting) it made sense.
>
> In the paranoid-schizoid position if you are being told you are doing well, if you are being rewarded for doing well, then you are good. If you are told you did something bad (however slight) and are being

punished (however mildly) then you are bad. And there are no degrees or gradations of good and bad. If you are good you are good and if you are bad you are bad. There is nothing in between. So, for a child who has been told for months that he is "good," suddenly perceives himself as being told he is "bad," this is literally crazy-making.

The paranoid-schizoid belief in a just world should not be confused with a more depressive position faith that justice will eventually prevail. A karma-style belief that the evil you do in the world will eventually catch up with you and the good you do in the world will eventually be rewarded is very much a depressive position function. A belief in karma implies that there is good and evil in each of us and that it is the balance between them that is important. This way of thinking is anathema to the all-or-nothing, splitting-based logic of the paranoid-schizoid position.

In the depressive position the qualities of good or bad are considered to be value judgments, *meanings* attributed to objects or actions. But in the paranoid-schizoid position good and bad are seen as qualities intrinsic to the objects or events themselves. As a value judgment or an attribution of meaning, good and bad in the depressive position are considered to be independent of consequences. Sometimes good is rewarded; sometimes it is not. Sometimes bad is recognized and punished; sometimes it is not. In the splitting-based paranoid-schizoid position good and bad are qualities inherent in the things themselves and, paradoxically, are qualities that are *revealed* by the consequences they receive. Thus qualities of good and bad are revealed truths rather than constructed judgments. But lest I sound too judgmental myself about the moral absolutism of the paranoid-schizoid position let me remind the reader that this is pretty much how children are taught right from wrong. A child learns that something is "right" because he is praised or rewarded for it. A child learns that something is "wrong" (the use of a swear word, for example) because he is punished or chastised for it, or simply receives a disapproving frown. Thus the reified moral system of the paranoid-schizoid position is, in some ways, closer to our original learning than is the depressive position system.

Before leaving this section I would like to give one more clinical example, this one of a client at a much higher level of functioning than the delinquent teens discussed previously.

Ellen entered therapy precariously but clearly in the depressive position. Her mother was being "unfair," "unjust," concepts that do not compute in the paranoid-schizoid position. Her mother was loving but "difficult," again a kind of ambivalence, a recognition of positive and negative qualities in the same object that is the hallmark of the depressive position.

But when I reframed "difficult" as "cruel," the paradigm shifted. "Loving-but-difficult" was bearable. "Loving-but-cruel" was not. The idea that the mother who loved her was also the mother who was cruel to her was more than Ellen could deal with and so she regressed back to the paranoid-schizoid position in which mother was all-good and merely lovingly and justly pointing out to Ellen her own badness.

Back in the paranoid-schizoid position Ellen felt all of the old self-hatred, the desire to self-harm, the impulse to apologize to her mother and beg her mother's forgiveness that she had felt as a child. This was, of course, enormously painful and Ellen would "talk herself out of it," remind herself that she was good, that she was loved by her husband, that her mother was controlling and manipulative. But having talked herself back into the depressive position she would again be confronted by her loving mother's cruelty, and the pain this caused was equally unbearable. So for days Ellen was caught in a nightmarish dialectic between two different paradigms, each with its own unbearable pain.

The logic of splitting VI: feelings that make sense, feelings that don't

We tend to think of feelings as fundamental to the human condition. We acknowledge that some people are "out of touch" with their feelings and we struggle to understand that other people (sociopaths, for example) are "incapable" of certain feelings. But object relations theory teaches us that there are a number of feelings that simply *make sense* in one position but not in the other.

Shame vs. guilt

If the word guilt is defined narrowly as the feeling one has when one realizes that one has hurt someone who doesn't deserve to be hurt, then guilt can only exist in the depressive position. In the paranoid-schizoid position, as we have said, if someone is hurt then they must deserve it. The absence of guilt among people in the paranoid-schizoid position is striking and disturbing. I have already described how the deaths of innocent bystanders (frequently children) in drive-by shootings are simply shrugged off.

Timothy McVey, the bomber of the Federal Building in Oklahoma City was said to have dismissed the children killed in the building's day care center as "collateral damage." I asked a client once who had been in the Special Forces in Viet Nam how he felt when he saw the bodies of Viet Cong he or his comrades had killed. "Good," he said matter-of-factly.

"Shame," on the other hand, is a much more powerful feeling in the paranoid-schizoid position than it is in the depressive position. Shame is defined here as the feeling one has when one has been caught doing something wrong. This makes perfect sense in both positions. It is more powerful in the paranoid-schizoid position because the black-or-white thinking of that position (splitting) means that if I do something bad then I am bad. It doesn't matter much whether I am caught committing murder of found with my hand in the cookie jar. It is revealed that I was doing something bad and therefore it is revealed that I am bad.

When we talk about "shame-based" people or clients we are talking about people who spend much of their lives dwelling in the paranoid-schizoid position. Shame loses its devastating (humiliating) punch when one moves into the depressive position. In the depressive position one can have the experience of being caught doing something wrong without the corresponding experience of being "bad." In the depressive position one can say, "Boy what I did was bad, but I'm still a good person." An expression of, "Oh my God, I'm so sorry!" is possible in the depressive position. In the paranoid-schizoid-position it is simply too mortifying.

Envy vs. jealousy

Again, let us define our terms narrowly. If we define jealousy as the feeling one has when someone one loves has something one wants, then jealousy also can only exist in the depressive position. In the paranoid-schizoid position if someone has something you want and doesn't give it to you, then they are withholding and selfish and therefore bad, and one does not love bad objects. The ability to love someone who withholds from you is a good sign that one is in the depressive position.

In the paranoid-schizoid position the comparable feeling is envy and envy (as defined here, and as Klein defined it) is an emotion involving hate. Envy is a socially unacceptable emotion and even people deep in the paranoid-schizoid position usually tend to know enough to hide it. Occasionally you will hear people admit, "I hate rich people in all their fancy cars," or, "I hate seeing lovey-dovey couples; it makes me so aware of my loneliness." One may be envious of a loving couple but when one feels envy one doesn't feel love. One feels hatred and the desire to destroy the person that one perceives as depriving or cheating us. Envy is what makes some men kill their ex-wives or ex-girlfriends when the ex finds a new partner. Envy is the feeling behind "If I can't have you no one can!"

Emptiness vs. sadness

Melanie Klein was fascinated by different kinds of anxiety. One particular kind of anxiety she observed had to do with the fear of permanent object loss. "If I let myself love this person he or she may die and then where would I be?" "If I let myself love this person will my underlying obnoxiousness (neediness, anger, etc.) drive this person away forever?" It was this particular anxiety – the anticipatory fear of the grief that C.S. Lewis (1976) tells us is the "price we pay for having loved," that gives the depressive position its name. If I allow myself to believe in the possibility of permanent object loss, then I am subjecting myself to the inevitability of loss and grief.

In the paranoid-schizoid position part objects are seen as coming and going randomly. The good breast is here, then it is gone (replaced by the bad breast) and then suddenly, without warning, the good breast will reappear. It is a position of chaos, of an absence of power or control, but it is a position free of anxiety over permanent object loss: "Here today, gone tomorrow, back again the next day." One might even say that internal objects are immortal. If I project the Bad Breast onto Rose, and then relentlessly attack and abuse her (as is the Bad Breast's due) and the real Rose gets fed up with this treatment and leaves (permanently), I have not really suffered a permanent object loss: Iris will show up and I can project the Bad Breast onto her.

As such, there is a strange absence of sadness in the paranoid-schizoid position. This is not to say that in the paranoid-schizoid position one never gets the blues, that one never feels sad or upset. But there is no deep grieving in the paranoid-schizoid position because there is never any need for grieving. Objects are never experienced as being truly lost. If they are momentarily gone, they will return in the next moment. We often speak of someone in the paranoid-schizoid position having an impulse or need to "kill off the bad object." But "killing" is really a word that has meaning only in the depressive position as it implies permanence. The best one can hope for, in the paranoid-schizoid position, is to temporarily *drive away* the bad object.

Thus, when I have a client in my office who is crying his or her eyes out, who is clearly, deeply, profoundly grieving, I secretly rejoice. This client (at least for the moment) has moved into the depressive position; this client is doing the work he or she needs to do.

The counterpart to sadness (deep, grieving type of sadness) in the paranoid-schizoid position is emptiness. Emptiness is the feeling one has when an internal object needs to be disavowed and projected out. This is true whether the disavowed internal object is good or bad. Both are part of the psyche and thus the absence of either will produce a sense of emptiness. When I am in the presence of the Good Breast (projected onto some hapless recipient), I will rejoice and feel blessed and feel alive in the presence of the other, but part of me will feel empty because part of me is missing (being carried by the other). Similarly, when I am in the presence of the Bad Breast (again, projected onto some hapless recipient) I will feel persecuted and miserable, but alive again in the presence of the enemy. But I will also feel empty, because whatever is personal about my rage, whatever is *me* about it, will no longer be me because it is being carried (in fantasy) by someone else.

Fear of nihilation vs. fear of death (loss)

This might be a slightly different iteration of the previous issue, perhaps its reverse (all facets of splitting overlap). If the predominant anxiety in the depressive position (its defining anxiety) is the fear of permanent object loss, then the corresponding anxiety in the paranoid-schizoid position is fear of nihilation. "Nihilation" is not a real word. It is a neologism that Thomas Ogden (1990, p. 75) coined because no other word quite fits. It is a derivative of the word annihilation, but the word annihilation implies ceasing to exist. The predominant anxiety of the paranoid-schizoid position, says Ogden, is the fear of never having existed in the first place. The paranoid-schizoid position is, as we have discussed, a position without history: without any sense of continuity. Part-objects come and go randomly, events happen spontaneously, there is no continuous flow of history provided by cause and effect, there is, in effect, no past or future, only a never-ending present.

Without a continuous flow of history one cannot cease to exist; one can only suddenly not exist and, in not existing, one never did exist. A frequent fantasy among the delinquents I worked with was the fantasy of "going out in a blaze of glory." I think that the impetus behind this fantasy is the sense that if one goes out in a blaze of glory, then one will have existed.

Shannon was a particularly bright gangster I worked with at the Center. Unlike almost all of the other gangsters I worked with, Shannon said that he knew that gangs were a "dead end" when he joined one. That knowledge did not dissuade him. He had become particularly "hard core" after his mother had died, a loss that devastated him. But Shannon had never grieved his mother's death. Instead, he had become hard, cold, and ruthless.

He had a relationship with a girl at the Center, at least as much of a relationship one could have in a highly supervised institution that actively discouraged such bonding. I hoped that Shannon would project his internal good-mother object onto his girlfriend and then, under that protective aegis, be able to work through (mourn) the death of his mother. This did not happen, and I remember witnessing their goodbye meeting and being struck by Shannon's cruel coldness in his goodbye. It was as he were saying to this poor, lovestruck girl, "Oh no! Don't even think anything is permanent."

A few months after Shannon's release I attended his funeral. He and some of his homeboys had been killed trying to rob a jewelry store. It must have been something of a suicide mission. The jewelry store workers, seeing their store suddenly rushed by a bunch of African-American teenagers, had reached for their guns even before the door was open. Shannon had died in a hail of bullets. His existence had been noted.

Helplessness vs. power (freedom)

Once again to the Myth of the Original Split: The infant bites the object it loves and the beloved object is suddenly a frightening and withholding object. The infant can't deal emotionally with the fact that he has just created this scenario, so the infant splits. "The good breast was just here and suddenly the bad breast is here in its place. Part-objects come and go randomly. This had nothing to do with me." So, an essential part of splitting is a rejection of power, of agency. Helplessness is an essential part of the splitting "mythology."

Let me emphasize that this has nothing to do with *real* helplessness or powerlessness. This has to do with the *experience* of helplessness and powerlessness. People in the paranoid-schizoid position have as much power and as much agency as anyone else. But they simply do not experience it. My client Sandra, presented earlier in this chapter, is a case in point.

When I began to work with Sandra on her sense of helplessness it was at first like we were speaking different languages (and in a way, we were. At the very least we were speaking from two different logical systems). Sandra could provide a dictionary definition of the words "power" or "empowerment," but they were like foreign words to her: she had no emotional connection to them.

As our work progressed her position shifted from a complete lack of understanding to anger and argumentativeness. "Yes," she said with clear irritation, "that's the way I experienced it. Law school just happened to me. I didn't want to go to medical school and I'm not good in math. So what else was there? I didn't have a choice. Law school happened to me!"

I believe that Sandra's anger had two components. One was the classical paranoid-schizoid experience of envy: I had something that intrigued her, something she wanted, and I wouldn't give it to her. For that she hated me. The other aspect of her anger had to do with frustration. She was beginning to realize that "the experience of power" was something she lacked and something she wanted. Ironically, of course, she felt *helpless* to be able to achieve this desired new condition. She was frustrated. But her frustration was a good thing. It was the first sign of her wanting to move into the depressive position, the first step towards the experience of agency.

The shift from the paranoid-schizoid position to the depressive position, from the experience of helplessness to the experience of empowerment, can, in the moment, be quite dramatic.

As I have said, the staff at the Center were frequently critical of the residents' "refusal to take responsibility." This "refusal" was due to two things. One was the residents' absolute inability to *experience* responsibility (agency). The other had to do with the implications of admitting to any transgression. In the paranoid-schizoid position there is no, "I did something wrong, but I am still a good kid." In the paranoid-schizoid position, "If I did something bad, I am bad."

When these kids would slip into the depressive position, however briefly, and "accept responsibility," it was amazing to watch. You could almost see the surprise on their faces. They had expected, upon admitting guilt, to feel like shit. Instead, they felt empowered; they felt free. They would stand straighter, inches taller than they had stood before. They would look you in the eye where they had previously stared morosely at the ground. They had a sense of power where they had previously felt helpless. Where they had previously felt themselves to be slaves to the fates, they had a sense of freedom: they could make choices and live with the choices they made, even if the choices were wrong.

The logic of splitting VII: omnipotence and magic vs. power and freedom

There is a confusing paradox here: Klein and Winnicott describe the paranoid-schizoid position as being one in which one experiences oneself as helpless, yet they also describe it as a period of "omnipotence." The resolution of this paradox has to do, once again, with the distinction between *experiencing oneself* as helpless and *acting as though* one were omnipotent.

The term "omnipotence" refers to the infant's (teenager's, adult's) belief/ fantasy that he or she can reconstruct the world to suit his or her purposes.

> If I cannot deal with the fact that the good breast and the bad breast are the same, I will act as if they were separate, unrelated objects. If I need you to be the good breast, that is who you will be. If I need someone else to be the bad breast that is who they will be. The "reality" of the situation be damned!

The paradox of this kind of omnipotence is that in order for it to work, it has to be completely unconscious. The conscious experience has to be, "No! That's the way it is! There is a good breast and a bad breast, and they are unrelated and come and go randomly and (most importantly) have nothing to do with me or my actions." If this process were to be in any way conscious, if one had to say, "No, I am going to pretend that. . . ." then the split would lose all of its power, would be rendered simply an exercise in "make-believe." So, the irony is that when one relinquishes the unconscious illusion of omnipotence, one gains the conscious experience of power.

Yet within the paranoid-schizoid position, there is an equivalent to (or, more accurately, a substitute for) the absence of power. This substitute is *magic*. To understand this logic, picture yourself as a native on a tropical island.

> I am aware that I have absolutely no power, that I am completely helpless, to control this volcano that dominates our tiny little island. Yet if I let myself believe that if I sacrifice enough goats (daughters,

captured enemies, etc.) then perhaps the gods that do have the power to control the volcano will have mercy on me. It's a long shot, it's a lottery ticket, but it's better than nothing.

A belief in magic gives one the hope that a higher power: a god, a ritual, an incantation, a spell, might somehow compensate for one's own total helplessness.

I divide magic rituals into two types: rituals of exorcism and rituals of supplication. Rituals of exorcism are rituals designed to drive away the bad object (the bad breast) in anticipation of the good object (the good breast) returning to take its place.

> I worked with an intern who was very bright, very intuitive, and very much in the paranoid-schizoid position. She would present a case to me and I would be dazzled by her insightfulness, the daring of her interventions, and the soundness of her insight . . . and everything would be fine between us. Then, I would make a critical comment, or even a suggesting for doing it somewhat differently, and she would attack me.
>
> I was always stunned. "What just happened?" "Where is this coming from?" But in the back of my mind was always the question, "How can she be doing this? How can she, an intelligent and insightful person, allow herself to take the risk of attacking me, her supervisor, a person who has so much power over her?"
>
> But from her point of view (from the paranoid-schizoid position) there was no risk. The good supervisor had disappeared and the bad (critical) supervisor had appeared in its place. The best one could hope for in this situation was recourse to a magic ritual of exorcism: attack the bad object and drive it away (in expectation that the good object will come back to take its place). This scenario, of course, makes no sense in the depressive position. In the depressive position the good supervisor and the bad supervisor are one-in-the-same. If you attack the bad supervisor you are also attacking the good supervisor. But in the paranoid-schizoid position the good supervisor and the bad supervisor are separate, unrelated (part-)objects. An annihilating attack on the bad supervisor has nothing to do with (will not alienate) the good supervisor. To the contrary, an attack on the bad supervisor will make an opening for the good supervisor to return and step into.

Rituals of supplication are the opposite. They are designed to woo back the good object by rituals of sacrifice, appeasement, or seduction.

Let me create here a fictional character whom I will call "Typical American Hubby" (TAH, for short). TAH comes home from work one day and finds his wife enraged at him. She is so enraged that she will barely speak to him but after much cajoling he is able to discern the reason for her rage: he has forgotten their anniversary.

If TAH is in the depressive position his reaction will be something like, "Oh my god! I am so sorry. I have hurt the person I love most in the world, and I need to do some soul-searching to figure out why. In the meantime, I will buy her flowers and chocolates as a physical manifestation of my love for her and my sorrow at having hurt her."

If TAH is in the paranoid-schizoid position his reaction will be something like, "Oh my god! I forgot! Shit happens! Forgetting happens! Now, suddenly, my loving wife has gone away and my bitchy wife is here in her place. What can I do to woo my loving wife back? Let me try the magic ritual of flower-and-candy-buying. There is no guarantee. But it has had some success in the past, and it's my only option."

The reader will note that the behaviors are identical in each case. What is different is the experience of the behaviors. In the depressive position the experience is of having taking an action (or having failed to take an action) that has resulted in damage being done to a beloved object. What follows is (in Melanie Klein's terms) an *attempt at reparation*, literally, an attempt to repair the damage that has been done.

In the paranoid-schizoid position there is no experience of power, responsibility, or guilt. "Shit happened; forgetting happened! So now, damn it, this beloved but fickle good wife has disappeared and in her place is this bitch-wife. Maybe, just maybe, I can seduce my good wife back by this magic ritual of flowers-and-chocolate."

The logic of splitting VIII: the absence of ruth

"Ruth" is one of those classically playful Winnicottian words. We think that we don't have a clue as to what it means until we see it expressed in its negative and then we say, "Oh, of course!" "Ruth" is whatever it is one lacks when one is "ruthless." As such, ruth can only exist in the depressive position. In the paranoid-schizoid position ruth makes no sense.

Return once again to a conversation I had with many teenage gangbangers. I would say, "But surely you know that the ones you are so hell-bent on killing are teenagers just like yourself, with mothers and fathers of their own, girlfriends, perhaps even babies of their own. If it weren't for the colors they wore you wouldn't be able to tell them from your homeboys, from yourself." And my earnest, soul-searching stare would be returned by a completely blank stare. "You don't understand," they would say, "these are enemies." *Enemies*: the beginning and end of who they are.

In the paranoid-schizoid position all objects are part-objects, and part-objects are either good or bad. There is no ambivalence, there is no a-little-bit-good-a-little-bit-bad. It is all or nothing. And if something is all bad, then the only thing to do with it is to destroy it. Compassion does not fit into this scenario, understanding does not fit in, "ruth" does not fit in. If it is all bad, it should be destroyed, driven away, annihilated. What else does one do with evil?

One of the most disturbing experiences I had working in the Center was that of coming in one morning and discovering that two girls who had been bosom friends the day before were now mortal enemies. This was a case of history being rewritten: "I thought that you were good and now it is revealed to me that you are horrible." My interventions, my attempts at reconciliation, were futile. "Wait a minute," I would plead, "this was your best friend yesterday." Implied in my plea was the depressive position perspective that yesterday's person and today's person are pretty much the same person. But this is not the perspective of the paranoid-schizoid position. In the paranoid-schizoid position history can be instantly rewritten. "What I saw yesterday (and for months of yesterdays before that) was a fantasy, a fraud. I now see the truth. What I saw as good is in fact evil."

What was especially chilling was the ruthlessness that accompanied this switch. Intimate secrets, secrets that had previously never been shared with another living soul, were suddenly broadcast around the campus. And there were no doubts, no guilt, no remorse about these sudden betrayals. "She deserved it!"

> One such flipping of the script let to a physical fight between two former best friends in which one girl bit the other on the breast, so hard as to draw blood through two tee shirts and a bra. I interviewed the biter and eventually asked my own pressing question: "Why there?" As I was studying Klein at the time I half expected some inchoate response about "tearing the bad breast to bits." Instead, the answer I got was even more chilling: "I wanted it to hurt!"

What, then, does "ruth" mean? Ogden (1990, p. 197) says that it means "empathy," something that can only exist in the depressive position. To my mind, "ruth" is synonymous with the depressive position. It means seeing people as whole objects instead of as part objects. If one sees people as whole objects, then one cannot be ruthless. If one recognizes that one's "enemy" is merely another teenage boy, with hopes and fears, loves and hates, much like oneself, then one cannot participate in a random "drive-by" and remain emotionally unaffected.

Ruth is the ability to empathize with, to identify with, to recognize that we are dealing with whole, complex, *real* human beings, not with cartoon characters or video game fabrications.

The logic of splitting: summary

Table 5.1 presents a summary of the facets of the logic of splitting that have been covered in this chapter. I use the word "facets" because these are more than just the logical conclusions of splitting; they are inherent aspects of splitting. There may have been some overlap in my presentation. Indeed, when it came to providing clinical illustrations to the various

Table 5.1 The Logic of Splitting

Paranoid-Schizoid Position	Depressive Position
Splitting	Non-Splitting
Part Objects (Unidimensional)	Whole Objects (Multidimensional)
Ahistorical (Chronology)	Historical (Continuous Flow)
Random Events	Cause and Effect
No Object Constancy	Object Constancy
Experience of Reliving (Flashbacks)	Experience of Remembering
Denial of Responsibility	Experience of Responsibility
Experience of Self as Object	Experience of Self as Subject
No Experience of Agency (Power)	Sense of Agency (Empowerment)
Meaning Experienced as Objective	Meaning Experienced as Subjective
Concrete Thinking	Symbolic Thinking
Belief in a Just World	Acceptance of Injustice
Specific Feelings	Specific Feelings
Shame	Guilt
Envy	Jealousy
Fear of "Nihilation"	Fear of Death (Permanent Loss)
Helplessness	Power/Freedom
Omnipotence and Magic	Power and Freedom
Ruthless	Ruth (Empathy)

facets, I sometimes had a hard time knowing which facet a particular case best illustrated. But overlap is inevitable given that we are always talking about the same core issue (splitting) and each case could probably be used to illustrate *all* aspects of splitting.

Although it loses so much in explanatory detail, the previous Table offers the advantage of showing the entire, complex picture in a single glance. This single glace brings to mind several types of clients that we deal with clinically. Chief among these is the so-called Borderline Personality Disorder. To my mind, object relations theory in general and the study of splitting in particular, offer the best explanation for the Borderline Personality of any I have encountered. Most of the DSM V criteria for the Borderline Personality Disorder can be explained as facets of splitting. A "Borderline," therefore, is simply someone who spends a disproportionate amount of his or her mental life in the paranoid-schizoid position.

The other group whom this Table seems to describe is adolescents, not just delinquent adolescents with whom I have had extensive experience, but adolescents in general. There seems to be a confluence of stressors in adolescence that produce a powerful regression to the paranoid-schizoid position, even in the healthiest of teens.

But before moving on to the achievement of the depressive position, I wish to emphasize one final point: the paranoid-schizoid position is *not* a form of psychopathology. To be sure, as I just indicated, excessive paranoid-schizoid functioning is associated with severe character pathology. But "mental health" should not be equated with dwelling exclusively in the depressive position. Indeed, a life spent exclusively in the depressive position would be dull and gray. A quick glance at Table 5.1 suggests several reasons why. To me there is no "magic" in the depressive position. This is not to say that I am a believer in the supernatural. But it seems to me that life would be quite dull indeed without some sense of magic. Whether one defines magic in Coleridge's words as a "suspension of disbelief," or as the voluntary suspension of our critical judgments that accompanies (allows for) the emotional state we call "being in love," some sense of magic seems to add color to our otherwise black-and-white lives.

Many writers have emphasized the developmental importance of the paranoid-schizoid position. Ogden (1990, pp. 52–54) presents a clinical vignette of a very disturbed young man whom he describes as a "failure to achieve splitting." I personally received a powerful lesson in the adaptive value of the paranoid-schizoid position during a visit from my then three-year-old grandson.

My wife and I babysat our first grandson for three nights, the first time he had been away from both of his parents for such an extended period of time.

Our grandson has a congenitally sunny disposition. He is almost always happy. As long as his grandmother or I were playing with him, this delightful happiness seemed to continue unabated. It was as though the two good breasts provided by his doting parents were seamlessly replaced by the two good breasts provided by his doting grandparents. At one point I found myself with the disconcerting question of wondering, if his parents were never to come back, would he ever miss them.

Of course, he would and did miss them. He, as all of us, moved back and forth between the paranoid-schizoid position and the depressive position. He appeared to be more in the depressive position when he was playing by himself. In those times he would slip into a kind of sober melancholy. At one point, while he was playing alone, I lost sight of him and went frantically looking for him. He came wandering back around the corner of the house announcing that he had been "out looking for my Mommy and Daddy." He never sank into despair, but for a three-year-old, three nights is a long time.

What struck me about that visit was the obvious survival benefit of the paranoid-schizoid position. He never had to grieve, he never had to worry, he never had to fret. Benevolent caretakers replaced benevolent caretakers, good breast B substituted for good breast A, and all was right with the world. With a three-year-old, dwelling too much in the depressive position, with its anxiety about permanent object loss, could have been a disaster.

We drove our grandson to the airport to meet his returning parents. On our way to the lobby he held his grandmother's and my hands tightly and with obvious anxiety. Which of his (part-object) parents would he meet? Would it be the good parents whom he remembered or the bad parents who had abandoned him? The hugs and kisses of his returning parents reassured him that it was the former, and all was right with the world.

Notes

1 Melanie Klein seems to have used the term "bad breast" quite literally, believing that the infant relates to the mother as though she were a bunch of disconnected body parts. She believed that the infant relates to that specific part of the

mother's body before being able later to relate to the mother as a whole object. Studies, beginning with Bowlby's (1988) studies on attachment, have since discredited that notion. Nevertheless, the terms "good breast" and "bad breast" remain a convenient shorthand for "good mothering functions" and "bad mothering functions" and, somehow, better convey the primitive ecstasy of attachment to the good object and the rage and loathing associated with the bad.

2 I will number the facets, the logical implications, of splitting for didactic reasons. This should not imply, however, that these implications occur in any kind of sequential manner. In fact, the act of splitting leads to all the implications simultaneously and instantly.

6   The paranoid-schizoid position
Object Relations Units

Fairbairn contributed an important modification to Klein's original con-
ceptualization of the paranoid-schizoid position. Rather than consisting
simply of "internal objects," the psyche in the paranoid-schizoid position
consists of "internal object relationships." These are not of the voices of
internalized objects, but of the internal dialogs between the self and signif-
icant objects. Kernberg coined the term "Object Relation Units" (ORUs)
to described paired substructures of the psyche representing the internal
object, the self in relation to that object, and the characteristic affect that
defines that particular relationship. Ogden argues that internal objects
are not simply representations of unfinished business from the past. They
constitute structures of the psyche; they constitute who a person is. Either
component (self or object) can be projected out onto others. This makes
the analysis of the transference much more immediately important, and
much more complex, than in the traditional Freudian paradigm.

Splitting not only creates its own system of logic, it leads to a particular
structure of the mind. This structure, which constitutes the psyche in the
paranoid-schizoid position, is based on "internal object relationships." As
with so many things in psychodynamic theory, the definition of an "internal object" depends on who you ask and on when (in the history of psychodynamic theory) you asked the question. The original model for internal
objects was Freud's concept of the superego. Freud (1923, chapt. 5) said
that, "The super-ego . . . arises from identification with the father as a
model" (italics added). But of course, it is not the *real* father that is used
as a model. It is a part-object version of the father containing all of the
father's punishing and judgmental attributes, attributes, for that matter,
as seen in the mind of a four-year-old child. To Freud, "Its chief function

remains the *limitation* of satisfactions" (1940, chapt. 2, italics in original). Of course, although the superego originates through "identification" with the father (or, to a lesser extent, with both parents) it is never simply a memory trace or mental "representation." The superego is a psychic structure, one of the three, along with the ego and the id, in Freud's "structural model." As a psychic structure, it is capable of engaging in conscious and unconscious dialog with the ego, the id, and the external world; of shaping our thoughts, our behavior; and of producing powerful emotions.

Melanie Klein took this concept and ran with it, creating a model of the psyche that consists of not just one but multiple internal objects, interacting to form a complex, multifaceted psyche. Klein's model was made even more complex by Fairbairn who got Klein to (reluctantly) agree that what is "internalized" is not simply an object but an object relationship. Thus, the later Klein/Fairbairn model proposes a system of multiple paired structures, each pair consisting of one component representing an internal version of an external object and another component that represents the self in relationship to that object. Otto Kernberg (1976) refers to these paired object and self-representations as "Object Relations Units," or "ORUs" for short. An Object Relations Unit, says Kernberg (1976), consists of three components: an object image or representation, a self-image or representation that corresponds to the object in that particular relationship, and an affective state that characterizes the relationship.

Thomas Ogden (1990), building on the work of Bion, has proposed a conceptualization of internal objects that appears to be more in keeping with Freud's description of the superego, as quoted previously. That is, it appears to focus on the role of the external object as a *model*. Ogden's version of an internal object is partly in response to conceptual problems with what it means to "internalize" or "introject" an external object (a real, living, human being). In Ogden's conceptualization there is no simple internalization or introjection. Instead, there is an inchoate psyche struggling to create structures with which to deal with some powerful affects or experiences with the external world. Let us take, for example, rage/hatred. "How do I deal with, how do I make sense of, how do I respond to my own rage/hatred or, for that matter, the rage/hatred that I perceive being directed towards me?"

I worked for a while with a young neo-Nazi skinhead whom I grew to like. When I asked him why he was a Nazi he replied simply that that was the way he had been raised: his father was a Nazi. This (social learning theory) explanation might have sufficed, were it not that his mother had not been a Nazi and she too had raised him and, in fact, had been his primary caretaker. Thus, some form of identification with, or internalization of, the father would also seem to be at work (as opposed to simply having *learned* from the father).

I challenged him further, pointing out that this Nazi father who had "raised him" and from whom he claims to have learned so much, also used to beat him mercilessly, and who was, in every other context, someone my client said he hated. Now "identification with the aggressor" is an old concept, dating back not just to the early object relations theorists, but to Anna Freud (1936). Simply put, identification with the aggressor is thought to occur when the aggressor, however much hated and feared, is seen not only as the agent of abuse but also as the repository of power. Since the abused person is by implication powerless, the acquisition of power that is fantasized as coming with identification with the hated aggressor is considered well worth the price that may be paid in the self-hatred that may come with it.

Again, this new explanation may well have sufficed, were it not for something the client said later in treatment. We were discussing his hatred of blacks when he said, with considerable animation, "I hate them. I am constantly looking for reasons to hate them." This last sentence caught my attention. If being a Nazi was simply a learned behavior pattern or a way of feeling powerful, then why did he constantly need to be finding new reasons for so channeling his hatred?

The interpretation I finally made to him (which he at least partially accepted) was that this otherwise likable young man was simply full of rage, much of it, no doubt, stemming from his history of abuse. Nazism represented a *structure* for his rage, a subdivision of his ego through which his rage could be given form and expression and in which, in a distorted way, it made *sense*. His father provided not the structure itself, but rather a *model* for the structure. It was not that anything external had been transposed to an internal location. It was rather that the blueprints of an external structure (father/Nazism) had been used as a ready-made model for the creation of an internal structure (subdivision of the ego).

Thus, if one looks at the ORUs of this particular client one finds a complex mental structure (complex in the sense that it involves two substructures: aggressor and target of aggression) that have been created for the understanding of, and processing of, anger, hatred, and aggression. This complex mental structure (ORU) coexists with other ORUs designed to process other internal and external issues. My young Nazi client also had a mother who showed him love and who tried (unsuccessfully) to protect him from the abuse of his father. Thus, a second ORU was created to deal with the experience of receiving and giving love. That ORU consisted of an "internal object" mother who was loving but weak and a corresponding self component through which he understood himself to be lovable but vulnerable.

The structure of the psyche in the paranoid-schizoid position can be described as a set of internal Object Relations Units (ORUs), each modeled after an originally external (now an internal) relationship and each consisting of two paired, semi-autonomous sub-structures, one modeled after the experience of an external object and the other modeled after the experience of the self that existed in that originally external (and now "internal") relationship. A hypothetical model of a psyche in the paranoid-schizoid position might look something like that shown in Table 6.1.

There is no theoretical limit on the number of ORUs that can comprise a psyche. But in practical terms, the number is unlikely to exceed a half-dozen, and some ORUs will obviously predominate over others. If we can hypothesize a client for Table 6.1 and suppose that that client's mother was only occasionally abandoning then the "Loving Mother/Lovable Self" ORU will tend to predominate and the client will tend to carry the warmth of that relationship, the self-esteem and self-love that such a relationship would produce. We would expect some "abandonment issues" in this client, not merely anxiety and anticipatory grief around the loss of an object, but feelings of worthlessness that come from the perception that a loved one has chosen to throw you away. We would not be surprised to find a history of promiscuity in this client's early adulthood, followed by a shamed and joyless sexuality once monogamy has been chosen. And, of course, we would expect this client to be the first to volunteer (and to derive much satisfaction from her service) when she perceives another to be in need.

Before continuing, it may be worthwhile to address the question of what is meant by the term "psychic structure." I tend to be a visual thinker and

Table 6.1 Object Relations Units

	ORU-1	ORU-2	ORU-3	ORU-4	ORU-5
Object Component	Loving Mother	Abandoning Mother	Punishing Father	Seductive Father	Needy Parent
Self Component	Lovable Self	Trash	Bad Self	Nasty Self	Caregiving Self

my immediate impulse is to think of a structure in terms of a building. There is, indeed, some utility to this view. Nazism was a kind of safe house for my young client, providing a prescribed avenue for the otherwise chaotic and fearful feelings of rage, hatred, and violent impulses. This "safe house" even came pre-decorated, replete with swastikas, straight-arm salutes, and boots. But the building metaphor is of limited use. A mental structure is not something concrete and visually observable. It is a process, or, more accurately, a formula for a process. A "structure," as I see it, is basically an *algorithm* for the attribution of meaning to an ambiguous situation. ORUs provide just such an algorithm.

Internal ORUs provide a kind of Rosetta Stone through which meaning can be interpreted. As an example, let us look at the child's attribution of meaning to a received smile. Smiles are generally lauded in social relationships, from the mother-infant relationship to casual checkout line encounters, to the client-therapist relationship. Smiling at our clients is right up there with "maintaining eye contact" as axiomatic conduct for therapists. But a smile is only a "good experience" if it is perceived as such by the recipient. A smile has no inherent meaning of its own. If the child is to attribute meaning to the smile (or to any such ambiguous experience and, it may be argued, to a child *all* experience is ambiguous) then he must have an organized system for the attribution of meaning to do so. In the paranoid-schizoid position ORUs serve this function.

If the child is under the sway of an Object Relations Unit (ORU) characterized by a loving internal object, then the smile will be interpreted as loving. If he is under the sway of an ORU in which the internal object is seductive, then the smile will be experienced as someone trying to "come on to . . ." or "hit on . . ." her, i.e., as an attempted seduction. If the child is under the sway of an aggressive/rejecting internal object, then the smile will be seen as a sneer, an expression of contempt and distain. If she is under the sway of an abandoning ORU, then she will interpret the smile as the sad, wistful, guilty smile of an incipient farewell. And so on. I have, for example, a client who routinely asks me why I am "smirking" at her.

The paranoid-schizoid position's ORU structure not only allows someone to attribute meaning to (to understand) an ambiguous situation, it provides a built-in course of action.

Let me give my example of my (hypothetical) boss who suddenly and unexpectedly seems to be furious at me. The internal object (psychic structure) of my (hypothetical) alcoholic father provides an algorithm for understanding his behavior and assessing the threat. My boss is randomly raging and out of control as my father was when he had been drinking. This same algorithm tells me (correctly or incorrectly) that he is more bark than bite and that everything will return to normal once he has cooled down (sobered up), and that by tomorrow he may not even remember this incident. This algorithm also informs my view of myself in this situation via the self component of the ORU. I am not to blame, it tells me, so I need not feel any guilt. In fact, what I feel is a mixture of sadness and contempt. I am not in any immediate danger, yet it is best to lay low and stay out of sight. I am impotent in this situation. All I can do is wait.

Needless to say, the previous interpretation and the corresponding course of action may be grossly inappropriate to the given situation. My boss may actually be raging because he believes that I have made a terrible mistake, in which case hiding from him and not trying to explain things to him would be the worst possible course of action. But in the case of a perceived threat (and, in the paranoid-schizoid position threats may lurk anywhere) some understanding – any understanding – is felt to be preferable to confusion and cluelessness and some formula for action – any formula, accurate or inaccurate, helpful or hurtful – is felt to be preferable to cluelessness and its resulting helplessness.

A brief aside may be appropriate here regarding the word, "trigger." People tend to think of ORUs as being *triggered* by external events. In the example just given, it is tempting to say that my hypothetical alcoholic father/retreating son ORU was *triggered* by my hypothetical boss's rant. But this description misses an essential point. ORUs do not just passively *happen*. They are not stereotypical responses to a specific stimulus. Neither are they a *reflex:* doctor's hammer strikes knee; foot jerks forward. ORUs are psychic structures that exist primarily for the purpose of *attributing meaning* to ambiguous events. Again, my boss was uncharacteristically raging and I employed an ORU in the attempt to make sense out of this unexpected behavior. This is an active process, not a passive reflex. I may employ the same ORU with monotonous repetition, attributing the same meaning over and over again, but it remains an *active* process and at times an exhausting one.

To the extent that one is in the paranoid-schizoid position (and one is never *entirely* in the paranoid-schizoid position: one is always in a dialectic tension between the paranoid-schizoid position and the depressive position) one *cannot* engage in real relationships with the real, external world nor with the real, external people who populate it. That capacity is specific to the depressive position. In the paranoid-schizoid position one never encounters a real person. One deals instead with someone onto whom one has projected either an internal object or a corresponding self-representation. The word schizoid in the term "paranoid-schizoid" refers to the use of the defense of splitting. But it also conveys something of the extent to which one lives, in that position, in an isolated, almost autistic, world. One does not deal with real other people in that position. One deals only with one's own internal objects, projected onto the bodies of hapless others. Real, external people have, in this position, been reduced to what Winnicott (1968a, p. 221) calls "bundles of projections." The more we dwell in the paranoid-schizoid position, the more time we spend there, the more unreal and autistic are our lives. We can live with other people – husbands, wives, sisters, brothers, best friends – for years and never really know them, never really interact with them. Instead, we interact perpetually with figures from our past (figures alive and well in the present as ORU components, as structures of our minds), but never with the people right in front of us, the people supposedly sharing our lives. The essential role of the ORU as algorithm in the attribution of meaning is one of the (many) reasons why the paranoid-schizoid position is so difficult to move out of. But in fact, the attribution of meaning function is only one of two critical functions served by the structure of the psyche in the paranoid-schizoid position. The other essential function is the subject's ability (in fantasy) to change, manipulate, and control who he is and the nature of the world around him. Winnicott and the other early object relations theorists referred to this as "omnipotence."

Omnipotence, as described in the previous chapter, refers to an *unconscious* fantasy (it has to be unconscious to be effective – to be conscious would be to have it recognized as merely a fantasy) that one can recreate oneself and the external world at will through a series of defensive maneuvers. These include splitting, projection, identification, and projective identification.

The psyche in the paranoid-schizoid position is based on splitting, and it is based on the twin mechanisms of identification and projection. I have tried to describe the process of identification earlier. It is not really the taking of an external object and somehow *internalizing* it, making it part of the psyche. Rather, it is the creation of a split-off, semi-autonomous psychic structure that is designed to deal with a certain affect (rage, in the case of the neo-Nazi client described previously) by *modeling* that structure on an external object (for example, the client's neo-Nazi father).

I used the word *autistic* to describe the paranoid-schizoid position. This is accurate in the sense that, in the paranoid-schizoid position, the real, external world is never truly seen. The only things that are seen are internal objects superimposed on external bodies. But people in the paranoid-schizoid position *interact* with the real, external world all the time, which is to say, they do not withdraw into a truly autistic dream world. The mechanism of contact, in the paranoid-schizoid position, between the internal world of ORUs and the external world with which one must cope, is *projection*. If you, in the external world, are suddenly loud and appear angry then I will project onto you my angry father and understand you and respond to you accordingly. If you, in the external world unexpectedly have to work late, then I will project onto you my abandoning mother and understand you and respond to you accordingly. What your anger is really about, what your absence is really about I will never know (nor even *care* to know). Who you are, I will never really know.

Just to compound any existing confusion, it needs to be noted that the word "projection" has two overlapping but different meanings. So far, I have been using the word in the way Winnicott used it when he described external others, in the paranoid-schizoid position, as "bundles of projections." This is to say that projections can be simply a person's attempt to *attribute meaning* in the paranoid-schizoid position. "My boss is acting strangely; I project onto him the internal object of my alcoholic father, and I think I understand the situation."

But projection can take on a second function: one that is defensive. In unconscious fantasy unwanted or unacceptable parts of the self (feelings or internal objects) can be projected onto others and (in fantasy) *carried* by those other people. Aspects of the self that can be split off and projected onto others can be negative or unacceptable parts such as frightening aggression or guilt-inducing sexuality. Or they can be positive elements that are considered to be endangered by one's overall "badness" and thus more safely carried by someone else deemed stronger and better.

To splitting, introjection, and projection needs to be added a fourth defense mechanism that characterizes the paranoid-schizoid position. That is *projective identification*. Projective identification is unique in the lexicon of defense mechanisms. All other defense mechanisms involve one person alone; all are solo dances. Projective identification involves a delicate *pas de deux* between two people. When I *identify* with another person, that person may have absolutely no idea that he or she is being so used. If, for example, I see a man who appears to be much more comfortable with his sexuality than I am with my own, then I may start dressing as he does, start mimicking his mannerisms, use him as a model for ways to approach women. But he is very likely to have no idea that he is being used this way.

Indeed, if he notices me at all he may note that I tend to have the same taste in clothes as he, but he would have no reason to assume that I am consciously or unconsciously copying his behavior.

Similarly, if I *project* an aspect of myself that I am uncomfortable with onto someone else, that person is equally unlikely to be aware of what I am doing. Using sexuality again as an example, if I am uncomfortable with my own sexuality and unconsciously project it onto a certain woman, that woman is again likely to not notice me at all. If she does take note of me she is likely to notice that I seem somewhat interested in her but that I am at the same time shy and withdrawn around her, or possibly, that I seem to take offence at her. If she thinks about me at all she is likely to dismiss me as a kind of odd duck, someone who may have "issues with women." But she, herself, is in no way *changed* by my projection.

But *projective identification* is fundamentally different. Thomas Ogden (1990) describes projective identification as having two steps. The first is projection, which he describes as an unconscious *fantasy* – the fantasy that another person is acting as a *container* for aspects of the first person that, for whatever reason, cannot be safely contained by the first person. Ogden's second part is a *behavior*, an *act of manipulation* that is an unconscious attempt to force the other person to actually feel or behave in a way that the projection (fantasy) says that they *should* feel or behave. In practice this can be amazingly simple.

> The kids at the Center who had been abused by cruel parents would frequently project their abusive internal object onto some member of the staff, and would then behave in such a manner as to invite abuse. They would be slow to follow instructions, hostile or surly in their interactions, rude, disrespectful, and generally obnoxious. The more experienced staff, who were used to such provocations, tended not to respond emotionally but, of course, would have to give "consequences" for rule violations. The kids would then feel "picked on," unfairly treated, or otherwise abused.
>
> But even with the experienced staff, it was extremely difficult not to have *some* emotional reaction to this kind of constant provocation. I remember working in a boys' unit and realizing that I was the recipient of a very unpleasant projective identification with one boy who would simply roll his eyes every time I started to say something in group. This simple and barely noticeable act of disrespect had two effects on me. The expected one was anger, which I found fairly easy to control. The second effect was more powerful but more subtle.

I suddenly noticed that I was reluctant to speak up in group, to do my job as group leader. It required a very conscious effort on my part to overcome this reluctance.

Let me take a side note here to address some skepticism that may be arising in the reader's mind. Although I believe that the previous examples are simple and near to everyday experience, the critical reader may remain dubious about the entire concept of projective identification. "Wait a minute," the reader may be thinking. "Are you saying that in projective identification a person acts as if a part of himself is not really a part of himself but is instead a part of someone else and then acts in a way that appears to make this fantasy a reality, and that this is all done out of conscious awareness?" Yes!

In order to understand projective identification, we must understand that it is one more permutation of splitting. Remember that when we split (see Chapter 5) we destroy any experience of history, any experience of agency, any experience of self as subject. In the paranoid-schizoid position (when we split) self is experienced as object: things happen to us. Among the things that happen to us are feelings. This is reflected in the use of passive language, especially when talking about feelings. "He made me mad." "She turns me on." "That person is scary." This way of talking reflects an experience of feelings as being almost external to the self. Getting a feeling is experienced the same way we experience catching a cold or getting the flu. Feelings *happen to us*. If there are flu germs in the air I may find myself hoping that someone else catches them so that I don't. If I feel fear, and if I am dissociated from that fear enough that it feels like there is "fear in the air," then I might just as well hope that someone else feels that instead of me. I may even manipulate the situation a bit – do a little bullying – to make sure that eventuates.

One last comment on projective identification: there are times when parents can be observed actually (and appropriately) teaching their children projective identification, or something very similar. If a young child is discovered anxiously worrying about the family finances it is perfectly appropriate for a parent to say, "No, Honey! You don't need to worry about that. Let Mommy and Daddy worry about that. We can take care of things better than you can." This is very similar to the example given previously. The fear that is momentarily owned by the child (depressive position functioning) need not be owned by that child. It can be released into the air (paranoid-schizoid position functioning) where it can be picked up and owned by someone more capable of owning it and dealing with it than is the child.

Transference

When disavowed parts of the self (feelings or ORU components) are projected onto external objects it is called life in the paranoid-schizoid position. When they are projected onto the person of the therapist, it is called "transference" (transference will be dealt with more extensively in Chapter 13). Thus, object relations theory provides three hugely important contributions to our understanding of, and our work within, transference. First, it provides (through projection and projective identification) the *mechanism* by which transference and transference-like phenomena happen. Second, and at least as important, it provides a much richer and more complex model of transference than does classical (Freudian) psychoanalysis.

Throughout all of his writings on transference, Freud described it as being the transferring of feelings, thoughts, or conflicts from an unresolved relationship in the past onto a current relationship in which they are – by definition – inappropriate. Freud's formula is always the same: an object in the present is experienced as if he or she were an object from the past. "The patient sees in his analyst the return – the reincarnation – of some important figure out of his childhood or past, and consequently transfers onto him feelings and reactions that undoubtedly applied to this model" (Freud, 1940, chapt. 6). Transference *always* involves "some important figure [from the] past" being transferred onto the person of the analyst or therapist.

But object relations theory, with its formulation of Object Relations Units, presents a construct of the psyche (in the paranoid-schizoid position) as involving not just internal objects, but an internalized relationship with two component parts: the formerly external object and the (part-object) self that existed in relation to that object. Either of these two components – the internal object component or the corresponding self component – can be projected onto the person of the therapist or any other person for that matter. Again, in Freudian/classical psychoanalysis only a former object gets projected. In object relations theory what is projected can be either half of the ORU: the internal object or the corresponding self component.

> Rape is one of the most powerful (and most vile) manifestations of projective identification. In the rapist there is an internal dialog (ORU) between an abusive object and an abused self. The abused self component, in keeping with the logic of splitting, is convinced on some level that he deserves the abuse he received (belief in a just world),

and therefore, out of the physical abuse, develops an even more perni-cious self-loathing.

This is not a good place to be. And some men in this condition will "flip the script." They will identify with the abuser – that is to say, they will make that component of the ORU an overt, conscious part of their identities, and will project the self component of the ORU onto some hapless victim. And then, when projection becomes projective identification, they will act in a way that almost guarantees that the other person will actually feel the feelings (the fear, the helplessness, the degradation, the self-loathing) that the rapist is not only trying to dissociate from but actually trying to coerce someone else into "con-taining" those feelings for him. Rape is not just an act of aggression; it is an act of defilement and degradation. It is an attempt to get the victim to loathe herself so that the rapist doesn't have to loathe him-self. It is the projecting of a hated part of an ORU (the self compo-nent) onto someone else (the victim) so that she can contain it for him. The sadistic pleasure taken by the rapist during the commission of the heinous act is not just the infliction of pain and degradation; it is also the fantasy of being released from his own sense of degradation and self-hatred.

For an object relations oriented therapist, it is often difficult to know not only what ORU is being projected in a certain transference reaction, but which component of an ORU is being projected at any given moment.

Therapists are familiar with the kind of client who appears determined to make the therapist look and feel incompetent. All interpretations are not just rejected, they are summarily dismissed, often with an expres-sion of contempt. The complaint, "This really doesn't seem to be help-ing!" becomes a common refrain. The clients will arrive at sessions late, showing no sense of having missed out on anything important. I know of at least two clients who dropped out of treatment announc-ing that their money would be better spent on fancy cars.

This kind of behavior is easily identified as transference, but it is not always easy to know exactly what is being transferred. If the cli-ent was a parentified child, having spent his or her entire childhood taking care of a needy and genuinely incompetent parent, then what is likely happening in these cases is the emergence of righteous anger and resentment at the incompetent parent, with that component of the ORU being projected onto the unlucky therapist. If, on the other hand, the client is the child of a critical and bullying parent, then the client may be identifying with the critical parent and projecting onto the therapist the never-able-to-please, never-able-to-succeed self component of that ORU.

A thorough knowledge of the client's history is clearly essential for making such a determination. But at times, this is not enough. Many parents (borderlines and bipolars especially) will vacillate between helplessness and hypercriticalness with their children. I have had several clients who would weep in one moment about how mean their mothers were to them and how helpless they were in the face of their mothers' cruelty, and in another moment relive the anxiety that came with a deep sense of inadequacy at being unable to take care of these same helpless mothers. When I, in the transference/countertransference, am being made to feel helpless and inadequate, who am I?

It is a constant challenge for both client and therapist to identify exactly which component of what ORU is being projected out at any time. This is not an idle exercise. A cognitive/symbolic (linguistic) awareness of "what is going on" gives both client and therapist a framework that facilitates understanding of both past and current processes, and some sense of control over future processes.

"Lucy" (see Chapters 4, 7, and 12) was fond of me the way she was fond of her father. But I think that the real reason that I believed that I was a father transference figure to her was simple laziness on my part: I am a male. I assumed that had she been in therapy with a female therapist, that therapist would have been a mother transference object.

But in spite of her fondness for me (and for her father), I seemed never able to bring Lucy any comfort. She never internalized my fondness for her. To the contrary, everything I said seemed to her to be critical. I would ask what to me was an innocuous question: "So, how did that make you feel?" and she would respond with, "I'm afraid I don't have an answer to that question" that made me feel like a critical school teacher confronting a recalcitrant student who had not done her homework.

About a year into therapy I blurted out an awkward intervention that was a desperate attempt to break through whatever was being projected onto me: "Lucy, it makes me so sad that you are so relentlessly self-hating, so unable to find anything in this life that brings you pleasure." Lucy reacted to my impassioned words as though she had been slapped (slapped in a way she was used to being slapped) and suddenly I understood. I was not her benevolent but impotent father; I was Lucy's critical mother.

Lucy had been born with significant physical deformities and had been adopted shortly after birth by a woman who seemed to have been motivated by a desire to present herself to the world as a "Christian martyr," someone who took into her home babies that no one else wanted. But her mother's martyrdom did not seem to include warmth or love. The unspoken message Lucy picked up from her mother was, "if only you could be perfect, then I could love you," an impossible challenge for any child but especially cruel for someone with Lucy's deformities.

So when I said, essentially, "it makes me sad that you cannot be happy," what she heard was (I pictured an angry mother with her hands firmly on her hips), "Well it's pretty *sad* that you can't even be happy!" My new understanding – shared with Lucy – was an enormous relief to both of us. It explained so much! My hope – that she might have a modicum of happiness – was equivalent in her mind to her mother's demand that she be perfect: to her, both were equally unfathomable. Furthermore, with the implications of her projection, my ability to love her was dependent on her ability to fulfill this impossible task. My attempt to encourage her and cheer her on had the ironic effect of sending her deeper into despair and hopelessness.

The third monumental change that object relations theory provides to our study and use of the transference has to do with a different aspect of the question, "What is being transferred?" Freud initially despaired when he became aware of transference (as he had initially despaired when he became aware of resistance). He saw transference as a kind of resistance, formulating it as a defense against remembering, against making the unconscious conscious, and therefore as an impediment to the whole psychoanalytic endeavor. Freud, however, came to believe that in addition to being an impediment, transference could also be the therapist's greatest tool. No one, he said, could actually be killed "*in absentia*," (1912, p. 108) and therefore the transference allowed unfinished work from old relationships to be brought into the room where they could be analyzed and resolved *in vivo*.

In classic (Freudian) psychoanalytic theory "resolving" the transference has one of two effects. In the earlier topographical model, resolving transference allowed for a "remembering" (removal of the repression barrier), which allowed for a healthier flow of libido. In the later structural model, it allowed for a healthier development of ego due to improved reality testing. But in either case, the benefits of resolving the transference were indirect: they were a means to an end. In the object relations theory model, resolving the transference directly changes the structure of the psyche – of the mind. This is because what is projected outwards in the transference is not merely the ghost of an unfinished past relationship, but a component of the structure of the psyche – part of an ORU.

In classical psychoanalytic theory "resolving" the transference improves one's reality testing and this is certainly a positive thing. But in object relations theory resolving the transference is in itself a change in the structure of the mind. If a perpetual inner dialog (an ORU) is put to rest, if the relentless conflict between an abusive object and an abused self is finally resolved, ended, put away forever, then the psyche, the mind, has been forever altered. I am no longer the person I was. It is not just that some unresolved relationship of my past has been finally resolved and that I feel some benefits from that, it is that I am a different person: my mind, my psyche, is different from what it was before.

One last brief and personal note on dealing with transference: One of the most difficult things I had to come to terms with in my development as therapist was the extent to which my clients not only didn't see me, but didn't *want* to see me. "No, no!" they would seem (to my ears) to shout at me, "We don't want to know who you are. We refuse to know who you are. We need you to be somebody else, somebody from our past. We have unfinished work with that person and we need to do it on your bones!" Having grown up with two extremely narcissistic, self-absorbed, *unseeing* parents, this was personally excruciating to me. But this experience is echoed throughout the psychoanalytic literature. Jay Greenberg (1986, p. 144) writes, "Transference represents an assault on the analyst's sense of self, a point on which analysts as theoretically different as Levenson (1972), Racker (1968), Sandler (1976), and Searles (1965, 1979) have been especially eloquent."

Countertransference

Current object relations theory also offers a radically different notion of countertransference from that of Freud and classical psychoanalysis (countertransference will be dealt with more extensively in Chapter 13). Freud (1910b) defined countertransference as the unconscious, unresolved (neurotic) material in the therapist that is activated by the patient's transference. Since countertransference was defined as being *neurotic*, it was always considered to be a destructive force in therapy in that it would inevitably interfere with the therapist's "objectivity."

Object relations theory, and particularly the concept of projective identification, provide a very different view of countertransference. If projection is the psychological mechanism by which transference takes place, then the shift from simple projection to projective identification (the addition of the manipulative component) allows for a new understanding of countertransference. In this new light, countertransference is no longer simply the therapist's unresolved "neurotic stuff" triggered by the transference. It is much more complex.

If a client projects a disavowed component of an ORU onto the therapist and then manipulates the therapist to feel or act in a way that would be expected of that component, then the way the therapist is feeling or acting cannot be said to be simply his or her *own* neurotic stuff that has been somehow "triggered." In this model countertransference is *co-created* by both the therapist and the client. As such, it tells us as much about the client as it does about the therapist. As Bion (1952) put it, you know you are the recipient of projective identification when you feel like you are "being manipulated as to be playing a part, no matter how difficult to recognize, in somebody else's phantasy" (p. 149).

So what?

Classical Freudian psychotherapists were instructed to keep their countertransference in check. When they seemed unable to do this, they were referred back into their own therapies where they could "resolve" their own neurotic issues to the point where they would not "contaminate" their therapeutic work. But if, as object relations and intersubjective therapists, we remember Bion's words, then we recognize that the "script" we are following was indeed written (partially) by someone else, and that someone else is our client. And the scripts written by our clients are the grist of all psychotherapeutic work.

What enabled me to recognize, after all those months of frustration, that I was a mother transference object to Lucy instead of a father transference object? It was not my fondness for Lucy, nor my identification with her, nor native perceptiveness. It was my frustration. Lucy had projected her critical mother onto me and I was not able to recognize this until I had been able to fully identify with the role: to be totally impatient with her, to want to shake her and scream, "What's the matter with you? Can't you see that . . ." That was her mother's role with her, not her father's.

7 Stable character structure in the paranoid-schizoid position

In Chapter 5 I argue that the paranoid-schizoid position can be seen as the template for the notoriously unstable Borderline Personality Disorder. In this chapter I present a long vignette that demonstrates how extremely stable character structures can also occur in the paranoid-schizoid position.

Near the end of Chapter 5 I described the paranoid-schizoid position as being a template for the Borderline Personality Disorder. In the BPD, as in the paranoid-schizoid position, part objects come and go randomly. At one moment one is in the presence of the good object and then suddenly one discovers oneself to be confronted by the bad object. The good object is to be worshipped and protected; the bad object is to be annihilated. There is no sense of history. There is no experience of agency: "I am a straw, buffeted by the cruel winds that blow me hither and yon. One moment I am blessed and in heaven and you are an angel; the next moment I am cursed and in hell and you are the devil."

Yet the paranoid-schizoid position can also produce the opposite structure: a character structure that is stable, even immutable to the point of calcification.

"Joe" was such a character. Joe, a Latino adolescent gang member, caught my attention from among his peers by a series of oddities that initially made no sense to me.

When asked to describe himself Joe would say, neither proudly nor apologetically but simply as a matter of fact, "I am a bad kid." This clearly was not some *role* Joe felt he was playing, nor even something that he had *become*. Rather, it was simply, in his mind, *who he was*. It was as if "Bad Kid" had been stamped on his birth certificate. Now this may, of course, have simply been something that Joe was taught:

something he had been told so many times that it was engrained in his psyche. But Joe seemed determined to hold on to this identity. When his positive qualities were pointed out to him Joe would become defensive. "No," he would say angrily, "that's not who I am. I'm a bad kid!"

And of course, Joe made this a self-fulfilling prophecy. Joe was a bully, and a bully of the ugliest sort. He not only bullied the weaker boys in his unit, but he organized his peers into bullying teams, rendering the lives of his designated victims sheer hell. But although Joe clearly derived some sadistic pleasure from his bullying, this in itself was not a sufficient explanation for his relentless behavior. Joe gave the impression that he felt that his victims *deserved* the abuse they got. Joe also attempted to bully one of the male teachers in the school, a somewhat effeminate man who, Joe decided, must be gay and therefore must be weak. But this teacher was not weak. He had all the power in the relationship and he was not hesitant to use it. Joe lost every confrontation he got into with that teacher. Yet he would not (could not) stop. Bullying was a compulsion.

Although Joe defined himself as unifaceted ("I am a bad kid"), he was not unifaceted by any means. I once overheard two girls discussing a boy named Joe, describing him as a "sweetheart." "Wait a minute," I said, "is this the Joe I know?" They assured me that it was. How could Joe-the-Bully also be Joe-the-Sweetheart? When I asked the girls if one of them were dating Joe they both burst into laughter. Nonplussed, I pressed on: "Why is that notion so funny?" I asked. "Well, look at him!" they said. So, I did. In my mind's eye I pictured Joe. Joe was a Latino gangster. He was heavily built, had a shaved head, and though by no means a "pretty boy," Joe had a kind of virile good looks that many girl gang members found attractive. So I shared my reflections with the girls. The girls became more reflective. "Dating Joe," they finally concluded, "would be like dating your brother." So, Joe-the-Gangster, Joe-the-bully, and Joe-the-sweetheart were all, in these girls' minds, somehow asexual, not boyfriend material.

Finally, I returned to Joe and confronted him with his reputation. "Gee Joe," I said, "I hear that some girls around here think that you are a sweetheart." "Yea," Joe said blandly, "that's me but not me."

So how are we to make sense out of all this, out of these paradoxes and contradictions? How do we understand a boy who not only defines himself as all bad but vehemently defends that self-definition? How do we understand a compulsive need to bully even in a situation where one loses every attempt? How do we understand someone who is a bully to weaker boys but a sweetheart to the "weaker sex?" And if girls experienced Joe as a sweetheart, why did they not consider him to be boyfriend material? And finally, what are we to make of his "me-but-not-me?"

Joe's parents had divorced when he was very young, when his biological father, himself a gangster, was sent off for a long stay in prison. Joe's mother remarried a man who was a police officer, someone who, in Joe's mind was the incarnation of evil. To balance this part-object representation of evil, Joe's mother became the "good (part) object." More precisely, Joe's mother became the "loving-but-weak" part object while his stepfather became the "hating (hateful)-but-strong" part object.

Neither of these (internal) part-object representations accurately depicted the real (external) whole objects that were his parents. Joe's mother was truly loving, but her love had clear limits. And though she may have deferred to her husband on many things, she was far from the fragile flower that Joe saw her as being. His stepfather was somewhat rigid and authoritarian, but on the other hand seemed genuinely to care for Joe and bore him no particular ill will. But for Joe the split was absolute: his mother could do no wrong; his stepfather could do no right.

So complete was Joe's split of his parents that he would not acknowledge any bond between them, even the bond of marriage. The crime for which Joe had been convicted was stealing several things from his stepfather, including his gun and a credit card. With the credit card he had run up a bill of several thousand dollars buying things he mostly gave away to his friends. When confronted by the fact that his mother was equally liable for the debt he had run up as was his stepfather, Joe could only sputter the crudest denial: "No! I stole from my stepfather, not from my mother."

The objects Joe was dealing with were internal part-objects rather than external whole objects. And, as object relations theory predicts, for every split in the internal object representation, there is a corresponding split in the corresponding self component of the ORU. The self component that corresponded to the loving-but-weak mother internal object was a "lovable-but-weak" self (lovable because the mother loves him; weak because the mother is unable to provide any protection). The self component that corresponds to the hating-but-powerful stepfather is the "contemptible-and-weak self" (contemptible because he is the recipient of his stepfather's aggression and contempt; weak because he is defenseless against the perceived threat of the stepfather).

One of the first things one notices about this structure is that no matter which ORU is dominant, Joe is weak. In the mother/self ORU he is weak because his (internal) mother is unable to protect him. In the stepfather/self ORU he is weak because he is vulnerable to the (perceived) threat of aggression from the (internal) stepfather.

So, Joe did what countless others have done in his situation, and what many of us could be expected to do under like circumstances: he, to use Anna Freud's (1936) concept, "identified with the aggressor." Given a choice between being a victim and an aggressor, he wholeheartedly chose the latter. "I may hate the son-of-a-bitch," he unconsciously told himself, "but he has all the power and if I am to protect myself from weakness (victimization) I have to become just like him." Joe never claimed to like himself.

Identification with the aggressor solves one problem but it creates another: what to do with the "lovable" self component that exists in relation to the "loving" mother in the mother-self ORU. "If I am going to be a mean (but powerful) son-of-a-bitch like my (hated) stepfather, there is no room in me for anything that is lovable. So, I will take this lovable facet of myself and, not destroy it, but rather project it out onto something where it can be protected and cherished." And what better recipient for this projection than *girls* who, like the mother, are perceived as loving/lovable but weak. And by loving, caring for, and protecting these "lovable-but-weak" girls, Joe turns simple projection into projective identification: the girls "carry" and revel in the "lovable" projection with which they are so eager to identify but which originates in a disavowed component of Joe's self.

If the weak-but-lovable self component of the mother/self ORU is projected onto girls, who can then be protected and nurtured, what happens to the weak-but-contemptible self component from the father ORU? This also gets projected out, this time onto boys or adult males who are perceived as weak. And once again, simple projection becomes projective identification. Joe bullies the targets (recipients) of his projective identification to make sure that they not only feel weak, but that they feel *weak-and-contemptible*. He needs them to feel contemptible because, in his unconscious, they are *carrying* that feeling for him: if they feel it, he doesn't have to. And he needs to stay close to them – to stay somehow connected to them – to witness their misery, the hell he has made their lives. Because in witnessing their torture he can revel in the fact that it is they, not he, who are carrying those feelings.

Let us now recap the original questions I posed about Joe, the facets of his character that seemed to demand explanation. And let us see if the object relations theory formulation provides some plausible answers.

First: *Joe describes himself – without shame or embarrassment – as all bad.* He acknowledges no good in himself. What our schema suggests is that Joe has taken all internal experience of goodness and projected it – in order to protect and nurture it – onto external objects, in this case: girls. As I have indicated before, it is a common misconception that only undesirable traits get projected onto others. Object relations theory makes it very clear that desirable traits can and will be projected out if they are considered to be endangered by being kept within the self. This seems to have been the case with Joe. The only power – the only security – Joe was able to feel was through identification with a hated aggressor. This meant that any goodness in him was experienced as endangered by his own badness and aggression. To be kept safe, his goodness had to be projected out onto external objects where it could be kept safe.

One might also speculate that one of the reasons Joe seemed so sanguine in his *all-bad* identity was that the goodness in him was never experienced as being far afield. It was always close at hand, carefully protected in the girls he saw, and talked to, and cared for, every day. And he could get a kind of vicarious pleasure and satisfaction in seeing the goodness they were "carrying for him" so well cared for by his own ministrations.

Second: *Joe was highly resistant and defiant when it was pointed out to him that he had some good qualities.* Again, this is explained by his original Object Relations Units. The internal object in his mother-self ORU was experienced as being loving but weak. His corresponding self component was thus lovable but weak (unprotected). In both sides of this ORU lovingness/lovableness (goodness) was associated with weakness. And because of his other (father-self) ORU, weakness was experienced as an unbearable sense of vulnerability and endangerment. To be told he was good was, for Joe, to be told that he was weak and, for Joe, weakness was totally unacceptable.

Third: *Joe needed to feel like a bully, even when the other had all the real power.* Our conceptualization suggests that simple projection was not enough for Joe. He needed to make sure, to actually observe, to take a kind of sadistic pleasure in observing the misery of those (who, he believed) were carrying his shameful weakness for him. He had to make sure they carried those odious feelings for him. He had to use projective identification. And this need was so great that it took on the quality of a compulsion. He needed to get this particular teacher (someone who "should" be weak) to feel – if even for a moment – the shame and odiousness that Joe needed him to "carry."

Fourth: *How do we understand that, for some girls, dating "sweetheart" Joe would be "like dating your brother?"* I think the explanation for this may be found in the nature of Joe's caretaking. Joe had no role model for masculine caretaking and hence had no internal component in his psyche of masculine caretaking. Caretaking was a component of one of his Object Relations Units: it was a facet of his internal mother. So the only kind of caretaking that Joe knew how to do – was psychologically equipped to do – was something that must have been experienced by the girls as essentially motherly. I suggest that what the girls in their struggle to explain why they didn't see Joe as dating material really wanted to say was not, "Dating Joe would be like dating your brother," but rather, "Dating Joe would be like dating your mother." And, Freud notwithstanding, dating your mother would not be a highly satisfying experience.

Fifth: *What are we to make of, "That's me but not me?"* As I have indicated, splitting rarely occurs by itself. It usually happens in conjunction with other primitive defenses such as denial, projection, identification, and projective identification. Joe used all of these defenses. He used denial ("No, I only stole from my stepfather"), projection (of both the good and the weak facets of himself), identification (with the hated aggressor father object), and projective identification. Of all these defenses, projective identification is by far the most empowering. Projection and identifications involve pure fantasies. Projective identification involves real people in real relationships. Joe was able not simply to fantasize others carrying his feelings, he was able to actually observe, to take pleasure in, their appearing to feel what he needed them to feel – because he was able to make them feel that way.

But there is a problem. In order to transform a simple projection – the projection of his lovable-but-weak self component onto girls – into projective identification, he had to be able to act in such a way as to make sure that they (the girls) would really *feel* "lovable-but-weak"; he had to actively care-take them (mother them). He could not project this caretaking tendency onto anyone else, because no one else could be trusted to actually carry it through. If he needed to have the girls carry his lovable-but-weak self, he had to do it himself. But as we have already seen, Joe was unable to acknowledge any caretaking tendencies (goodness) in himself. So he couldn't again use projective identification. What was left was a much less satisfying defense, but it was all Joe had left: *pure splitting*. Joe used the classic *as if* mechanism and said (unconsciously), "I know that I am one, but I will act as if I were two. There is the "me" and there is this other thing that I can only call the "me-but-not-me. And when pressed

I will grudgingly acknowledge this other me, but I will distance myself from it (deny it) as much as possible."

I have presented Joe here in great detail because I believe that his case beautifully illustrates a character structure that is clearly in the paranoid-schizoid position but is not in the least bit "borderline." Joe's character structure is not only stable, it is rigid and immutable. Joe was as resistant to therapeutic interventions as anyone I have ever worked with. Efforts to help him "feel better about himself," to have a "more positive attitude about himself" were experienced by Joe as efforts to undermine his power and sense of security. Efforts to get him to renounce his sadistic treatment of other boys were felt by him to be efforts to get him to re-own and re-experience his own sense of weakness and loathsomeness. Interventions designed to help him integrate into a whole self as opposed to two part-object selves were similarly threatening to his internal psychic structure. Joe's paranoid-schizoid psyche was obviously dysfunctional and led to self-defeating patterns in his own behavior and sadistic behaviors towards others. But Joe was willing to pay those prices. He acknowledged that his psyche did not work well, but it worked well enough for him. And he knew, intuitively and unconsciously, that to give up his character structure, to grow, to mature, to become "healthy," to move into the whole-object depressive position, would have required him to feel much more pain and vulnerability than he was willing – or believed himself able – to feel.

8 Resistance and holding onto bad objects

Chapter 8 reexamines the Freudian concept of "resistance" in light of object relations theory. This, in turn, leads to a reanalysis of the entire concept of the unconscious. In this chapter I argue that while in Freudian theory the unconscious is defined primarily by its contents, object relations theory tends to think in terms of unconscious processes. This leads to a significant difference in how the task of the therapist is conceptualized in terms of working through the resistance.

The case of "Joe" (preceding chapter), which was presented as an example of stable character structure in the paranoid-schizoid position, could just have well served as an example of resistance in psychotherapy. "Resistance," along with the *dynamic unconscious* and *transference*, were what Freud considered his three main therapeutic "discoveries." Both the concept of the dynamic unconscious and the concept of transference have undergone much debate and evolutionary pressures in the hundred-plus years since Freud introduced the terms. But the concept of resistance has remained remarkably unchanged, remarkably steady, across the course of what Ogden calls the "psychoanalytic dialog." "Resistance" is a specific manifestation of the basic human (animal) tendency to avoid pain. It is specific to the therapeutic situation in that it refers to the impulse to avoid the pain that would be necessary to achieve therapeutic change. Joe was an unhappy soul. Joe did not like himself, not a whit. Joe recognized that his gangster path would lead him into prison or into an early grave. Yet the pain of his everyday life seemed a trifle to him compared with the pain he had worked to escape and back into which he felt himself in constant danger of falling. He knew, intuitively, that to work in therapy, to work to change, would involve getting back in touch with that deeper pain. And he chose not to.

People often come into therapy with a naive hope that their therapists will be able to take away all their pain. Consciously or unconsciously, they think, "I will be loved; I will be seen; I will be heard as I have never been loved, seen or heard before. And the pain of having not been loved, seen or heard will disappear." There is a crisis in almost every successful therapy in which the client realizes that working through current pain involves first getting deeper into old, buried pain. It gets more painful before it gets less. The reluctance to feel this pain is what resistance is all about. Freud recognized this over a hundred years ago. All of us rediscover this in our practices every day.

Before going on to an object relations theory understanding of resistance, let me briefly recap Freud's perspective on it. Freud's first "discovery" was of the dynamic unconscious which he defined primarily as repressed materials including memories, feelings, and impulses. Freud postulated that repression blocked the normal flow of libido (sexual energy) much as a beaver dam blocks the flow of a stream. And the blockage of the normal flow of libido results in neurotic symptom formation just as a beaver dam results in the stream flooding to form a beaver pond. Tear down the beaver dam and the beaver pond disappears and the stream resumes its normal flow. Tear down the repression, Freud reasoned, and the neurotic symptom will disappear and libido will resume its normal flow. It was an elegant theory. It was logical. It made sense. And it didn't work.

Freud quickly realized that his patients resisted his attempts to tear down their repressions. It was as if they could hear him, nod in agreement, and then suddenly forget or ignore what he had just said. He would find himself successful in forcing the abandonment of a certain symptom, only to have an entirely new symptom arise in its place serving, he recognized, exactly the same function. Some patients even, when confronted by the "truth" of their symptomology, abruptly terminated therapy.

Freud was nothing if not scrupulously honest, and he prided himself on his scientific rigor. He had formulated a theory that predicted a certain outcome, and that outcome did not happen. He would have to either abandon or seriously modify his theory. At first he despaired. And then he had what many consider to be one of his most brilliant insights. Repression happened, he reasoned, for a reason; it was not a random event. Repression happened because the repressed material was too threatening, too painful, too shameful, too whatever, to be allowed into consciousness. Repression and resistance were two sides of the same coin. Repression happened when certain unbearable feelings acted to send some thoughts, feelings, or impulses into the unconscious. Resistance happened when *those exact same unbearable feelings* acted to keep the material repressed, counteracting the work and the goals of psychotherapy. What Freud recognized is that working through the resistance and working through the repression are exactly the same thing. With the discovery of resistance early psychoanalysis underwent a major technical shift: the analyst's task was no longer to force or pry unconscious material out of the unconscious and into consciousness. Rather, it was to gradually work through the resistances, after which the unconscious material would appear on its own. This was a radical shift in psychotherapeutic technique, but it allowed Freud to preserve intact the essence of his theory.

The object relations theory of resistance is essentially the same as the classic, Freudian theory: the unconscious is unconscious because it is believed that its contents would be, in some way, unbearable if allowed into consciousness. And thus, as with Freudian psychotherapy, the work of object relations theory psychotherapy is the gradual, patient, empathic, working through of the resistance. What is different about object relations theory, in distinction from Freudian theory, is the way it sees the *unconscious*.

One of the most obvious and most important differences in their respective definitions of the unconscious has to do with the different ways Freudians and object relations theorists structure the psyche. As was described in Chapter 5, the classic Freudian subdivision of the psyche into id, ego, and superego is supplemented (not replaced) in object relations theory by the concept of a compartmentalized structure of Object Relations Units (ORUs) each of which consists of a complementary internal object relationship identified as between a specific (part-object) Other and the specific facet of self that existed in relationship to that Other.

The original components of the ORUs (self and other) can be modified, or even reversed, by a process of internal projection and identification. Thus, with the case of "Joe," we saw that what was originally experienced as a facet of self (despicable weakness) was projected onto Others and denied in the self, and what was originally experienced as a facet of an Other (his stepfather's sadistic power) could be identified with and experienced as "That's who I am." And, with Joe, we saw that this kind of structure could be extremely resistant to change.

In doing therapy, each time we encounter resistance in one of our clients, we are encountering a little bit of Joe. Joe shouted out his resistance with a proud, almost gleeful defiance: "I'm a bad kid. That's just who I am." Others may whisper their resistances with hopeless despair. "I am a helpless person. I have no power. You have all the power. You must do it for me." "I am alone in the world. I am a freak of nature. I will form relations with others only until I discover that crucial difference that separates me from them, differentiates me from them and from the rest of humankind. And I will be alone again." "I am an unloved child, an unwanted child. No one can ever love or want me. It is due to some unknown flaw in me. But it is my fate."

The befuddled therapist will shake his or her head and want to ask, "Don't you ever get tired of this identity?" The answer is yes, the client is usually bone-weary of it. It is awful. It is miserable. It is worse than anything, anything except . . . and this is the question: what is it that is worse than this addiction to a bad object? What is the nature of this powerful, life-destroying force that we dispassionately label *resistance*?

In Freudian theory, what were repressed were thoughts, feelings, and impulses that were judged by some part of the psyche to be too threatening to be allowed into consciousness. Freud considered that the bulk of such thoughts, feelings, and impulses were sexual in nature. But after 1920, Freud, with the introduction of the death instinct, included aggression as a category of repressed material. Taken together, the Freudian unconscious can be said to be defined by its *contents*. The Freudian unconscious consists of the thoughts we cannot allow ourselves to think, the feelings we cannot allow ourselves to feel, the memories we cannot allow ourselves to remember, the impulses we cannot allow ourselves to experience.

In contrast, while not totally rejecting the model of the Freudian unconscious, the unconscious in object relations theory is primarily comprised not of *content* but rather of *mental processes* that cannot be allowed into consciousness. As we have seen, the object relations theory model of the psyche is an extraordinarily complex web of internal objects, part objects (splitting), projections, projective identifications, and so on. As I noted earlier, all of these psychological processes *need to be kept unconscious if they are to be effective.*

When Joe projected his weak, contemptible internal object onto certain males and then bullied them to make sure that they felt as bad as he thought they ought to, he was unconsciously trying to get them to "carry" for him a facet of himself. This process *had to be unconscious* for two obvious reasons. First, if the process had been conscious Joe would have been aware that he was attempting to get others to carry a facet of himself that was weak and contemptible. Yet the entire purpose of this elaborate defense mechanism was to deny the existence of any weakness or contemptibility in himself. The only way the maneuver could be effective psychologically was if the maneuver itself was kept unconscious. Second, a conscious awareness of what he was doing would have been tantamount to an awareness that he was engaged in a fantasy, that he was playing a kind of mental game with himself and others. I do not mean to suggest that conscious fantasies and mental games cannot be powerful. But they are not nearly as powerful as the self-deception that is enabled by keeping the process unconscious, by allowing oneself to believe that one's fantasy is in fact truth.

The same thing can be said to be true for all defense mechanisms, and for the same reasons. Let us briefly revisit the *as if* mechanism that under-lies the basic defense of splitting. Splitting is the psyche saying to itself, "I know that I am dealing with a single object, but I will function *as if* there are two, independent but diametrically opposed objects." If this thought were allowed into consciousness the "oneness" of the object would be acknowledged and thus the split undone. And, if the thought is allowed into consciousness, then the power of an experienced "truth" would be reduced to the power of a mental "game."

This shift in focus from *content* to *process* leads to a subtle but impor-tant shift in the way the object relations theory therapist interacts with clients and in particular in the way the therapist offers interpretations. A classical Freudian therapist might say something like "You seem to be transferring your idealized mother onto me." The object relations theory therapist might tell the same client, "You seem to be working very hard to see in me only the loving, the nurturing, and the good." Again, the dif-ference between these interventions is subtle. One addresses content; the other addresses process. They may be considered to be two different facets of the same thing. But object relations theory considers that the focus on process more directly addresses the issue of resistance. Consider the object relations theory interpretation: "You are working very hard to see me in a certain way. You seem to *need* to see me in a certain way. What is the nature of this need?" The focus is on the nature of the need itself rather than the content of the need. Not that the content of the need is not impor-tant! But the nature of the need is the essence of the resistance.

Interestingly, there is no such term as "counterresistance" the way there is "countertransference." But whatever would be referred by such a term is to be found in every therapy session. Therapists routinely collude with – or have to maintain exhausting consciousness and self-discipline to avoid colluding with – their clients. This is no great mystery. We tend to grow very fond of our clients and it pains us to see them in pain. And the pain of our clients frequently touches our own pain. Whatever a client happens to be working on – betrayal, abandonment, abuse, neglect, loss – will trigger memories of our own versions of these issues and, being as human as our clients, it is in our nature to try and avoid pain.

Interns, in a psychodynamic training program, often come to supervision sounding like behaviorists: "My client never learned how to express such-and-such a feeling." "My client never learned how to be intimate." As though the task of the therapist were simply to "teach" the client these "skills" without any consideration of transference and countertransference, resistance and counterresistance issues. At other times interns overvalue their own importance to their clients. A client bemoaning his or her aloneness in the world will be countered with, "But I'm here for you! Don't hesitate to reach out to me." Although this intervention sounds narcissistic, I doubt that it is simply an overvaluation of the importance of a specific fifty minutes out of a ten-thousand-minute week. It is, at least as importantly, the therapist's collusion with the client to avoid pain. "No," the therapist is implying, "you don't have to feel that much pain. It is too much for you to bear. And it may be too much for me to bear."

But it is not just interns and novice therapists who engage in counterresistance. Senior therapists must be constantly on guard as well.

> Celeste, mother of two, divorced for a little over a year, was weeping bitterly in a session over the injustice of the different parenting roles she and her ex-husband had assumed. She (the primary caretaker) made sure the kids did their homework, that their clothes were clean, that they were clean, that they were well-fed and well-rested. Her ex, who had the kids every other weekend, would take them to Disneyland, feed them meals of guacamole and chips, allow them to stay up until midnight on school nights, and neglect their homework.
>
> Celeste was sure that her kids would grow up to resent her for her discipline and adore their father for his indulgence. "Celeste," I wanted to say, "your kids are not blind. They are not dumb. They sense your love for them and they see, on some level, that their father's indulgence is a form of neglect and indifference. They are not stupid!"
>
> I had this speech scripted in my mind. I wanted to say it. I was tempted to say it. I thought hard about it. And I bit my tongue. Instead I took a deep breath, steeled myself, and said something to the effect of, "You are deeply convinced that nothing you offer your children will be appreciated by them. I don't think this is really about your children. I think that on some level you are convinced that nothing you have to offer another person – any person – has any value. And I think you have probably felt this way your whole life."

To paraphrase Tolstoy's oft-quoted opening line in Anna Karenina, all happy people are alike in their happiness. But each unhappy person is unhappy in his or her particular way. So it is difficult to discuss resistance in a general way because it is difficult to generalize about resistance. Each resistance is unique. Nevertheless, object relations theory and intersubjectivity both predict that certain issues will be of particular relevance to resistance.

Sources of resistance

Each of us has our own unique pain which we deal with (and run from) in our own particular ways. Each of us has our own secret shame which we hide from others (and ourselves) in our own unique ways. Each of us has our own idiosyncratic fears which we acknowledge or hide, acquiesce to, cover over, or overcome. Each of us has our own resistance or, at least, our own motivation to resist. And as Freud recognized, the empathic understanding of, the appreciation of, the shepherding into consciousness of that resistance is the essential work of psychodynamic psychotherapy.

Freud offered sexuality (and later aggression) as a common template for understanding resistance, so too does object relations theory offer a set of categories (issues) around which resistance and can be expected to crystalize. The following list of categories is not meant to be exhaustive. Nor are the individual categories listed meant to be mutually exclusive. As with all the concepts discussed in this book, there is tremendous overlap.

Resistance as maintenance of the ego

As was discussed in Chapter 6, ORUs – internal object relationships – are not simply "unfinished business" from past external relationships. Many of us will rehash past conversations or arguments (sometimes years later) making retroactive points – victories in hindsight – by saying in our imagination what we *should have said* in the moment. "Dang! If only I had said this or that instead of hemming and hawing, it would have clinched my argument!" Such internal dialogs may be called many things (obsessive responses to narcissistic injuries?), but they are *not* ORUs (though they may be part of an expression of an ORU). An ORU is a structure of the psyche; it is an organizational unit of the mind; it is part of who we are. As such, it is not easily given up.

The adolescent gangsters I worked with vehemently defended what they acknowledged was a dysfunctional lifestyle. Some, like "Joe," would never budge beyond "That's who I am!" Others, like "Frank," (Chapter 7) started out from the same place ("My *name* is Francisco G. but *who I am* is

Frank-from-F13") but were eventually able to allow for a substantial shift in their identities. But among this latter group, there was a universal point of hesitation: "Wait a minute! If I stop being this and this and become something else, I won't recognize myself, I won't know who I am."

> In a boys' group one young gangster seemed to be considering the possibility of leaving his gang but was hung up on what he would wear if he didn't dress like a gangster. Dutifully, the other boys in the group offered suggestion after suggestion of different dress styles. To each suggestion the boy seemed to writhe in pain at the very notion: "Oh no, man, I couldn't dress like that!" In the moment I thought the discussion was absurd and disingenuous, but I now see it differently. This boy saw dressing like a gangster as part of being a gangster and being a gangster as part of who he was, and he could not conceive of anything else.
>
> Another boy argued with the staff over the prohibition against wearing red. "No, man, I'm not 'showing my colors' (he was from a Blood gang); I just really like red." Again, I and the staff thought he was being absurd. But from his point of view he was speaking a profound truth: he really did love red. Being a Blood was who he was. Red was part of who he was.

For those rigidly locked in the paranoid-schizoid position, giving up an ORU can be experienced as a kind of amputation or even death.

> One young gangster was expressing genuine anguish at the things he had done and the things he had seen done; his "homeboys" who had been killed and the unseen faces of those he may or may not have killed in drive-by shootings. When I gently suggested that he might want to think about a different lifestyle, he almost shouted at me: "No! That's just who I am." It was a part of himself that he acknowledged to be ugly and despicable but, from his perspective, it was *part of who he was*.

Even with "healthier" clients personal change involves a loss of some part of their identities.

> Bethany, a young psychology student, entered therapy determined to do whatever it took to change. There was essentially nothing about herself that she didn't dislike, and she was willing to go to any painful

place if it would get her out of who she was. Most clients will have an occasional respite session in which they take a momentary break from the painful work that constitutes therapy. But not Bethany. When I suggested that her relentless work might be a residue of her need for self-punishment, she adamantly disagreed, "No! I don't want to stay in this place for one second longer than I have to. Don't suggest that I waste any time getting in out of it."

After a few years of very hard and very productive work, Bethany began to allow herself to share with me some of her triumphs. One of her bosses at work had been short and critical with her and Brittany had decided that this woman probably didn't like her. But instead of retreating into the orgy of self-hatred that used to characterize her responses, Brittany found herself thinking very differently. "No, of course she doesn't like me: that's who she is. I tell her when I think she is wrong and she is somebody who doesn't like being corrected, especially by subordinates. Come to think of it, I don't like her very much either."

As soon as she had finished telling me this story the broad smile on her face disappeared and was replaced by a look of considerable discomfort. "This is more than a little weird," she said. "I am becoming somebody I don't know."

Resistance as maintenance of the good and the bad

I believe that Thomas Ogden (1986) has described the essence of splitting as simply and as eloquently as has anyone:

> The infant must be able to split in order to feed safely without the intrusion of the anxiety that he is harming his mother, and without the anxiety that she will harm him. It is necessary for an infant to feel that the mother who is taking care of him is fully loving and has no connection whatever with the mother who "hurts" him by making him wait. The anxiety arising from the thought that the nurturing mother and the frustrating mother are one and the same would rob the infant of the security that he needs in order to feed safely. Similarly, the ability to desire safely would be lost if the infant, while feeding, experienced himself as the same infant who angrily wished to control and to subjugate the breast/mother in her absence. While feeding, the infant must experience himself as loving in an uncomplicated, uncontaminated way in order to be able to feel that he can want without damaging.

(p. 54)

The need/desire for a purely good object – and a purely good self – are not restricted to infancy.

> An extremely intelligent young college student with a history of abuse presented at her college counseling center with depression and para-noid tendencies. She described a tumultuous history of previous therapy experiences, marked by flip-flopping between idealizing and vilifying her therapists. It seemed to take very little to turn this young woman against her therapists. A wrong turn of phrase, an unwelcomed glance, a suggestion that the client did not agree with, and a previously idealized therapist would suddenly be seen not just as bad and incompetent, but as malicious and being "out to get" her. These flips would sometimes happen several times a week. She would frequently leave a session angry and simply not show up for her next appointment. Or, she would call and cancel her next appointment and then, without calling back to reschedule, would simply show up at her regular appointment time, expecting to be welcomed into the session without question.
>
> Her therapist at the counseling center, recognizing her fragility, made a decision to tolerate this highly provocative behavior that, at most ther-apy settings, would simply have been labeled unacceptable and grounds for termination. Needless to say, the "work" of nearly every session was to uncover what it had been that had so upset the client in the previous session. And the "reasons" were consistent: any deviation from perfec-tion by the therapist was unbearable to the client. The slightest misat-tunement on the part of the therapist – a failure to understand, a missing smile when a smile was expected, an unwanted challenge – was experi-enced by the client as abandonment, neglect, and betrayal.
>
> And, as Ogden suggested, it was not just her therapist she could not stand when imperfection was revealed, it was herself. She hated who she was in those moments as much as she hated who she per-ceived her therapist to be. Her therapist had been "revealed" as a mali-cious betrayer and in her presence the client felt herself to be an angry, unlovable, terrified child. Both perceptions were equally intolerable. What she "needed" (what she felt she could not live without) was feel-ing like the perfect child in the arms of (at the breast of) the perfect mother. Nothing else seemed remotely adequate.

Ogden goes on to write that it is not just the good breast/mother that needs to be kept "pure," it is the bad breast/mother as well:

> Splitting not only safeguards the infant's need to give and receive love; it also safeguards his need to hate. If the object of the infant's

hate is contaminated with facets of the loved object, the infant will not be able to hate it safely. (The assumption that the infant has a need to hate is not dependent upon the Kleinian assumption of the presence of powerful, constitutionally determined destructive wishes. For instance, one could postulate, as did Winnicott (1949, 1950) and Fairbairn (1952), that hate arises from excessively frustrated need and that is essential for normal development that the infant, child, or adult be able to experience this feeling without being frightened by it.)

(pp. 54–55)

I have already discussed (Chapter 6) the young neo-Nazi I worked with who needed a target for his considerable rage and hatred, a target he could hate in a pure, uncontaminated (and almost gleeful) manner. Other clients have shown a need to maintain a hate-object, often at considerable cost to themselves.

Terry, a gay male in his twenties, was financially entirely dependent on his father, in spite of the fact that his father and he otherwise expressed nothing but hatred and contempt for each other. This mutual hatred seemed to go back as far as Terry could remember. He remembered as a toddler his father angrily yelling at him to "walk like a boy, not a girl!" And he could not recall the first time his father had pronounced him a "failure."

Terry seemed determined to make that epithet a reality. He trained as an interior decorator but insisted that he "could not" make decisions about color, fabric, wallpaper, etc. He tried to move into floral work but proved himself "all thumbs." And Terry took these failures with equanimity, expecting them and almost seeming to welcome them. And all the while his father paid for everything: his food, his apartment, even his therapy.

What emerged in the course of therapy was his realization that, for Terry, failure was a kind of revenge. His entire life was a behavioral shout: "You call me a failure; so be it! You want to see failure? I'll show you failure. I'll be such a failure that you will have to take care of me for the rest of my life."

But as I have been indicating, even the most sophisticated of us spend some time in the paranoid-schizoid position and as long as we are there we will need someone to hate purely as much as someone to love purely.

Max was an intelligent, sensitive, and insightful professional who would occasional take up considerable therapy time talking about his issues with a female colleague, Jody. Although Jody appeared to be fond of Max, Max saw Jody as being both "brilliant" and "castrating" (words that might just as well have described Max's mother). Over time, Max's perception of Jody gradually changed. He recognized that she was "very smart," but not intimidatingly brilliant (not necessarily smarter than Max himself). And he also came to realize that although she occasionally displayed a sharp, cutting wit, she was at heart a kind person and that she had nothing but good will towards Max himself.

What bothered Max was the realization that while his *perceptions* of Jody were changing, his *feelings* towards her were not. In her presence, Max found himself remaining a frightened, intimidated child, desperately wanting to please and impress her but mute for fear that she would scorn and humiliate him. In hindsight he would question her judgments, but in her presence he would passively accept everything she said as though it were spoken *ex cathedra*.

Max recognized that he was being unfair both to Jody and to himself in this relationship and was very disturbed by the fact that this awareness seemed to make no difference to either his feelings or his behavior. By this time he also recognized that Jody was a mother transference object to him, but this knowledge too made no difference.

Then, in one session, Max reported that he had had what felt to him to be "almost like an auditory hallucination." He had been ruminating about his relationship with Jody, berating himself for being so "unfair" to her, when he heard a voice in his head that sounded "like an angry, pouting child." "No," this voice had shouted, "I'm not going to change my feelings. I'm not ready to stop hating her!" (Max had previously never been aware of any feelings of "hatred" towards Jody). Interestingly, as soon as Max heard this voice inside him his feelings and behavior towards Jody changed almost instantly and became more mature and appropriate.

Resistance as maintenance of a dialectic

A category overlapping with the one just discussed is the need, in the paranoid-schizoid position, to maintain the dialectic of good and bad. In splitting, ambivalent feelings towards a whole object cannot be tolerated and an "as if" mechanism is invoked. The splitter says, unconsciously, "I know that this is a single object, but I will act *as if* it were two, unrelated part-objects, one good and one bad." Thus, splitting necessarily involves the creation of a dialectic of good and bad. One cannot have good without bad and one cannot have bad without good. They negate each other but they also create and sustain each other. To give up one is to give up the other.

> Candice, an intelligent and sensitive college student, presented with a history of multiple therapy experiences, all of which ended when a previously idealized therapist was summarily rejected as being uncaring or even hostile and persecutory. Most of these previous therapists seemed to have been very fond of Candice and some appeared to have gone to extraordinary lengths to keep her in therapy and to be helpful to her. But Candice would hear nothing of this: they were all uncaring and unloving and all had somehow "turned against" her. She would acknowledge nothing *good* about any of them.
>
> In the course of her work it became clear that to acknowledge any "good" in these "bad" objects would have been to give up the split, to have allowed herself to see them as whole objects, loving but human and flawed, objects that drew feelings of ambivalence. And to give up the split would have meant losing the other side of the split: the unambivalently loved, purely good mother – the good breast. And the fantasy of finding the good breast, of reuniting with the good breast, was a driving force in Candice's life. It was a fantasy that protected her from sinking into a profound depression of despair and hopelessness. To her, the maintenance of the idea of the good breast was well worth the endless series of disappointments that came with her recreation of the bad breasts.

The good/bad split is not the only dialectic in the paranoid-schizoid position that needs to be defended and maintained. Each ORU consists of a dialectical relationship. The internal *object* component of the ORU defines and maintains the internal self component and *vice versa*. With most people in the paranoid-schizoid position, complementary (good and bad) ORUs are of relatively equal weight and the relative balance can allow for the eventual giving up of the split and the integration of good and bad part-objects into whole objects. But when the psyche is seriously out of balance, a negative ORU can become self-perpetuating.

> "Lucy" (first presented in Chapter 5) entered the paranoid-schizoid position with a clear split. The bad breast was projected onto Lucy's critical and hating adoptive mother in whose presence Lucy felt

inadequate and hateful. And the good breast was projected onto her weak, passive, but loving adoptive father in whose presence Lucy felt vulnerable but lovable. These complementary ORUs "worked" until Lucy was about 10, 11, or 12 when her "passive but loving" father came to her . . . and raped her . . . and continued to molest her every time the mother was out of the house until Lucy left for college at age 18.

Whatever "goodness" Lucy experienced within the original father/ daughter ORU was superseded (though never entirely replaced) by an ORU consisting of a lecherous/abusive father and a "nasty little girl" self. Lucy was left essentially hating herself under either mother or father ORU.

Given this winless choice, Lucy opted to live predominantly in her mother/daughter ORU: an ORU that left her feeling hateful and unlovable, but which nevertheless offered some hope – her mother's message had always been, "If you were only perfect I could love you."

For months I struggled (foolishly) to get Lucy to let go of this noxious maternal "introject." Lucy professed no love for her mother. She recognized her mother's dynamic as a "Christian martyr," who had adopted "damaged" children whom no one else wanted, as a sign of her own moral superiority. But Lucy could not (would not) let go of her mother's critical – hateful – voice. The maternal voice was one pole in a dialectic tension with the other pole which was a pathetic, inadequate, contemptible child. And this self-image – the inadequate, contemptible child – however odious it was, was the only self-image Lucy had. To give up the noxious mother she would have had to give up the loathsome child and that was all she had. Outside of that ORU (or of the comparable one with her father) she had no existence.

Resistance and insufficient witnessing

An intern once reported to me a client declaring adamantly: "I'm fucked up and I'm going to stay fucked up! I'm not going to let my parents off the hook." The intern and I were both flabbergasted. This was such a blatant and conscious statement of what could easily have been an unconscious process. I originally saw this as an addiction to hate, but I now see it differently. To be sure, the statement was that the client was not ready to give up her hatred of her parents. But this was not an addiction to hate. Rather, it was a statement that the damage she believed she had received from her parents had not yet been sufficiently witnessed and appreciated. When she felt that her injuries had been sufficiently validated, then she would be willing to let go of her hatred and allow herself to "get well."

> A different client, an intelligent, insightful, and "higher functioning" client than the one presented by my intern, presented with essentially the same issue. Chronically depressed and self-hating, she began a session with the following assessment: "I have decided that my mother did the best she could, but it wasn't good enough." She said this with a numb expression and a voice filled with hopelessness.
>
> I immediately countered that I saw it differently. "No," I said, "I don't think your mother did as well as she could have, but I think it was basically good enough."
>
> The client reacted as though I had slapped her.

What I was trying to convey in my "reframe" was the following: "I think there is plenty of fault to be found in your mother's mothering, so it's fine with me if you are still angry at her. But you can be angry at her without deeming yourself *irreparably damaged* which is what seems to be implied by your statement." Since I considered this to be an entirely positive reframe, I was puzzled by her negative response.

But it was not my support of her that made the client feel slapped. It was my seeming to let her mother (as the client quoted previously said) "off the hook." I had never (to my awareness) defended her mother, nor encouraged her to "see things through her mother's eyes." Indeed, my conscious efforts were in the opposite direction: to encourage her to give full vent to her hurt and rage. But clearly my efforts had been insufficient. Clearly, my client felt that I had insufficiently witnessed and appreciated the hurt and damage she had experienced by her mother's emotional abandonment. And she was willing to experience herself and to present herself as doomed and beyond repair if this was what it took.

Resistance and "heroic loyalty"

In the last section I presented two clients who were unwilling to give up their rage at, or hatred of, their parents. Frequently, the opposite seems true: clients will do anything but criticize, "badmouth," or otherwise show negative feelings towards their parents. Psychoanalyst Stewart Aledort calls this "heroic loyalty."

When parents project some unbearable part of themselves onto a child, and then manipulate the child to carry that feeling or that trait for them, it is typically an act of desperation, and almost always a sign of profound weakness. And when the child (unconsciously) agrees to carry the projection, there is an equally unconscious awareness of the weakness from which it comes.

> Morgan described his father as being intelligent and aloof, relating to the world (or avoiding the world) primarily through the defenses of arrogance, contempt, and condescension. His father had never achieved a level of success in his career that might otherwise justify his arrogance. But he would not/could not acknowledge failure. Instead, he projected his grandiose self onto his son. His son would be the success, the brilliant star, that he, himself, could not be, and therefore he would never have to deal with his failure.
>
> Morgan, as intelligent as his father but far more insightful, grew to see this clearly. Morgan was tortured by his own perfectionism. He saw how it interfered with his relationships and even with his career. He recognized how the agony he suffered when he was less than perfect was unnecessary and self-defeating. He saw clearly that when he re-projected this perfectionism onto his wife, that this was cruel, unfair, and destructive to the relationship. He recognized the perfectionism as having been jointly created by himself and his father. He saw in this how his father had used him. He even was able to see in this his father's weakness. But he was unable to have any feelings about any of this. His insights were purely cerebral. "No," he would say blandly, "I don't seem to be able to have any feelings towards my father."
>
> This was *heroic loyalty*. On a conscious level he saw everything clearly. But on an unconscious level he preferred to contain the noxious and self-defeating perfectionism and grandiosity himself, rather than relinquish it back to his father, whom he perceived as being too weak to be able to bear it or deal with it himself.

Resistance and the tantalizing object

An earlier vignette involves a reference to what Fairbairn (1952) referred to as the "tantalizing object." The message Lucy received from her mother was, "If you were only perfect, I could love you." The tantalizing object represents an interesting divergence from the Kleinian model. In the Kleinian model, objects (part-objects) are good or bad. Good objects are available and giving; bad objects are maliciously withholding and unavailable.

Fairbairn's tantalizing object is a good object that is unavailable. But unlike the bad object, the tantalizing object does not communicate, "I have infinite bounty, but I withhold from you because you are unworthy, and I take a sadistic pleasure in my justified withholding." Instead, it says, "I have infinite bounty, but I withhold it for your own good. You need to try harder. When you have met my demands, my bounty will be yours."

> The tantalizing object is maddening, frustrating, enraging, but power-fully addictive. One pleads with it: "Wait, wait, don't go away. Give me one more chance. I'll do better. I'll be better. I'll give you what you want. Pleasing you is so close (yet so elusive). And when I am finally able to please you, nirvana awaits."
>
> This was a good part of what kept Lucy addicted to her cruel and critical mother: the mother held out a devil's bargain – "Love awaits! It is you, not I, who is the problem. If you can only become what I require you to be then all will be well and my love will come shining down upon you." Lucy's mother's criterion for love was perfection. If there can be degrees of "impossibility," then this was even more impossible for Lucy than for most people. But this did not keep Lucy from trying. And oh, how she tried! It was extremely important to Lucy that she be seen as a *good person*, that she not be found wanting, that she be *perfect* in every way. Early in her treatment she required hospitalization for suicidality after her best friend expressed concern that she might be "putting on a little weight."

The tantalizing object walks a fine line. It has to give just enough to keep the object "hooked." But if it is too withholding it runs the danger of flip-ping into the "bad object," its maliciousness revealed. The tantalizing object has to stay very close, its bounty always dangling like a carrot on a stick, just out of reach; the object has to feel its presence, see it, smell it, taste it, feel its breath, but rarely actually get it. But not always. In cases of severe trauma or deprivation, a tantalizing object can become reified into an immutable force.

> Charlene, a delinquent teenager at the Center, had a mother who had been absent for most of Charlene's life. A severe drug abuser, the mother had essentially lived on the streets, supporting her var-ious habits by prostitution. In the moments when she did return to her daughter's life, she would shower the young girl with affection, apologies, promises, and pull towards fusion. When Charlene was a

teenager she had "bonded" with her mother by going into the streets with her, prostituting together, and then using their profits to buy and use drugs together. When Charlene was in the Center she had not seen her mother for over a year and had no idea where she was, or even if she were alive or dead. Regardless, she spoke of her mother with a kind of enraptured awe. "My mother is my life. I don't think I could live," she said, "if my mother were to die."

Resistance in service to an essential part of the ego

In the paranoid-schizoid position, the psyche is essentially *compartmen-talized*. Different ego functions are assigned to different pigeonholes, each of which is then labeled in terms of one or the other component of an origi-nally external relationship. Sometimes an essential ego function gets put in a particularly ugly pigeonhole and gets labeled as "bad."

In the early part of our work together both Lucy and I were convinced that she was hopeless. Lucy appeared to be relentlessly self-hating and required multiple hospitalizations for suicidality (Lucy was the one who became suicidal after her best friend remarked that she was "put-ting on a little weight"). I saw Lucy three times a week not because I had any real hope of improvement but because it seemed the only way to keep her alive.

But Lucy did get better. After two years on disability she found a job as an assistant manager at a movie theater. In our first few ses-sions after beginning her new job Lucy presented as someone I did not know – and as someone I did not particularly like. The Lucy I knew, in spite of her depression, had a sense of humor and an infectious laugh. And the Lucy I knew identified with the child who wanted to be perfect, who wanted to be loved, and I found her easy to love. This new Lucy was angry, sarcastic, and contemptuous. "Well," she would almost spit out, "my so-called manager – she thinks that good managing involves . . ." and then go on to describe some incident in which the manager was simply following company policy, all the while Lucy's face being contorted with disdain and contempt.

It took me a while to finally recognize the person in the room with me. The voice I was hearing was that of Lucy's critical, rejecting mother. And I didn't like her any more when she was Lucy than I had when she had been an internal object beating Lucy up. But what Lucy had done (unconsciously) made perfect sense. With the inadequate child/critical mother ORU Lucy had always identified with the inadequate child and projected the critical mother object onto those around her (myself included). But somehow Lucy had sensed that the pathetic child identity could not function as an assistant manager: strength was needed. And the only source of strength in her ORU (or among all her ORUs) was the hated internal mother.

So, Lucy *flipped* the identification. Instead of identifying with the self component of her dominant ORU she identified with the object component and the inadequate, pathetic child component was projected onto her manager. This was exactly what "Joe" had done early in his life, and for very similar reasons. *Strength* was needed and the only strength to be found was through identification with the aggressor. The difference between Lucy and Joe was that for Lucy this switch was a temporary adaptation to a particular situation while with Joe it became his permanent identity.

Resistance to the loss of a symbiotic relationship

When a part of the self – either a feeling, an impulse, or a part of an ORU – is projected onto another person, a special bond is created (in fantasy) between the projector and the other person. The boundaries between the projector and the recipient are (unconsciously) seen to be diminished and the experience is one of partial fusion. One person is seen as *carrying* a part of another person for the purpose of safekeeping that disavowed part. The two people are seen (in unconscious fantasy) as being psychologically joined, as being a kind of psychological Siamese twins. The *bond* that is created by this unconscious process can be extremely powerful.

> For many years I was part of a supervisors' group along with Emma, a therapist I liked and esteemed. But there was a certain issue over which Emma and I constantly disagreed, and this disagreement eventually became the focus of a schism in the group. This issue was "negative transference" within the supervisor/supervisee relationship. When I was the object of an intern's negative transference I could only see, and only deal with, the intern's fear of me. When Emma was the object of an intern's negative transference she could only experience the intern's hatred of her.
>
> Of course we were both experienced enough therapists to "know" that fear and hatred are often two sides of the same coin. But each of us seemed locked in our particular perspective, partly out of a

sense of needing to defend our positions against the outrageousness of the other's position. I saw Emma as being cruel and judgmental in her labeling of the interns and she saw me as being naive and easily manipulated in my obliviousness to the obvious.

Clearly (though clearly only in hindsight) we (and the group) were splitting, though it took us an unconscionably long time to become conscious of this. When we finally did, the splitting lost much of its power, as unconscious processes do when they are allowed into consciousness. But in addition, Emma and I made concerted efforts to prevent a return of the splitting. I pushed myself to not only be aware of, but to actually *experience*, the hatred behind a negative transference and Emma did the same thing with fear.

The result was a much more harmonious group and much better supervision for the interns. But in one subsequent group I suddenly found myself wanting to attack Emma along the old battle lines. I was also aware that my urge to attack was not being provoked by Emma but was coming from something entirely internal to me. I was very disturbed by this experience and took some time to figure it out.

What finally felt true was that I missed the unconscious *connection* I used to experience with Emma. When we were splitting I had the experience of carrying a part of her and of her carrying a part of me. While the conscious part of the experience was of anger and contempt, the unconscious experience was of an intense connectedness or bondedness. When I had "reconnected" with my own issues around anger I was much more whole, much more autonomous, but I also felt much more alone. Emma was still my friend and my colleague, but she felt more separate from me and I missed and longed for the fantasized connection with her.

Resistance as a defense against unbearable pain

Melanie Klein had an especial interest in anxiety. The "depressive position" got its name from the particular form of anxiety that marks that position: anxiety pertaining to the prospect of permanent object loss. In the depressive position, whole objects (external objects) can die. They can die of old age, they can be killed, or they can be driven away so that they are functionally dead. And (in the depressive position) when something is dead, it is dead and it can never come back.

This is not true in the paranoid-schizoid position. In the paranoid-schizoid position part-objects are interchangeable and part-objects (good and bad objects) come and go randomly. No loss is forever. This is one of the huge attractions of the paranoid-schizoid position. The paranoid-schizoid position has many of its own anxieties, but permanent object loss is not one of them. To those who have had multiple (real) object losses in their lives, this difference can be decisive.

> Angela was a 16-year-old Latina whose bright smile and childlike demeanor belied her serious drug problem. Angela was the type of drug addict of whom the staff said that if she saw a pill in a dust ball in the corner of a room she would dive for it and swallow it, dust ball and all, without stopping to see what it was, before the staff had a chance to stop her. Angela was a third-generation substance abuser. Her grandfather had been one of the major methamphetamine dealers in the community. And her mother was essentially lost to drugs and had been out on the street for as long as Angela could remember, doing prostitution to support her drug habit. Angela's only contact with her mother was when the mother would periodically show up at home with a new infant in her arms, deposit the baby with some willing relative, and disappear again to the streets.
>
> I arrived at the Center one morning and was stopped in my tracks by the sound coming out of one of the front offices. It was the sound of weeping and wailing such as I had never heard before. It sounded as if someone's heart had been ripped out and shredded. It was Angela. Angela had just learned that her mother had done it again. She had shown up at the family home, new baby daughter in her arms, and had left the infant with a relative and instantly disappeared again.
>
> Angela was weeping. She was weeping for her new baby sister; she was weeping for herself; and she was weeping for the mother who she momentarily realized (could not deny) would never be a mother.
>
> An hour later Angela was out on the playing field laughing and playing with her peers, as though she didn't have a care in the world. Reality had momentarily forced her into the depressive position. Permanent object loss had hit her like a brickbat. But the pain of that position had been too much. The *reality* of the depressive position had too little to offer her and the *escape* of the paranoid-schizoid position was irresistible. Angela had taken a momentary foray into the depressive position, followed by a full-scale retreat into the paranoid-schizoid position.

Part III

The depressive position, intersubjectivity, and the discovery of external objects

9 The psychological "third"

Chapters 9 through 15 deal with the problem of how one leaves the paranoid-schizoid position and enters the depressive position and, in the process, how one disavows internal objects and discovers external objects. Chapter 9 shifts out of object relations theory and into intersubjectivity theory long enough to introduce the concept of the "psychological third." In relational and intersubjective theories the only way out of the binary relationships that comprise ORUs is the introduction of some form of internal or external "third." It can be argued that all the different ways of emerging from the paranoid-schizoid position – all the different ways of discovering external objects and the external world – involve some variant of the psychological third.

In the first three chapters we encountered the paradox that an infant can learn a huge amount about the external world by itself but cannot learn about his or her own inner workings without some kind of external mirror. The mother serves as the earliest mirror, first through her provision of the holding environment and the mirroring function of her eyes in particular, and then through the provision of her own external ego (fantasized by the infant to be, in part, its internal ego) in the "mother-infant unit."

Modern relational and intersubjective theorists postulate that a similar external mirror is needed for the infant to be able to emerge from the fantasy of the mother-infant unit, from the "omnipotence" of the paranoid-schizoid position, and to accept the separateness and autonomy, the *alterity*, of its mother – to accept its mother's externality to itself and its own externality to its mother. This second external mirroring function is what is called the psychological "*third*."

There are many kinds of psychological thirds. There are inner thirds and intersubjective thirds, and subcategories of each. But basically, a psychological third is simply an object (internal or external) that offers a third perspective.

A psychological third (a third perspective) is what people seek when they go into therapy. If I am locked with my spouse in a frustrating and repetitive clash of perspectives, each of us taking turns uttering a plaintive, ". . . but my experience is . . ." which is met by "Well yes, but *my* experience is . . ." then a couple's therapist might offer a way out of this fruitless ping pong game. The couple's therapist cannot simply say, "Your spouse is right and you are wrong," because that is merely choosing between two perspectives rather than offering a third. Nor can the therapist simply offer his or her own perspective as a kind of trump card. It is as easy to get locked into a three-way stalemate as it is a two-way. In order for the therapist to function as a true psychological third, the third perspective must be co-created by all parties. It is not just a *different* perspective, it is a *new* perspective, co-created, intersubjectively created.

The same is true with individual psychotherapy. If I am locked in a two-way battle between me and an internal object, if my internal abandoning parent delights in taunting me with my worthlessness and the corresponding self component of that ORU responds with useless and pathetic objections, then a therapist might be helpful. And again, the therapist cannot simply say that one side is right and the other wrong. A new perspective (a new truth) has to be co-created by the interaction of our two subjectivities if I am to be released from this endless-loop tape.

Why is a third perspective necessary? There is the perspective of the infant and the second perspective provided by the mother. Why do we need a third? The answer is that a dyadic system always runs the risk of being a closed, and therefore immutable, system. If I have one perspective (one opinion) and you have another, then what can we do but argue forever. I have no data to present (nothing external to our closed system) that would change your mind and you have nothing external to present to me that would change my mind. We could "agree to disagree" but that would effectively foreclose our relationship (around that issue). If we are to continue to have a relationship (around the issue) all we can do is argue. If I am a small child who announces that I am hungry a half-hour before dinner and you are my mother who tells me that I will have to wait, then you are the bad breast who maliciously tortures me. You can tell me otherwise, but who believes the bad breast? I can wish for the return of the good breast who used to feed me on demand, but this is to wish for a *different* relationship rather than a wish to alter a current relationship. In order to be able to alter a relationship – to be able to *grow* within a relationship – one needs to be able to step out of that relationship and see it from a third perspective.

The theories of Klein and Lacan posit that the original "third" is embodied in the person of the Oedipal father. With the arrival of the Oedipus complex the mother-child *dyad* transforms into the Oedipal *triangle*: the third is introduced into the child's psyche. The pre-Oedipal child can happily maintain the fantasy that he or she and mother are forever united, that there is a unique connection between them, that the umbilical cord has not been completely severed. The father may be emotionally important to the child, but primarily as an auxiliary or substitute mother. However, with the arrival of the Oedipal triangle, the father becomes something other than just a substitute mother: he becomes the mother's partner. The issue here is not the rivalry that the father represents, nor the castration anxiety/penis envy that Freud focused on. Rather, the issue is more in how the mother is seen. With the arrival of the Oedipal father, the mother is recognized as having a partner of her own (other than the child), a lover, a friend, a confidante, a mate. The mother is seen as having a *life* of her own: she is external to the child.

Most modern relational and intersubjective theorists tend to reject the father-centric model of the third. Current infant research has simply placed the infant's capacity for a psychological third far before the traditional time period of the Oedipus complex. Benjamin (2004) postulates that a nascent psychological third is inherent in the earliest mother/infant relationship, even in the period often referred to as a period of "oneness."

> In my view of thirdness, recognition is not first constituted by verbal speech; rather, it begins with the early nonverbal experience of sharing a pattern, a dance, with another person. I . . . have therefore proposed a nascent or energetic third – as distinct from the one in the mother's mind – present in the earliest exchange of gestures between mother and child, in the relationship that has been called *oneness*. I consider this early exchange to be a form of thirdness, and suggest that we call the principle of affective resonance or union that underlies it the *one in the third* – literally, the part of the third that is constituted by oneness.
>
> (pp. 16–17, italics in original)

Benjamin's ideas here are completely in keeping with those of Winnicott. As I argued in Chapter 1, Winnicott said that the holding environment represented the child's first encounter with an Other. This is because the holding environment is not a simple one-way teaching experience. It is a system that allows for *mutual learning.* In the holding environment the mother learns how her baby is different from all other babies (perhaps most importantly, how her baby is different from how she was as a baby). She learns what kind of holding is too tight and what is not tight enough. She learns when Baby needs to be picked up and when Baby needs to be put down.

And, in the holding environment, the infant begins to learn about the mother, most importantly, that she is there: that she is consistent, reliable, and predictable. This is why Winnicott says that the Primary Maternal Preoccupation ("almost an illness") is so important for the infant. After a while, the infant can begin to tolerate some inconsistency in its mother, some empathic failures, but this is because the infant has, by this time, has come to know that *she is there* – he has come to know her rhythms.

And, in the process of discovering his mother, in discovering her separateness, he has started the process of discovering himself, his separateness, his independent existence as an Other to the Other of his mother.

It is the *mutuality of learning* that keeps the extraordinarily intimate system of the holding environment from being the kind of "closed dyadic system" described at the beginning of this chapter. And this quality, this capacity for openness, for change, for learning, is almost entirely dependent on the person of the mother.

This is one reason why Winnicott was so insistent that *mothering cannot be taught* (see Chapter 2). But perhaps we should modify Winnicott's statement: mothering cannot be taught *by anyone except the infant.* When the mother raises her infant "by the book," she is alienating herself from what her infant has to teach her about himself/herself. And when the mother is alienated from what her infant has to teach her, the infant fails to learn about himself or herself and becomes self-alienated. When a mother feeds her infant by the clock and in prescribed amounts, the infant has a harder time learning about hunger and satiation. When the mother fails to notice the way her infant arches his back when held in a certain way, the infant doesn't learn that he has the power to influence his environment and to communicate with his caretaker. When a mother relates to her baby as though he is *an infant* rather than *her unique infant*, the baby acquires little sense of having a unique self.

When, for whatever reason, there is a failure of *thirdness* in the child's early development, whether it stems from the mother's own inability to come out of herself enough to function as a third or the Oedipal father's inability to fill that role, then the role of the third necessary for psychological development ends up being *embodied in the person of the therapist*. This is the essence of what is now called relational or intersubjective psychotherapy.

As with Winnicott's mothering, this aspect of the therapist's role cannot be taught. This, of course, is not to say that there is not a great deal of formal learning that is necessary to become a competent therapist. Rather, what I am saying is that there needs to be a dialectical relationship between what our theory tells us and what our clients are telling us. To rely only (or excessively) on theory – or on some "manualized" treatment – is to treat the symptom rather than the person (or, in the case of CBT, to treat the behavior rather than the person – which, of course, is what they say should be done). Treating the symptom or the behavior rather than the whole person may be appropriate when this is all the client wants. If a client wants help with a certain discrete phobia that is problematic, then that client certainly has the right to a specific, focused type of treatment. But, in my judgment, few clients are so constituted. Indeed, I would argue that one of the great disservices provided by the *Diagnostic and Statistical Manual* is the artificial breakdown of the human psyche into (supposedly) discrete "disorders," defined by an apparently arbitrary number of symptoms.

> I began my own psychotherapy unconscionably late for a young therapist. When I finally did seek out help, I interviewed two different therapists. When asked by the first therapist why I was seeking help I answered, "Because I don't like myself; I don't like who I am." He nodded and responded, "Perhaps you are depressed."
>
> Part of me liked this answer: it let me off the hook. I might not have to get into all the messiness of who I was. I might simply have a "depressive disorder" that could somehow be "alleviated," maybe even with medication. But mostly I was angered by his suggestion. I, I thought, had the courage to face something ugly in myself. Why was this therapist so eager to make excuses for me?
>
> When I presented the same complaint to the second therapist he simply nodded and waited for me to say more. I chose the second therapist.

Inner thirds

In the quote by Jessica Benjamin at the beginning of this chapter Benjamin (2004) "propose[s] a nascent or energetic third – as distinct from the one in the mother's mind – present in the earliest exchange of gestures between mother and child." What Benjamin refers to as "the one in the mother's mind" is a different kind of third. It is an internal third, one that is part of our psyches (that we carry with us into all relationships). It is distinct from the intersubjective third that arises out of the particular relationship we are engaged in.

Inner thirds are essential to healthy functioning. They are the depressive position equivalent of the internal objects of the paranoid-schizoid position. The difference between the internal objects of the paranoid-schizoid position and the inner thirds of the depressive position ("intersubjectivity," in Benjamin's terms) is that the former are "part-objects" with whom one can only engage in an endlessly repetitive, closed-loop type of role-taking (what Benjamin (2004) calls a "complementary relationship" or a "doer/done-to" relationship). Inner thirds are internal whole objects: inner objects with whom one can have an actual conversation, a conversation that moves one forward to new ground rather than being endlessly stuck in the same spot.

To illustrate this, let us contrast one particular kind of inner third, what Benjamin (2004) calls a "moral third," from its equivalent in classical psychoanalytic theory: what Freud called the "superego." The superego is, in object relations terms, an internal part-object. As such, it is incapable of thought or true dialog. It is capable of arguing (endlessly and pointlessly) with other parts of the psyche such as the ego, it can shame and criticize, but it is impervious to reason or to persuasion. In contrast, the "moral third" is an internal subject and is therefore capable of thought, reasoning, pondering, and therefore is capable of change. The superego is limited to telling you that, "You are bad. Your thoughts are dirty. Your impulses are shameful." But a "moral third" is like having one's own internal moral philosopher with whom one can have a productive dialog about what is right and what is wrong.

In the case of the mother, her inner thirds could be her internal version of her own mother (as an internal subject, not an internal object); whatever (non-dogmatically held) theory of childrearing she gleaned from books, peers, or classes; and other important "Others" in her life such as husband, friends, jobs, etc. Again, what is crucial here is that these inner objects be what she can have an actual dialog with, what she can continue to learn from and grow from, even in the absence of the actual (external) Other. If the internal object is a part-object: if her internal mother is an idealized "good breast" whom she has to slavishly emulate or a "bad breast" whom she must obsessively be *better than*, then these do not constitute *inner thirds* (they are inner *objects* rather than inner *subjects*) and can provide little benefit to her or to her child.

Psychotherapists own inner thirds frequently include their own thera-pists, their theories, important mentors, and whoever else made an impact on their lives. As with Winnicott's mothers, there must be a capacity for dialog with each of these inner representations rather than a slavish devo-tion towards, or rejection of, them. One can continue to learn from one's own therapist long after the actual therapy has terminated (Schedler, 2010). But one can also get stuck trying to "be the kind of therapist my therapist was" or, in the opposite direction, obsessively need to prove one's self "warmer" and "kinder" than one's own "cold, detached" former therapist.

I strongly believe that a sound theoretical foundation provides an essen-tial inner third. This is especially true when one discovers oneself caught in, and struggling to emerge from, a "complementary relationship" (Ben-jamin) or "subjugating third" (Ogden). It is in these moments, when one is struggling to recapture one's sense of self, one's subjectivity, that the ques-tion, "What just happened?" can be best answered with the help of theory.

But theory can also be a cruel slave driver. It is extremely painful to review the psychoanalytic literature of the 1950s and read case material in which it is now clear that women were browbeaten and shamed into "acknowledging" their continuing and unresolved "penis envy" because they reported being incapable of a "vaginal orgasm." It wasn't until 1966 that pioneering sexologists Masters and Johnson called into question the very existence of a purely vaginal orgasm.

Some clients will object when they perceive their therapists to be over-relying on their own inner thirds (especially inner thirds derived from the-ory). But though we can appreciate when this happens, we cannot rely on our clients to do this work for us. Therapists need to develop the habit of previewing their interventions. If a particular interpretation "sounds right" but *feels* "textbookish," it is probably wrong.

Mothers' (or therapists') inner thirds provide them with invaluable tools for the mother/infant (therapist/client) relationships. But they also provide a more direct benefit to the infant (client). Many relational theorist (c.f. Benjamin (2004), Green (2004)) point out that when a mother engages her infant from the position of a subject (whole object) she engages with her whole self, including her inner thirds. Thus, the mother's inner thirds become part of the infant's discovery of the mother. Green (2004) one-ups Winnicott's (1951) famous dictum, "There is no such thing as an infant" (outside of the mother-infant relationship) by asserting that:

> There is no such thing as a mother-infant relationship. I intend this statement, of course, as a reminder of the role of the father. While it is obvious that the baby in the very beginning is related exclusively to

the maternal object, this is no reason to conclude that the father has no existence whatsoever during that period. It is also obvious, at least to me, that the good enough quality of the relationship with the mother hinges on the mother's love for the father and vice versa – even if the child's relationship to the father seems minimal in comparison to the bond with the mother in the earliest period of life.

(p. 101)

Thus, who a mother is, in relation to her infant, will be determined at least in part by who she is in relationship to the infant's father (both as an inner third and an external, intersubjective third). A mother with an abandoning husband will tend to be an insecure and resentful mother. One with a supportive husband will more likely be confident and giving. Even her sexual relationship with the baby's father may affect her relationship with her infant. What conscious or unconscious ambivalence might she have when she first presents her breasts to her husband's new rival?

Thus, once again, we have a paradox, a dialectic. The infant desperately wants to believe that he/she and mother are still one, that their relationship is unique and exclusive, that theirs is a relationship of "oneness." Yet to the extent that the mother remains true to herself in her relationship with her child, to the extent she relates to her infant as a subject, the infant is being constantly reminded that this is not true. Or, more accurately, as with the (later) transitional object, both (mother is mine alone/mother has other relationships) have to be true at the same time.

The old Freudian paradigm of the therapist as an objective analyst is increasingly being replaced by the notion of the therapist as a subjective partner in an intersubjective relationship. And, as a subject, the therapist necessarily and inevitably brings into the therapeutic relationship his or her own inner thirds. Much has been written recently readdressing the old debate about "self-disclosure" by therapists. Whatever effort we make as therapists to remain anonymous or neutral to our clients, our clients know us or, at least, know what is important about us. They may not know if we are married, but they know if we are able to empathize over relational problems. They may not know how many children we have or even if we have children, but they know whether or not we can feel their pain over the loss of a child. In short, they know our inner thirds.

Seemingly out of the blue, one of my especially sensitive clients suddenly remarked that she "liked" my wife. Although I wear a wedding ring I was nevertheless nonplussed. I was sure that I had never said anything about my wife in our work together. It turned out that what she liked was my "feminine side," but somehow she could not disassociate this from either my relationship with my wife nor the actual person of my wife. She added a little later that she was "not so sure" about my mother. What this referred to was that she was not sure that I could have empathized the way I did to her own mother's egregious mothering if I had been the product of an Ozzie and Harriet or Brady Bunch kind of family. This client *knew* my inner thirds.

Why is this important? Why should our clients give a damn, or need to give a damn, about our inner thirds? The answer is the same as that for the infant and its mother. The infant's powerful need to *deny* the subjectivity of its mother, to maintain the complementarity of the mother/infant relationship, is counterbalanced (dialectically) by an equally powerful need to engage the mother intersubjectively and in doing so, to discover its own subjectivity. Benjamin (2004) traces the concept of intersubjectivity back to its philosophical roots with Hagel (1807) who states that one cannot become aware of one's subjectivity until *one sees oneself being seen by an Other*. Being seen by someone who is not experienced as an Other, by someone who is experienced as an object rather than as a subject, is essentially the experience of being mirrored. Now the crucial importance of good mirroring for the development of the child has, I hope, been well discussed in this volume. But the experience of being mirrored alone does not enhance one's sense of subjectivity. An object is something that things happen to, and mirroring is one of the many things that can happen to an object. One can be mirrored, one can be surrounded by mirrors, and still be an object: still be alone in the world (that is, alone with one's projections).

Experiencing oneself being seen by an Other is different from the experience of being mirrored because an Other is a subject rather than an object. This means that the Other sees one according to his or her subjectivity rather than providing some kind of more or less accurate reflection of who one is. When one sees oneself being seen by an Other the experience is, "This is how I look to another, which is different from the way I look to myself." This is the essence of subjectivity: "Who I am" is subjective. I am one thing to myself and another thing to someone else. This does not involve an assessment of who is right and who is wrong (though there is always a dialectical tension between wanting to be seen subjectively and wanting to be mirrored objectively). But questions of accuracy, of perceptions being correct or incorrect, fall within the mirroring/objectivity end of the dialectic tension. At the subjective end, another's experience of me is neither right nor wrong; it is simply different from my own.

Of course, if the Other's experience of ourselves is too much at odds with our own then we are likely to not recognize ourselves in the other's view, and the mutative effect will be nil.

> Over the years I have had a number of clients whom, after months or years of work, I have come to love. And, loving them, I find them eminently "lovable." Yet being *lovable* is so far from the self-concepts of these clients that while they recognize my love for them, it has no effect on them. The more cynical ones dismiss it as an artifact of my profession (it is something I *have* to do, part of my job description). The more trusting ones will believe it more, but attribute it to what they believe to be my huge heart rather than to any inherent lovableness in themselves. In both cases I am not experienced as a subject. I remain an object, something to hang their projections onto.
>
> But sometimes, if the dissonance between my perception of my clients and their perceptions of themselves is manageable, then I may momentarily be seen as a subject, which allows for a momentary experience of subjectivity in themselves, and subsequent growth.

The co-created third

In the beginning of this chapter I remarked that the psychological third necessary for the growth of our clients frequently resides in the person of the therapist. This statement needs refining: it is not so much the *person* of the therapist that is important as it is the *subjectivity* of the therapist. If the therapist acts like an object, and is experienced by the client as an object, then it is likely that the therapeutic couple will become stuck in the closed dyadic system we have already described, the "doer/done to" kind of relationship that Benjamin calls "complementary." Complementarity was, in fact, the original model for psychodynamic therapy (and still is for CBT therapists). The therapist was the expert and the client the layman. The therapist was "healthy," the client "neurotic." The therapist was "developed," the client was "fixated." And (in the case of CBT) the therapist thinks logically while the client is plagued by "cognitive distortions." Of course there is, and needs to be, some truth in this complementarity. The therapist needs to have some expertise to guide his or her interventions and through which the client can acquire some sense of security. Therapists should have worked to achieve as much self-awareness as possible if they are to be able to help their clients do the same. But if the therapeutic relationship is exclusively complementary, the client will have no avenue by which to escape the "done to" position.

If the client is to achieve subjectivity, then the therapist too must be a subject and, in particular, the therapist's subjectivity must be part of a shared intersubjectivity, co-created by both the therapist and the client.

Returning to our "psychological third residing in the person of the therapist" statement, we can say that it is of no use for the therapist to be a subject outside of the therapeutic relationship. It does the client no good if the therapist is a subject with his wife or her husband, with colleagues, friends, or whomever. The client needs the therapist to be a subject in the therapeutic relationship, in the relationship with the client. The therapeutic relationship needs to be "intersubjective." And for this to happen, the subjectivity of the therapist needs (in part) to encompass the person of – the subjectivity of – the client.

Intersubjectivity theory, therefore, implies that Winnicott's assertion that a client cannot have the same analysis with two different analysts does not go far enough. Intersubjectivity theory suggests that a therapist cannot be the same therapist with two different clients. So too it would rewrite Yalom's (1997, 2002) credo, "Create a new therapy for each patient." Intersubjectivity theory requires us to create (become) a new self (subjectivity) for every client.

I am speaking in hyperbole here (but only somewhat). I obviously cannot, and do not want to, create an entirely new me with every client I see. I carry into each therapy session a consistent and necessary sense of self. Nevertheless, I am a different therapist (a different person) with each of my clients. With some I am more intellectual, with others more emotional. With some I am actively engaged in a dialog, with others I am quiet. With some I am more accepting, with others more challenging. In short, who I am with a client depends on who the client is and on what the client brings out in me. Who I am in the room – my subjectivity – is co-created by my client and myself.

This is very different from making a "diagnosis" and then formulating a "treatment plan" based on that diagnosis. That approach is tantamount to objectifying the client (turning the client into an aggregate of symptoms) and in objectifying the client the therapist too becomes an object (a follower of a script, even if the script is written by the therapist).

It has to be this way. Only a subjectivity that is co-created can be influenced and changed by another. When I allow my subjectivity to be co-created by my client, I am setting up a paradigm in which my client's subjectivity can be co-created (altered) by me. Without such a paradigm – without co-created subjectivities – the client will perceive the therapist to be a kind of alien force, one that can only be resisted or yielded to. As Benjamin (2004) put it, instead of a psychological third, "he becomes a persecutory invader, rather than a representative of symbolic functioning, as well as a figure of identification. . . . The only usable third, by definition, is one that is shared" (pp. 12–13).

The intersubjective third subject

Let us return still again to the basic reason for this chapter, the observation that the *person (the subjectivity) of the therapist* may, at times, function as the psychological third that allows for emotional and psychological growth. We have seen that in order to facilitate growth, the third has to function as, and be perceived as, a subject rather than as an object. Any person who functions as, and perceives himself/herself as, an object is not likely to facilitate growth in another. To the contrary, they are likely to get stuck in the kind of "doer/done to" relationship that Benjamin (2004) despairs of. We have also seen that in order for a psychological third to be effective it must be "co-created," in the case of psychotherapy, by both client and therapist.

At this point our discussion takes us to yet another clarification (modification) of the term "psychological third" and of our initial assertion that the "person of the therapist" (the subjectivity of the therapist) fills in for any other missing "third." If the psychological third – the intersubjective third – needs to be co-created by the subjectivities of the client and the therapist, then the third *cannot be* the subjectivity of the therapist. The person of the therapist – the subjectivity of the therapist – is an essential component in the creation of an intersubjective third, but it cannot be the intersubjective third itself.

This means that the intersubjective third, in therapy, is a kind of disembodied subject or, more accurately, a subject that flits back and forth dialectically between the person of the client and the person of the therapist. This is what Thomas Ogden (1994, 2004) calls (in psychoanalytic treatment) the "analytic third." The analytic third, to Ogden (2004), is "the jointly created unconscious life of the analytic pair" (p. 157). And Ogden leaves no doubt: the analytic third is a third *subject*, and as a subject it is capable of generating thought.

Thus, in Ogden's view, psychoanalysis (and by extension, psychodynamic psychotherapy) consists of a situation in which there are two people and three subjects: the client as subject, the therapist as subject, and a third subject – the intersubjective third – created out of, and maintained by, the intersubjective relationship of the first two.

The idea of a third subject, created by and maintained by but distinct from the subjectivities of the two people in the relationship, may strike us as bizarre, but this is because it is not usually applied to dyadic relationships. In the theory of small group functioning, it is commonplace. The idea that "the whole is greater than the sum of the parts" dates back to the early work on group therapy pioneered by Kurt Lewin (1947) and Wilfred Bion (1961). Lewin introduced the term "group dynamics" and was the first to argue persuasively against the prevailing view that a "group" had no particular existence beyond the aggregate of its individual members. Today Lewin's views are taken for granted and young group therapists are trained to attend to the "group dynamics" and "group process" over the personal dynamics of the individual group members.

Thus, concepts like the *analytic third* may seem less bizarre and more easily comprehensible if we consider that what Ogden and others may be doing is applying long-established principles of group dynamics to a long-neglected group form: groups of two. This is not to diminish how radical and important Ogden's contributions are, nor to deny that they have tremendous clinical importance. Ogden, for example, turns the traditional way of dealing with the transference-countertransference matrix upside-down. He asserts (1994, 2004) that the traditional task that the therapist assumes, of trying to sort out "How much of this stuff is mine and how much of it belongs to my client?" is misguided because it ignores the intersubjective third. A more productive approach, he implies, is to look at the interaction between the two individual subjectivities and the co-created intersubjective third.

> In both the relationship of mother and infant and the relationship of analyst and analysand [therapist and client], the task is not to tease apart the elements constituting the relationship in an effort to determine which qualities belong to whom; rather, from the point of view of interdependence of subject and object, the analytic task involves an attempt to describe the specific nature of the experience of the unconscious interplay of individual subjectivity and intersubjectivity.
>
> (Ogden, 2004, p. 168)

From my perspective, this is exactly the task group leaders have taken on for the past half century. Nevertheless, as a change in technique in individual psychotherapy, it is a tectonic shift.

The concept of an intersubjective third, a new subject co-created in the unconscious interaction between two subjects, a new subject that is capable of thought and of experience, may be a radical new idea or a radical application of an established idea. Regardless of which of these it is, the concept of the intersubjective third is, to my mind, crucial to the theory of therapeutic change. Indeed, I would argue that without a co-created, intersubjective third, personal change would be impossible. Let me reiterate my explanation.

> If I, a client, alone in my subjectivity, believe myself to be a worthless piece of trash, then that belief is immutable. Alone in my subjectivity, there is nothing to change my belief, nothing to move me off center.
>
> If I, a therapist, alone in my subjectivity, see my client as worthy of my love, my respect, my caring, then I am helpless to persuade my client of his or her own worth. I have my view; my client has his or her view. As I stated earlier, all we can do is argue or agree to disagree.
>
> But if I, the client (but this time a new "I," an "I" that has been co-created by me and my therapist out of the unconscious interaction of our individual subjectivities) come up with a new idea – that maybe I was thrown away not because I am inherently trash, but rather because of some tragic flaw in my caretakers – I, the client, cannot dismiss this notion as the dutiful professional babblings of my therapist, because the idea has been co-created and I am one of the co-creators.

When I was first struggling to understand the concept of the intersubjective third, I very much wanted to see it as a "We." It seemed to make so much sense. There is the first subject, "I," there is the second subject, "You," and there is a third subject "We" that is co-created by our interaction. And a "we" (just as a group) can generate new thoughts and experiences. But Ogden (2013) expressly rejects that formulation, writing that "I don't think of the analytic third as having a quality of 'us.' Rather I think of it as having a quality of I, a third I in the analytic intersubjectivity." I now understand Ogden's position as reflecting the *experience* of the analytic or intersubjective third. The intersubjective third is experienced differently (asymmetrically) by each participant. But each participant experiences it as an "I," a new "I" that did not exist before the intersubjective relationship and may not exist outside of it. Indeed, when I hear someone describing an aspect of his or her therapy in terms of "we think that . . ." or "my therapist and I think that . . ." my heart sinks a bit. The experience of an intersubjective third is not of a "we" or an "us," it is of a new "I" and therein lies its power.

Ogden emphasizes that the intersubjective third is an unconscious process. He also stresses the role of *reverie* in accessing that unconscious material. Ogden borrows the word reverie from Bion and expands on it. Reverie is closely akin to "daydreaming" and related to the French word *rêve* or dream. Interestingly, the word reverie is more directly related to the Middle French word *rêver*, to wander or, delirium. And, indeed, it is the mind-wandering, dream-like quality of reverie that appeals to Ogden. As Freud saw dreams as the "royal road to the unconscious," Ogden sees reverie as the royal road to intersubjectivity. Ogden claims essentially that nothing that happens in a therapy session is random. Everything that occurs occurs out of the intersubjective field. When the therapist's mind "wanders off," it is wandering in a direction determined (unconsciously) by the immediate intersubjective relationship. Analysis of the therapist's reverie, of his mind's "wanderings," can be an invaluable indicator of what is happening in the therapeutic relationship.

For several excellent examples of a therapist's examination of his/her own reverie the reader is referred to Ogden (1994) and for a particularly detailed example to Ogden (2004). My own example has already been given in Chapter 4 in the role of play in the filling of Potential Space. Let me give it once again:

> Caitlin was a very bright, insightful, and hard-working young woman in her early thirties. The only child of a bipolar mother and an abandoning father, Caitlin was working in one session on a number of different issues that appeared to have a common relatedness to having been a parentified child and thus not having really been allowed to *be* a child.
>
> Near the end of the session a chain of associations led her to the movie *Men in Black* which she explained as a quest by the protagonists for a lost universe. At the end of the movie the lost universe was discovered. It had been present all along, inside a small glass ball worn around the neck of a cat.
>
> At this point Caitlin began to weep quietly and to repeat over and over the phrase, "An entire universe inside a tiny ball!" After a while she looked at me and asked me if I knew what she was talking about. To my surprise, I said that I thought that I did, not in any way I could articulate, but on some kind of intuitive level. Then, after some reflection, I decided to share with her my own association. I said that it reminded me of the awe I sometimes feel when I look at a small child, especially a preverbal child. There is an entire universe of thoughts

inside their little minds which is unable to be expressed verbally and, therefore, frequently unappreciated. Caitlin responded to my association with a radiant, child-like smile. "Yes," she said, "That's it! The small little ball is the child's tiny little head."

I presented this vignette in an earlier chapter as an example of mutual play in the "overlap of the play space" of the therapist and the client. What Ogden adds to Winnicott is the observation that this mutual "play" involves a form of unconscious communication. I did not "interpret" the meaning of Caitlin's associations. The process was much more complex, and largely unconscious. Caitlin's associations (reverie) led her to an image that clearly had enormous emotional significance to her but a significance which she was unable to give symbolic representation to (unable to put into words or formulate into a conscious thought). My "understanding" of her words was equally unconscious (unformulated). I was then able to allow my reverie to carom off or her reverie and then she was able to do the same with me, until a conscious, symbolic (verbal/conceptual) understanding of meaning was achieved.

One final example demonstrates, I believe, not just the use of psychological thirds, but the gradual shift from external to internal thirds:

> I described Hester in Chapter 1 as being initially so withdrawn that I approached her as one would approach a chipmunk with a peanut in an outstretched hand. Over several years of therapy Hester improved to the point where she was able to attend and do well in college. But still she struggled with isolation.
>
> In one session she reported having been extremely upset when she emailed one of her favorite professors (who had become something of a mentor to her) and did not hear back for many days. She was sure that she had unknowingly done something horrible and that the professor had washed her hands of her. Her anxiety around this was exacerbated by the fact that she had received a notice from Student Aid that she had failed to file a (minor but) necessary form and that she was in danger of losing her financial aid and being terminated from her classes.
>
> The second of these issues was now less anxiety provoking because she had mentioned the problem to an acquaintance who had looked at her quizzically and commented, "But that's such an insignificant form!" "She wasn't even trying to make me feel better," Hester said. "It was just a matter-of-fact statement."

So I addressed the original issue. "What do you think you might have done to alienate your professor?" I asked. "That's just it." She exclaimed. "Somehow I knew that you would ask that question so I have been racking my brain and I can't think of anything I might have done that would turn her against me." This mental exercise had clearly calmed her significantly (though not entirely) after her initial reaction of despair and hopelessness.

This vignette presents two examples of the use of psychological thirds. The first third was the external (intersubjective) third provided by the perspective of her acquaintance who pronounced the whole crisis "trivial." It was important that this person was not perceived as trying to make her feel better. That would have diminished her power as a third. No, she was perceived as providing a disinterested evaluation: the evaluation of an outsider, and thus a third.

The other third was, of course, myself. But what interested me (and delighted me) was that she had anticipated my thinking and had begun and carried out a fairly successful internal dialog with me long before speaking with me in person. In our early sessions I often had the impression that Hester would get so lost in her own world that she literally forgot that I was in the room with her. Over the years I had gradually evolved into an external third that she valued and used. Now, clearly, I was in the process of further evolving into an inner third.

10 Projective identification and the subjugating third

This chapter focuses on the work of Thomas Ogden on projective identifi-cation. Ogden argues that, paradoxically, projective identification is both a hallmark of the paranoid-schizoid position and a vehicle out of that posi-tion. In this chapter I catalog a number of different ways in which projec-tive identification leads to character changes in both the projector and the recipient of projective identification.

Projective identification has already been discussed in Chapter 5 as one of the defining defense mechanisms of the paranoid-schizoid position. Indeed, I believe it fair to say that saying that someone uses projective identification and saying that someone is in the paranoid-schizoid position are pretty much the same thing. Projective identification is the defense mechanism that allows for the *Groundhog Day* type of endless repeti-tion of past relationships to the exclusion of one's ability to be actually engaged, in the moment, with the real person in front of one. To the extent that one is in the paranoid-schizoid position, one deals only with internal objects projected onto external objects, never with the external objects themselves.

So it is not surprising that, when Thomas Ogden (1994, 2004) lists projective identification as one of the major vehicles for psychological growth, as a form of a *psychological third*, Jessica Benjamin (2004) calls this "confusing" (p. 10). A psychological third, after all, is something that allows us to move out of "complementary" or "paranoid-schizoid" functioning rather than being the chief mechanism by which that type of functioning is maintained. But Ogden insists, with increasing adamancy, that projective identification serves both, albeit contradictory, functions. To my mind, Ogden's formulation is reminiscent of Freud's eventual understanding of the "repetition compulsion." Freud had fretted about the repetition compulsion throughout most of his career since it seemed to contradict his axiomatic belief in the "Pleasure Principle." In *Beyond the Pleasure Principle* Freud (1920) suggested that the repetition compulsion may represent an attempt at mastery. This view was adopted by many Ego Psychologists, including Fenichel (1945) and by object relations theorists such as Casement (2014) who suggested that the repetition compulsion always involves an "unconscious wish" (p. 118) for a different outcome.

The *unconscious wish* that Ogden suggests lies behind all projective identification is the wish that the "recipient" of the projection is better equipped to deal with the projected material than is the "projector." And, going further, that thus protected and enhanced by the recipient, the projected material will ultimately be reclaimed by the projector as his/her own so that the projector will become more complete, less self-alienated.

What Ogden suggests is that projective identification is not done randomly. It is guided by an unconscious wish that the outcome of a new iteration of a past relationship will have a different outcome than did the original (now internalized, currently being re-externalized) relationship. When I project my unacceptable anger onto another person and then unconsciously provoke that person in an effort to force him or her to really be what I am projecting, I am doing so (suggests Ogden) in the unconscious hope that the recipient will somehow tame my anger to a point where I can reidentify with it and become a stronger, more fully integrated, more fully human person. Similarly, if I project my goodness (which I perceive to be endangered by my overwhelming badness) onto someone else for safekeeping, I am unconsciously hoping that the goodness will be strengthened in its surrogate womb (or that in its proximity my badness will be reduced) so that I can ultimately reidentify with it and become a stronger, more fully integrated, more fully human person.

The trick, of course, is that for all of this to work, I have to choose my recipient well. If the recipient of my projected anger is less able to handle anger than I am, then my provocative behavior will be met by a rage reaction that might be more terrifying than the unconscious anger that I had tried to safeguard in a surrogate body. Similarly, if the goodness that I believe is endangered in my psyche is projected into someone with sadistic power issues, then I may find myself entrapped in some kind of cult. In either case, my being stuck in the paranoid-schizoid position (or in Benjamin's complementary relatedness) will be exacerbated. In such cases, projective identification may have produced characterological changes, but changes for the worse.

Although originally proposed by Melanie Klein, projective identification was formulated as currently understood by Winfred Bion and other
object relations theorists. It has been a lifelong study of Thomas Ogden.
In Bion's presentation, it is a fairly simple three-part process: the projector projects out (in unconscious fantasy) an unacceptable part of himself
(either positive or negative) and simultaneously manipulates (behavio-
rally) the recipient to actually become what in fantasy is being projected;
the recipient "identifies" with (accepts) the projection and simultaneously
"metabolizes" the projection; the projector then reidentifies with (re-owns)
the metabolized projection. In the remainder of this chapter I present nine
(an arbitrary number) different facets of this process in which change
occurs. It will be noted that these nine points of change include change for
both the projector and the recipient.

1   *The projector projects out (in unconscious fantasy) a part of his psyche
    and manipulates the recipient to "become" what is projected.* The par-
    enthetical "in unconscious fantasy" is meant to describe the process, not
    to minimize the psychological event. The projector actually believes –
    convinces himself – that he no longer possesses a certain part of his
    psyche. Another way of saying this is that *his self-concept has changed.*
    He really believes himself to be – and in some ways acts as if – he were
    a different person. We can see this in the so-called "passive-aggressive
    personality." When a person projects his own anger and aggression onto
    others and then manipulates (provokes) them into anger and aggression,
    he is likely to have no idea at all about his own anger/aggression and
    will be genuinely baffled when people try and point it out to him. "But
    I don't feel anger," he will truthfully say. "I just have this problem with
    forgetfulness. I just can't ever seem to get anywhere on time. I can't
    get organized. Why don't people understand? Why does everybody get
    angry at me all the time? I don't do it on purpose." If passive-aggression
    is a character type, then projective identification is the mechanism by
    which this character type is created and maintained.
2   In doing so the *projector becomes depleted, self-alienated, becomes
    less than a whole human being.* This is one price to be paid for projec-
    tion. Whatever the satisfaction I get from freeing myself (in fantasy)
    from an unwanted part of myself and believing (unconsciously) that
    someone else is carrying that unwanted part for me, the price I pay is
    that I become less human. Human beings are whole creatures. They
    are endowed with a broad spectrum of emotions, impulses, urges,
    thoughts, fears, and desires. To deny, to become alienated from some

part of oneself is to lose contact with some essential part of what it means to be human. That is no small thing! If we are in denial about some aspect of ourselves that does in fact exist, then we have minimal to no control over that part. Denial of hatred is *not* a good thing if it means that we are more likely to act out that hatred unconsciously. The number of people who kill in the name of hatred is miniscule compared to the number who project out their hatred and kill in the name of love. The Crusaders killed thousands in the name of "love of God." Jihadists kill thousands in the name of "love of Allah." Millions have been killed in the name of "love of country."

3   In the unconscious fantasy that the recipient is containing some disa-vowed part of the projector, the projector is creating a *fantasy of con-nectedness* that harkens back to the mother-infant unit. Winnicott's "mother-infant unit," it will be remembered, represents a particular moment in the dialectic of oneness and separateness that is shifted heavily towards the pole of oneness. The infant *knows* that mother and itself are separate but opts to *know* the opposite, that it and mother are one. These dialectically opposing "knowledges" create their own, cor-responding conflicting feelings: there is tremendous relief and sense of safety in the oneness with a corresponding sense of suffocation at the inhibition of autonomy. Projective identification creates an experience of connectedness that recaptures some of that lost sense of oneness.

The connection between the projector and the recipient is obviously a highly asymmetrical one. One feels empowered, the other disem-powered. One feels relieved of an onerous burden, the other feels bur-dened and intruded upon. Nevertheless, each feels a powerful, primal connection; a semi-fusional type of connection that neither may want to relinquish. This aspect of projective identification may be a basis of what Cohen, Mannarino, and Deblinger (2006) and Carnes (2010) have termed "traumatic bonding" and its closely related phenomenon, the "Stockholm Syndrome."

The reader may remember April (Introduction), a third-generation gang member, was in a kind of Romeo and Juliet relationship with a boy from an enemy gang. But unlike Shakespeare's couple, April's relationship was marked as much by abuse as by love. April told the story of his return home one night when she was six or seven months pregnant. Her boyfriend was high on drugs and insanely jealous. He accused her of cheating on him saying he was sure the baby was not his. He beat her severely and shortly after this beating April miscarried.

What struck me was that April told this story without anger, shock, grief, indignation, or any such feeling. She told it as an example of how much he loved her. Her message was, "He is driven mad by his love for me!" She could never imagine leaving him. The bond between them was too strong.

4   The recipient accepts the projection, which is to say, *he has the unconscious fantasy that he is the "container" of someone else's feelings.* As Bion (1952) says, he feels himself to be playing a role in a script written by someone else. By definition here, the recipient is a changed person. He is experiencing something that he has never experienced before, something that is jointly created by himself and an Other. By Benjamin's definition, by Ogden's, by any definition, this is a psychological *third*. And the psychological change that can be produced by an encounter with such a third can be enormous. I have already discussed (Chapter 6) the psychologically destructive aspects of rape. Rape is an act of projective identification (the physical aspect of rape being the "manipulation"). In rape the perpetrator projects his own self-disgust and self-loathing, his fear and disgust of his sexuality, his fear and disgust of his own feminine side, onto his victim and he makes sure that she feels it. Rape victims report that it takes months or years to finally reject that projection, and some never do.

As a young therapist I worked with a teenage girl who had been gang-raped. She reported the experience as being one of the most traumatic of her life and she still could not recall it without disgust and self-loathing. "But why do you hate yourself?" I asked naively. "They are the ones who did something wrong. They are the ones who deserve your hatred." She replied with icy anger. "You don't get it! You are lying there naked and they are standing around laughing at you, spitting on you, telling you how ugly you are, how disgusting you are. And it goes on forever!"

I could only hope that she would not carry that projection with her forever.

But not all projective identification is destructive. Ogden argues that projective identification is the basis of empathy. Ogden (1994) even suggests that projective identification is an essential component of every human relationship. Without projective identification, understanding another person's feelings, understanding another person's psyche, would be a purely intellectual exercise. Empathy, compassion, true affective understanding involves getting into another person's head and heart and allowing that person into your head and heart. It involves being willing to project yourself into them and allowing yourself to receive their projections. This, I believe, is why therapists become therapists.

Working with adolescent gang members was an exercise in working with machismo – male machismo and female machismo. These were young toughs, proud to call themselves "thugs." They acknowledged no fear and actually felt very little fear. They despised and rejected all weakness. None of them expected to live past 20, and they had convinced themselves that they didn't care.

One of the split off and self-alienated feelings that they projected onto me was sadness and for the 20 years I worked with this population I contained this sadness. And I was glad to carry it because it made me more than who I had been before. It brought me into contact with a world I had never known and could barely imagine. Paradoxically, it filled me with awe and admiration and gave me a new appreciation for the word, "survivor." I quickly came to know that if I had had to walk a mile in the shoes that any of these kids had grown up in, I would have gotten about a hundred yards, curled up in a gutter, and died. This projective identification I carried, this empathy I contained, enabled me to work with what otherwise would have been a population of monsters.

5 Both projector and recipient are changed by the element of *coercion* in projective identification – the projector is empowered by it, the recipient disempowered. This is one reason why relationships based on projective identification tend to have a battle-like quality to them. The projector enjoys the empowerment and fights to hold onto it while the recipient resents the disempowerment and struggles to free himself of it. This is especially true when the projection is particularly noxious and the degree of coercion particularly severe (as in rape), but it is also true when the projection is positive.

Susan, a senior member of an interns' process group, expressed a particular dislike of feeling idealized by the younger interns. She presented this as an aftermath of her family dynamics in which idealization was always accompanied, cheek-by-jowl, by murderous envy. When someone put you above himself, he was sure to take you down.

The group struggled to persuade Susan that their good opinion of her was not tainted by envy. They did not see her as having something that they did not, something that she somehow deprived them of by possessing it. Rather, they saw her as a role model, someone who had skills they hoped to emulate and learn from.

Susan's fears were somewhat assuaged, but her negative feelings towards the idealization remained. She felt coerced, she said; she felt constricted. She felt inhibited in her ability to confess her self-doubts, her feelings of incompetence, the confusion she felt when with certain clients. In object relations terms, she felt reduced to a part-object – a good part-object to be sure – but still a part-object. The disavowed part of herself – the doubts, the insecurities, the ignorance – were not parts that made her feel particularly good about herself, but they were parts of herself . . . and she wanted them back. She wanted to be seen as *whole*.

6   In Bion's conceptualization of projective identification the crucial moment comes when the recipient *metabolizes* the projection. This implies that the projected material is somehow processed/digested by the internal, psychological workings of the recipient and thus reduced to a form more palatable (more digestible) for reidentification by the projector. My understanding of metabolization is that it is an extremely simple, commonplace process: it is making the projected material one's own.

A quick restatement of Bion's famous dictum: you know that you are the recipient of projective identification when you feel yourself to be playing a role in a script written by someone else. The recipient of projective identification experiences feelings as not quite being his/her own. Feelings are experienced as a kind of intrusion, as alien to who one really is. Sometimes such feelings are barely acknowledged as one's own and are rather seen as aspects of the projector: "He is so enraging. She is so sexy. He is so revolting." "Metabolizing" is the process through which feelings that are originally experienced as alien and intrusive are gradually owned and acknowledged as one's own.

The "manipulation" that is the behavioral component of projective identification is often wonderfully simple. I was the leader of a group of delinquent adolescent boys when I noticed that, for some time, one of the boys rolled his eyes every time I began to speak. I noticed his behavior as I simultaneously noticed two of my own reactions. First, I had a strong impulse to slap the kid. Second, I found that I was increasingly reluctant to speak up in group. Neither of these reactions felt like "me." I do not claim to be above occasional fantasies of physical violence, but such fantasies are not usually triggered by eye rolling. Second, I have, over the years, become quite comfortable with my role as therapist and group leader and if I have something to say I rarely hold back.

My first act of metabolizing was to own my anger. My anger was my response to an act of subtle but overt disrespect. Now, I do not like being disrespected any more than do most people. But in recognizing the cause of my anger and in owning it as my own (as justified), my anger instantly became proportional to the degree of provocation. I was annoyed, but I was aware of no impulse to strike anyone. When I was able to accept my anger as a response to a *behavior* (freed of the element of projective identification), then my anger became an appropriate response to that behavior.

I then made a conscious effort to metabolize my pull towards silence. "I am an experienced psychologist," I said to myself. "Why should I allow myself to be cowed by some smart-assed kid? If I have something to say, I will say it."

Needless to say, this second attempt needed much more work. In fact, I had not metabolized the projection at all; I had merely turned it on its end. Instead of allowing him to dismiss me with his eye rolls, I had dismissed him as a "smart-assed kid." Many projective identifications are falsely "resolved" in this way. "You want me to be the victim? Hell no! You be the victim and I will be the perpetrator."

To successfully metabolize my reaction to being dismissed, I had to do a considerable amount of work on my own historical issues with feeling dismissed as a child. *Arrogant dismissal* was my family's collective defense mechanism. If it wasn't in my mother's milk, it was certainly in the air I breathed. This adolescent boy was a "smart-assed kid," but that was not all he was. He was a young man who, for whatever reasons, found me, everything I stood for, and everything I said, to be threatening. And he tried to deal with those threats the same way I had dealt with threats for most of my life: with arrogant condescension and dismissal. I had been able to metabolize dismissal into empathy, and I was in a position to work with him again.

7 As the theory goes, the change in the recipient of projective identification (the metabolizing) allows for a change in the projector (the reidentification with the self-alienated material). To the frequent

question, "How can I get my clients to reaccept their projections?" I always answer the same thing. "We can't. We can only make it safe enough for them to want to do it themselves."

A student therapist was working with a recovering addict. The client had been a successful executive making well into six figures annually. He had then gotten into drugs and had lost first his job, then his home, and then his wife and family. At the time of the session the only thing he had in the world was a friend who was letting him sleep on his couch.

The client arrived at one session sputtering with rage. He was sure that his friend was about to turn him out. For most of the session he raged against the heartlessness of his friend, against the injustice of the world, against the perniciousness of drugs. And his rage always seemed on the brink of violence. The young therapist sat across from his client, spittle literally hitting him in the face.

When I ask my students what is being projected here a few of them always answer "rage." Rage was certainly being broadcast here. It was being dumped, heaped on the hapless therapist. But in the sense of projective identification, it was not being projected. Projective identification is when an *unacceptable* feeling is asked to be carried by another. And rage was hardly unacceptable to this client. Indeed, he basked in it. It was the only experience of power he had. What was unacceptable to this client was fear and it was *fear*, through the constant, underlying threat of violence, that the therapist was being forced to hold.

And I am pleased to say that the young therapist did his job well. He did not try to reassure the client about a future he could not possibly predict. He did not say to the client, "Calm down! Get a hold on yourself. Stop yelling!" Had he done so I am convinced that the client would have bolted from the session, sure that his therapist was as unable to contain fear as he was. Instead the therapist sat through the session processing (metabolizing) his own fear, recognizing it as an appropriate reaction to his current situation rather than a primal terror he was containing for his client. And, by the end of the session, when the therapist was able to speak to his client about how terrified he must be, the client was able to move past his defensive anger and acknowledge his fear.

8   According to Bion's original schema, when the projector reidentifies with his/her projection, the self-alienated has been reclaimed and the work is done. But I believe that there is much more to be said. At

the end of a successful working-through of a projective identification, both parties are likely to experience a sense of satisfaction. The projector has reintegrated a portion of himself or herself from which he or she had previously been alienated and, as a result, feels like a more whole, integrated human being.

The recipient experiences a sense of relief and liberation. For as long as the projective identification has held sway, the recipient has felt, at least in part, like a marionette being made to dance to an alien tune. The resolution of the projective identification represents the cutting of the strings and the re-experiencing of freedom of movement, not to mention freedom of thought and freedom of feeling. The recipient is once again his or her own person: autonomous and whole.

But at the same time, both the projector and the recipient may experience a deep sense of loss. The pathological and dysfunctional elements of projective identification are well known and much discussed. It is what Benjamin calls a "complementary" relationship in which each party is defined by – and reduced by – its split opposite. Ogden calls it a "subjugating" relationship and it does, indeed, involve the partial taking over of one person by another. Yet Ogden also says that his conception of analytic intersubjectivity (explicitly including projective identification) "represents an elaboration and extension of Winnicott's (1960a) notion that 'there is no such thing as an infant [apart from the maternal provision] (p. 39n)'" (2004, p. 168).

As Ogden suggests, projective identification represents an extraordinarily powerful kind of connectedness that harkens back to the mother-infant unit. As I discussed in point number 3 listed above, the sense of connectedness contributes powerfully to the prolonging of projective identification, even in cases where the particular pathology is dramatic. But even in incidents of "healthier" projective identification (Ogden (2004) says that the pathology of projective identification is defined not by issues of intensity but rather by how long it goes on without coming to resolution), there may be a sense of deep loss and grief even when projective identification has been "successfully resolved." Indeed, the siren call of that potent connectedness lures us back into such relationships over and over again, despite our awareness of the shipwrecking rocks we know we head for.

9   Finally, with the successful resolution of a projective identification, both the projector and the recipient will have had an experience with an Other that is profound and life changing. To be sure, while they are still caught up in the midst of the process, neither will be experiencing

the other fully as an "Other." The projector will experience the other – *needs* to experience the other – at least in part as an extension of himself. The projector needs to experience more than a simple connection with the recipient. The projector needs to believe (in unconscious fantasy) that the recipient is a kind of remote extension of himself so that he can get vicarious satisfaction out of experiencing the other as carrying disavowed parts of himself for him. As with "Joe" who described an aspect of himself as "Me-but-not-me," the projector in projective identification has to experience the disavowed parts of himself as "mine-but-not-mine." "They are not mine because I have given them to you to keep for me, but they can still be mine through the connection (fusion) I feel with you." Thus, the recipient cannot be allowed to be experienced as an *alterity*, as a truly separate, autonomous Other.

Similarly, the recipient in projective identification feels himself to be positively invaded, possessed even, by the disavowed aspects of the projector. "This isn't the way I think. These aren't feelings I recognize as my own. This is not the way I normally behave. I don't get this angry. I don't feel this kind of arousal. I am not familiar with this kind of anxiety." The projector is experienced not just as not an Object, but as an intrusive force that is not even completely external.

But as the participants emerge from the projective identification both will recognize, at some level of consciousness, that they have shared an episode of extraordinary intimacy with another human being. The (former) recipient will have had the experience of having felt another person's feelings, thought another person's thoughts, reacted according to another person's character. It is as though he or she had been invited into another person's psyche and had dwelled there for a while, as though he or she had walked awhile in another person's shoes. This is an extraordinary and quite literally mind-altering (life-altering) experience. When one emerges from another person's psyche one is not the same person as one was before. Ogden (2004) writes of this experience:

> The recipient of the projective identification is engaged in a negation (subversion) of his own individuality in part for the unconscious purpose of disrupting the closures underlying the coherence/stagnation of the self. Projective identification offers the recipient the possibility of creating a new form of experience that is other-to-himself and thereby creates conditions for the alteration of the person whom he has been to that point and whom he has experienced himself to be. The recipient is not simply identifying with an other

(the projector); he is becoming an other and experiencing (what is becoming) himself through the subjectivity of a newly created other/third/self (p. 189).

The former projector has also had a mind-altering experience. Projectors entrust parts of their psyches into the care of another human being. The entrusted parts of the psyche may be frightening and dangerous, shameful and embarrassing, or treasured but endangered. But in any case, they are all parts of the projectors' psyches. Again, this is not an experience of complete alterity. Complete alterity has to be denied so that the projectors can maintain some experience of partial ownership. But it is a crucial step towards the experience of alterity, and alterity is in part discovered through the resolution of projective identification.

At the beginning of this chapter I mentioned that the number nine, given as the number of potential changes that can happen through a cycle of projective identification, was arbitrary. Ogden observes that projective identification is never unidirectional. In every relationship that involves projective identification, the projector is also a recipient and the recipient is also a projector. Projective identification is always bidirectional. Thus, the nine potential points of change just listed should perhaps be doubled as there are always two overlapping projective identifications going on simultaneously.

A client projects onto me the father she never had and relates to me in an adoring, solicitous way. In accepting this projection (identifying with her projection) I am simultaneously projecting onto her the daughter I never had.

Another client – an abused adolescent – projects onto me his critical and punishing father and then provokes me with disrespect and misbehavior. As I identify with his projections I am also identifying with my own critical and rejecting father and projecting the worthless self component of that ORU onto my client.

Yet another client projects onto me her abandoning parents and then makes demands on me that make her feel to me like a millstone around my neck. As I identify with those projections I am simultaneously identifying with my own abandoning parents and (unconsciously) projecting onto my client the feelings of being an unwanted burden that I carried in relation to my parents.

Thomas Ogden, in his later writings, has sung a virtual paean to projective identification. Projective identification, says Ogden, is not simply the unconscious pit we struggle mightily to avoid and, having unwittingly fallen, we need to scramble out of as quickly as we can. It certainly can be such, depending on our success at emerging. But what is generally considered to be a pit may in fact be a passageway to a new place.

> Projective identification can be thought of as involving a central paradox: the individuals engaged in this form of relatedness unconsciously subjugate themselves to a mutually generated intersubjective third for the purpose of freeing themselves from the limits of whom they had been to that point. In projective identification [both subjects] are both limited and enriched; each is stifled and vitalized. The new intersubjective entity that is created, the subjugating . . . third, becomes a vehicle through which thoughts may be thought, feelings may be felt, sensations may be experienced, which to that point had existed only as potential experiences for each of the individuals participating in this psychological-interpersonal process. In order for psychological growth to occur, there must be a superseding of the subjugating third and the establishment of a new and more generative dialectic of oneness and twoness, similarity and difference, individual subjectivity and intersubjectivity.
>
> The two subjects entering into a projective identification (albeit involuntarily) both unconsciously attempt to overcome (negate) themselves, and in so doing make room for the creation of a novel subjectivity, an experience of I-ness that each individual in isolation could not have created for himself. In one sense, we participate in projective identification (often despite our most strenuous conscious efforts to avoid doing so) in order to create ourselves in and through the other who-is-not-fully-other; at the same time, we unconsciously allow ourselves to serve as the vehicle through which the other (who-is-not-fully-other) creates himself as subject through us. . . .
>
> In projective identification, one unconsciously abrogates a part of one's own separate individuality in order to move beyond the confines of that individuality one unconsciously subjugates oneself in order to free oneself from oneself. . . .
>
> The projector and the recipient of a projective identification are unwitting, unconscious allies in the project of using the resources of their individual subjectivity and their intersubjectivity to escape the solipsism of their own separate psychological existences.
>
> (Ogden, 2004, pp. 188–191)

11   The use and destruction of the object

This chapter is unique in this book in that it focuses on a single article – a highly controversial and misunderstood article by Winnicott that seems to have as many different interpretations as readers of the article. I offer my own interpretation of what I think Winnicott is saying and I discuss some important clinical implications.

So far, we have traced the entry into, and the transition out of, the mother-infant unit that had provided both an escape from unbearable anxiety and an auxiliary ego to help the infant deal with the internal and external world. We followed the child's path, aided by transitional objects, into the paranoid-schizoid position and we chronicled some of that position's powerful benefits: the unconscious experience of omnipotent control, freedom from the fear of permanent object loss, and freedom from the pain and confusion of ambivalence.

But at a certain point, says Winnicott, children become more and more interested in the real, external world, the world beyond their fantasies and projections, a world outside of their "omnipotent control." They know that they will have to pay a huge price to live in this world, but they are also intrigued and excited by it. So they decide, in entering this brave new world, that it would probably be nice to have some company in it. This entails the "discovery" of external objects.

In one of the last papers he wrote, "The Use of an Object and Relating through Identifications" (1968a), presented at the New York Psychoanalytical Society in November, 1968, a little over a year before his death, Winnicott postulates the simultaneous, bi-faceted "destruction" of the internal object and "discovery" of the external object. Winnicott's biographer, F. Robert Rodman, noted that the audience and discussants in New York "had a great deal of difficulty understanding the paper (as has been the case for new readers ever since)" (Rodman, 2003, p. 330). Rodman's parenthetical comment seems to apply to experienced readers as well. Indeed, Rodman's own explanation of this elusive work seems to differ substantially from those of other Winnicott scholars, including Thomas Ogden and Steven Tuber. Rather than trying to decide which of the various interpretations of *Use of an Object* is "correct," let me simply offer my own, to stand or fall as it will.

Regardless of their differences, all interpreters of this article focus on a dramatic but cryptic paragraph.

> The subject says to the object: "I have destroyed you," and the object is there to receive the communication. From now on the subject says, "Hullo, object!" "I've destroyed you." "I love you." "You have value for me because of your survival of my destruction of you." While I am loving you, I am all the time destroying you in (unconscious fantasy). . . . The subject can now use the object that has survived.
>
> (Winnicott, 1968a, p. 222)

We seem to have here yet another Winnicottian paradox. Nearly everyone who writes on this article refers to this paragraph. And all agree (despite numerous other disagreements), that the article is about the "destruction" of internal objects and the "discovery" of external objects. Yet what is striking (at least to me) about the paragraph is that in it, Winnicott clearly refers only to a single object ("the object") rather than to two different objects. Of course, he discusses two very different kinds of "objects" in the article: internal objects and external objects. Internal objects are *mental constructs* that tend to be projected onto whomever we (in the paranoid-schizoid position) are dealing with. Indeed, Winnicott describes the recipients of such mental constructs as "bundles of projections." External objects are real, whole, alive people, external and autonomous from ourselves. And it is intuitively obvious that for the child to *discover* external objects, internal objects must be let go of (Winnicott prefers the word, "destroyed"). Yet in the much-cited quote referred to previously there seems to be a single subject who is destroyed, who survives the destruction, and who is then loved and used.

I think that this can be understood better in light of Winnicott's seemingly offhand aside that the "armchair philosopher [who might criticize his theory] needs to come out of his chair and sit on the floor with his patient" (pp. 89–90). I assume that what Winnicott is saying here is that in order to understand his thesis we need to be able to see through the eyes of the infant (since it is infants, not Winnicott's patients, who sit on the floor).

From the viewpoint of the infant, there is only one object: the object in front of him. This object has always been perceived as being within omnipotent control (an internal object projected onto an external body). But the infant, says Winnicott, is entering the "change to the reality principle" (p. 222). It is tempting here to introduce Freud's term, "the stone wall of reality." But Winnicott's view of reality was sunnier than Freud's. Winnicott recognized that the acceptance of reality meant giving up the fantasy of omnipotent control. He saw reality as potentially frightening, as constricting, but he also saw the infant's entry into reality as the opening of the door to a cornucopia of experiences. He would have appreciated Mahler's description of the toddler's experience as being a "love affair with the world" (Mahler, 1972). But for whatever reason, fear or excited anticipation, Winnicott seems to have seen the infant as needing a partner in this endeavor, someone belonging to a "shared reality" (p. 221). As I interpret Winnicott, therefore, the "I love you" with which the infant greets the newly discovered external object is short for,

> I love you because you have met my need for an external object with whom I can share reality and who might be able to protect me from the more frightening aspects of this newly acknowledged reality and who (by virtue of being external to me and different from me) might expand my experience and enrich my life.

So what is the role of "destruction" in this process? I think the answer is exceedingly simple. If I am an infant dealing exclusively with objects within my "omnipotent control," then I can do anything in the world I want with them and they will respond according to my desires and my expectations. If I destroy an object that is under my omnipotent control, then it will be destroyed (at least until I decide to recreate it). But if I destroy an object and it refuses to be destroyed, then it must be beyond my omnipotent control, it must be an *external* object, it must be *real*. There can be (in my powers of imagination) no other test of "reality." This, I submit, is why the "survival" of an object after my "destruction" of it becomes an "ongoing" (p. 90) issue. Every time I need to reassure myself of an object's externality, of its ability to protect me in times of danger and keep me company in times of joy, then the only way I can do this is by *destroying* the object (for the umpteenth time) and reassuring myself that, by having survived my destruction of it, it is beyond my omnipotent control; it is external; it is real.

Mary was an extremely bright, extremely sensitive, young woman in her early thirties, with whom I had been working for about three years.

I was very fond of Mary and respected her enormously. These were feelings which I neither broadcast nor made any effort to hide. They were part of our "frame." And I knew that Mary's feelings towards me were equally warm, though her view of me was highly idealized.

Mary began a particular session with me by asking that I be especially attuned to her as she was planning on being especially vulnerable. I made the mistake of agreeing to her request without spending any time identifying exactly what it was she wanted from me. Whatever it was she wanted from me, she did not get it in that session and she left feeling angry and betrayed and I left feeling stupid and frustrated.

The next session Mary came in sputtering with rage. Somehow, she told me, she had managed to hold onto the knowledge that I cared about her and that she cared about me, otherwise she would have skipped this session and never come back. I forgot my Winnicott and compounded my initial mistake with a series of ill-advised interventions. I apologized for my failure but my apology was compromised by the fact that I still wasn't certain what I had done wrong and therefore I didn't know exactly what I was apologizing for. I tried to interpret her reactions to my failure but my interpretations fell on deaf ears. At one point I observed that she seemed torn between her need to punish me and her conviction that no amount of punishment would be sufficient. She grudgingly acknowledged this interpretation but was unmoved by it.

When I say that I had forgotten my Winnicott, I am referring to Winnicott's statement, in "The Use of an Object": "The analyst feels like interpreting, but this can spoil the process, and for the patient can seem like a form of self-defense, the analyst parrying the patient's attack. Better to wait until after the phase is over, and then discuss with the patient what has been happening."

(p. 92)

Mary's rage at me continued unabated for three weeks. Then, at the beginning of the fourth week, it suddenly disappeared. Mary refused to process with me where it had gone or to do any more work on what it had been about. "No," she said, "I have other things I need to work on." And I, relieved to be out of the line of fire, did not push the matter as much as I should have.

A few months later Mary was working on her fear of being "overwhelmed" by the intense affect of one of her close friends. "Do you," she asked me, "ever get overwhelmed by the feelings of your clients?" I responded with some vague statement about trying to stay, as much as I could, in touch with the feelings of my clients. A few minutes later I realized with a start that my response had been condescending and that it had not addressed her question. "Excuse me," I said, "I think the answer I just gave you was only half of the truth. Yes, I do sometimes get overwhelmed by the feelings of my clients. In fact, that may have been what happened when I failed you so badly a few months ago."

Mary listened intently and responded that she was amazed that she had been thinking about the same incident just before I spoke (Winnicott's "direct communication"). She went on to say that she could barely remember why she had been so angry at me and that she probably hadn't quite known at the time. What she did remember clearly was cutting her feelings off. She had, she said, looked into my eyes at a certain point and seen that her attack on me was "hurting" me (that she had been in danger of successfully destroying me).

This perception had enraged her even further. I was not "supposed" to be hurt. I was supposed to listen empathically, to try to understand, to admit responsibility, but *not* to be hurt. To be hurt meant (to her) that I might leave her, that I would retaliate, that I would not survive her destruction of me. Rather than risk this, she had to stop her attack and cut off her feelings.

The fact that it was I who brought up the issue again meant that I had survived. Furthermore, my response this time was attuned to her needs rather than my own. I empathized with the pain I had caused her rather than apologizing for my misbehavior. I interpreted my own transgression rather than her reaction to it and my self-interpretation was offered as a gesture of identification (see Benjamin, 1998) rather than as an excuse. I had demonstrated myself to be an external object (I had survived her destruction of me) and she was, once again, able to "use" me.

I want to stress here two points that I think have been overlooked or misunderstood in "The Use of an Object." The first is about the destructiveness of the "destruction" of which Winnicott writes. Steven Tuber (2008) has written a book subtitled *A Winnicott Primer* in which he presents an interpretive analysis of each of Winnicott's major writings. In his chapter on "The Use of an Object" Tuber presents an interpretation of "destruction" that is at the mildest extreme of Winnicott's admittedly broad and generally benevolent attitude towards "aggression." Tuber (2008) writes:

As we have noted, through the back-and-forth of mother-baby interaction, a spontaneous gesture occurs on the baby's part. The mother stays by and large the same in the midst of this spontaneous gesture.

Over time, the baby increasingly has the experience that even when he does something that feels viscerally distinct, the mother *stays the same*. If the mother stays the same while the baby feels different, then she over time increasingly feels, from the baby's point of view, outside of the baby. Being outside of the baby means that for that moment the mother has been "destroyed" as an extension of the baby.

(p. 86)

Thus, in Tuber's analysis, "destroying" becomes the occurrence of "a spontaneous gesture" and "surviving the destruction" becomes "staying the same over time." Ogden adopts a similarly non-aggressive interpretation of "destruction." Ogden (1986) writes: "The act of faith that takes place in giving up ("destroying") the internal object" (p. 195), thus seeming to equate "destroying" with "giving up." There is much in Winnicott to support such a non-violent interpretation of "destruction." Winnicott says, "*There is no anger* in the destruction of the object of which I am referring, though there could be said to be joy at the object's survival" (p. 226, italics in original). A page earlier he states that, "The word 'destruction' is needed, not because of the baby's impulse to destroy, but because of the object's liability to not survive, which also means to suffer change in quality, in attitude" (p. 225).

But this last quote clearly does not mean to imply that the baby does not *have* an impulse to destroy. To the contrary, a page earlier Winnicott says, "It is legitimate, however, to say that at whatever age a baby begins to allow the breast an external position (outside the area of projection), then this means that destruction of the breast has become a feature. *I mean the actual impulse to destroy it*" (p. 225. italics added). Elsewhere, he again refers to destruction as an impulse: "the fact that the first impulse in the subject's relation to the object (objectively perceived, not subjective) is destructive" (p. 223). A few pages later Winnicott says, "Without the *experience of maximum destructiveness* (object not protected) the subject never places the [object] outside" (p. 224, italics added). In speaking of psychoanalysis, Winnicott says that positive changes, "depend on the analyst's *survival of the attacks*, which involves and includes the idea of the absence of a quality change to retaliation" (p. 224, italics added).

Some interpreters imply that the words "destruction of" could just as well be interchangeable with "replaced by" or even "fades away." But by my rough count Winnicott uses the word "destroy" or "destruction" 47 times in this essay, "attack" 10 times, and "survive" or "survival" 19 times. One entire page out of a nine-page essay is devoted to a discussion of the psychoanalytic theory of aggression. If Winnicott had wanted to substitute a less aggressive synonym for "destruction" he had ample opportunity to do so. Instead, he is quite specific: destruction is an "impulse," it is an "experience," it is not simply the inadvertent result of some benign process. We have no reason not to take him at his word when he says, as quoted previously, that the ideal is "the experience of maximum destructiveness" (p. 224).

My thesis here is that what is lost in an attempt to declaw Winnicott's concept of the destruction of the object is the heart of what he is trying to convey: that the discovery of externality lies in the *act* of attempting to destroy and the survival of that destructive act by the object. Winnicott does say that the destruction of the object takes place "in (unconscious) *fantasy*" (p. 222). But he also makes it clear that this involves an actual action, a real attack on the real object, that a fantasy or hallucinatory substitute simply will not do. This is made most clear in a footnote: "In fact, the baby's development is immensely complicated if he or she should happen to be born with a tooth, so that the gum's attack on the breast can never be tried out" (p. 225, fn). An actual *act* of aggression is necessary, even if it is little more than the infant aggressively gumming its mother's breast.

I think we need to take Winnicott at his word when he says at the outset of his essay that, "What I have to say in this present chapter is extremely simple" (p. 219). If an object is experienced as being within a subject's omnipotent control (an internal object), then when the subject destroys that object, the object should be destroyed. That's what "omnipotence" means. If a subject "destroys" an object and the object is not destroyed (survives the destruction), then clearly the object is outside of the subject's omnipotent control: it is an external object. I think Winnicott's argument is as simple as that. What is needed for the "discovery" of externality is a *destructive act*, an attack, enacted upon the person of the object in question. If the object in question behaves as predicted by "omnipotence" and is in fact destroyed (disappears or retaliates) by the destructive attack, then the object is an internal object. If the object in question fails to behave according to the predictions of omnipotence and survives the destruction, then the object must be external.

Contrary to Tuber's (2008) assertion that it is the mother's (the Object's) job to be predictable, I read Winnicott as stating that the mother (the Object) must be unpredictable. The m(Other) must defy one specific prediction above all; she must refuse to be destroyed by the omnipotent command to be destroyed (by the prediction that a destructive act will in fact destroy her). It is only through her refusal to be predictable (to the predictions based on omnipotent thinking) that she can be recognized as external, that she can be "used." The word "refuse" is used here guardedly. The mother (or therapist) does not need to refuse to be predictable. She cannot be otherwise. She is an autonomous human being, not under the omnipotent control of the infant (client). This is a great relief to both child (client) and mother (therapist). But when it comes to the subtle acts of aggression and destruction of which Winnicott is speaking, the mother (therapist) needs a certain determination to not allow herself to be destroyed.

A client told me the story of his mother who made the opposite determination. When he was in his early twenties, his mother told him that she had an "apology" to make. She told him that once, when he was a toddler, he had been squirming in her arms wanting to be put down. "When I put you down I took a kind of oath that I would never pick you up again. And I never did."

Winnicott seems to be setting up destruction (or, more accurately, the survival of destruction) as proof of externality, as the equivalent of Descartes' "thinking" as proof of existence. Descartes confounded his hypothetical Deceiving Demon by the realization that a demon could be deceiving him about every perception he had except for the perception of his own existence, and that was by virtue of the fact that he was thinking about it. Hence: "I think therefore I am." Interestingly, Tuber also makes reference to Descartes. But he makes a direct transposition of the Cartesian "I think therefore I am" into a Winnicottian "I destroy therefore I am" (2008, p. 92). I think that there is a great deal of truth in this portrayal, especially in light of the clinical vignette that Winnicott (1968b) presents as meant to serve as a "clinical illustration" to his "Use of an Object" article. But unlike Tuber I see the subjective implications of destructiveness not as a direct expression of what Winnicott is saying here, but rather as an indirect result of the inevitable dialectic between subject and object. What Winnicott is directly saying in this essay is: "I destroy and therefore you are" ("I destroy you (and you survive my destruction) therefore you are (an external rather than internal object)"). And – dialectically – because you have existence independent of me, then I have existence independent of you.

Thus, paradoxically, if the object allows itself to be destroyed (as an external object, as a subject) then the child (client, subject) is also destroyed (as a subject, as something external to other external subjects) and can continue to exist only in the paranoid-schizoid position, as an object in a world of objects. Its subjectivity, its agency, its existence in a real, externally defined, objective world, is destroyed along with the reality and externality of the object.

Winnicott does not say, in "Uses" that this assaultive form of destruction that I have been describing is the *only* way that an external object can be discovered. Indeed, this would seem to me to be highly unlikely. Anytime an object fails to act according to the predictions of omnipotent control, it stands the chance of being recognized as external. This kind of "failure" would have to be properly dosed. If the failure (the difference between the predicted behavior and the actual behavior) was too great the dweller in the paranoid-schizoid position would simply "flip the script." The object he had thought to be a "good object" would now be recognized as a "bad object" or vice versa, one internal object would be replaced by another, one bundle of projections for another bundle of projections.

But if the dose were small enough this flipping mechanism might not be triggered. "The Rock of Gibraltar" might be experienced as slightly less solid, the "Fickle One" slightly more constant, the "Ice Princess" slightly warmer, etc. As each part-object became less split (more whole) it would become more "real" and therefore more external. This is similar to what Kohut describes as the process involved in "transmuting internalizations." Kohut suggests that the growth of the Self is facilitated by "dosed" empathic failures. If the empathic failure is too great, it leads to "disintegration of the Self" and narcissistic rage. If, however, the empathic failures occur in small enough doses the selfobject function is internalized and the subject is able to soothe itself (Kohut's selfobjects themselves do not get internalized. It is the selfobject *function* that is internalized). What I am proposing here is the mirror image of that process: dosed failures in the predictability of internal objects leads to their rejection in favor of external objects.

But what is different about this kind of passive, non-aggressive discovery from the acts of aggression that (I believe) Winnicott is describing in his article is that the former are out of the immediate control of the subject. The subject cannot simply *will* an object to behave in a certain way at any given time. What the subject can do, however, when it needs immediate (unconscious) verification of the externality of an object is put it to the acid *test*: "destroy" it and see if it survives destruction. And the subject can do this any time, and as often as, such a need is (unconsciously) felt. Once again, in the vignette I gave earlier in this chapter, *Mary tried her best to destroy me, hoping all the while that I would survive her destruction of me. When it began to seem to her that I was in danger of failing to survive, she abruptly called off her destructive attack. By revisiting the issue myself I demonstrated to her that I had indeed survived her destruction and she was able to use me as an external object.*

The second topic that I believe has been underappreciated in "The Use of an Object" is the idea of the "ongoing" destruction of the object. Winnicott died shortly after the publication of "The Use of an Object" so, tragically, he was never able to develop this idea further. But Winnicott introduces this idea with characteristic boldness and authority.

> In other words, because of the survival of the object, the subject may now have started to live a life in the world of objects, and so the subject stands to gain immeasurably; *but the price has to be paid in acceptance of the ongoing destruction in unconscious fantasy relative to object-relating.*
>
> (p. 90, italics added)

In the summary at the end of his essay he restates this even more dramatically. "The object is always being destroyed. This destruction becomes the unconscious backcloth of love of a real object; that is, an object outside the area of the subject's omnipotent control" (p. 94).

The implications of this idea – that *destruction* needs to be ongoing, needs to become the unconscious backcloth of all love – are huge.

> Max and June were a couple in their mid-fifties, both established professionals. One of Max's complaints about June was that she would frequently speak to him "like I was some kind of slightly slow child" (later he refined this to: "No, it's more like she is a little girl talking to one of her dolls"). Max inevitably snapped back angrily at June, telling her she was being condescending and offensive.
>
> I tried to frame both action and reaction in terms of their respective backgrounds. Max was the child of two arrogant and condescending parents who had little use for the opinions of anyone who did not have a Ph.D., let alone those of a child. His reaction to June's manner was a simple transference reaction.
>
> June had experienced multiple losses and abandonments in her childhood. Her mother had died when she was five, and her father, a cold, austere, and critical man, had remarried a woman who could never quite develop maternal feelings for June.
>
> My interpretation of June's behavior was that in times of stress she needed to "use" Max as an external object, for support, comfort, companionship. But because of her history, she could never really trust that he would be there for her as a strong, external partner. So she would test him. She would test him by destroying him. She destroyed

him with her condescension and her dehumanizing of him. And Max inevitably allowed himself to be destroyed (to *retaliate* with his sharp, angry retorts). Thus, Max was never able to prove his externality to June, to make himself "useful" to her. Instead, Max remained forever a carrier of June's projections (an internal object to her), and continually accepted (and confirmed) the role of the whiny and petulant little boy that she projected onto him.

June accepted and validated my interpretation, but it seemed to have little direct effect on her. In contrast, Max was markedly changed by my interpretation. No longer taking her condescension so personally, he was able to curb his anger and his sharp retorts. He learned to respond to her condescension with patience and humor rather than anger. And he learned to recognize her behavior as a sign of her stress rather than as an indication of her contempt for him. In short, he learned to *survive* her destructive attacks. And these changes, in turn, allowed June to begin to see him as an external (non-abandoning, non-retaliatory) object, as an adult partner whom she could "use."

At this point I would like to address and clarify Winnicott's interesting and confusing choice of words in his title, "The Use of an Object and Relating through Identifications." Winnicott spends very little space in the article talking about the second half of the title. "Relating through Identifications" seems to be his starting point, his baseline, that aspect of human functioning which he says in his opening paragraph has already benefited from the "full attention" (p. 218) of psychoanalytic theorists. Relating through identifications refers to how we relate in the paranoid-schizoid position. It is one person saying to another, "Oh, I can relate to what you just said," or, "I can identify with you on that." Now this is definitely a kind of relatedness and an important one. It is something one frequently sees in new therapy groups, even with very sophisticated members. What is really being said is, "It sounds like one of your internal objects is a lot like one of my internal objects, so I can relate to you. We have something in common."

This is an important but very limited form of intersubjectivity. If I can relate to (identify with) you, if your internal objects echo my internal objects, then we are joined in a sense of commonality and we are both comforted by that because neither of us is alone in the world. But if, on the other hand, your internal objects are sufficiently different from mine then you are unrecognizable to me; you are alien to me. And in the paranoid-schizoid position, there is no way to bridge that mutual alienation. "Using" an object, on the other hand, is a much higher form of intersubjectivity.

> A few months into a psychotherapy group the leader announced that a new member would be joining the group. "Oh my God!" was the general reaction. "We have worked so hard to get to know one another, to get to trust one another. This is going to be *so* disruptive." One member, Leanne, chose to challenge her peers. "I don't understand," she said. "I don't have the same fear of change. So, what if someone new is coming? Why should that undo the work we have already done?" The group felt attacked by Leanne and responded by attempting to ostracize her.
>
> It took several weeks to work this through. Leanne was able to recognize and admit that there had been an element of attack in her statement but insisted that that was only a part of what her statement had been about. She had genuinely been confused by the group's reaction and had been trying to engage the group so that she could move beyond her own limited reactivity. She had been trying to engage because she wanted to grow.
>
> The rest of the group was able to recognize that Leanne's assertion of her difference from them was not a statement that they were "wrong." What they had heard was, "My internal objects are different from your internal objects and therefore yours must be invalid." Once they were able to recognize that along with the attacking element of her statement was a genuine desire to understand their subjectivities, they were able to join her in trying, on their part, to understand her subjectivity. The group had shifted (momentarily) from a static and unproductive attempt to relate through identifications to a much more productive and growth-enhancing form of using each other through engagement.

In a very short article written a few months before "Use of an Object," Winnicott, 1968b) makes it clear that he does not mean the word "use" as a disparaging description of a kind of manipulative, anti-social behavior: calling somebody a "user" or saying that somebody callously "uses" people. Just the opposite! To use someone, in Winnicott's sense, is to engage that person, to recognize and celebrate not just the similarities one feels with another person but their differences as well, to recognize and respect that person's "otherness," their alterity. Indeed, Winnicott closes this article poignantly: "and it is perhaps the greatest compliment we may receive if we are both found and used" (Winnicott, 1968b, p. 233).

An intern presented the following case of a family in therapy. The identified patient was the wife/mother who was in a severe depression. Her own parents had died a couple of years earlier and she had taken over the family business. This business had clearly represented a substitute for her lost parents. The continued success of the business meant that her parents were somehow still alive and her running of the business represented her continued connection with them.

Her acute depression began not with the immediate deaths of her parents but with the subsequent failure of the family business at the height of the Great Recession. "She needs support," I said to the intern. "She needs to feel less alone in the world and she needs someone to be with her as she grieves her parents. Who's available in her family?"

Her two adult daughters had felt alienated from their mother their entire lives. The mother had been so closely bonded with her own parents that she had never allowed herself to bond with her own children – she had never allowed herself to become a mother. Her daughters, therefore, remained hostile and resentful. They saw her as a part-object (abandoning and unavailable) and they functioned as part-objects to her (angry and rejecting). Neither was in a position to be able to be *useful* to their mother.

What then of the husband? The intern explained to me that this man was profoundly religious and that he had a particular religious belief that, because everything was "God's will," one should be "happy" about everything. His wife, he believed, should be happy that her parents were "in a better place" and she should be "happy" that God had relieved her of the burden of running the business. My heart sank. This man was a living part-object. In his eternal optimism he was less useful to his wife than were his angry daughters.

12 Interpretation

"Interpretation," the bedrock of Freud's clinical approach, has become the subject of much controversy in both object relations theory and relational and intersubjective theories. In this chapter I attempt to cool the often overheated rhetoric on the subject and offer a view of this intervention that respects and acknowledges its dangers and shortcomings while recognizing its contribution to our therapeutic work.

This is the fourth chapter in this section which deals with factors and processes that effect change. Unlike the processes discussed in the three preceding chapters, which tend to be unconscious as much as conscious, and passive as much as active, interpretation involves a conscious and deliberate action by the therapist.

Psychoanalyst Owen Renik perhaps said it best: "It seems to me a fundamental principle of analytic collaboration that an analyst's aim in offering an interpretation is not to have it accepted by the patient, but rather to have the patient consider it in making up his or her own mind" (Renik, 1993)

Sigmund Freud, the father of all psychodynamic/psychoanalytic theories, saw the role of the therapist in terms of a single function: interpretation. Indeed, Freud saw this as the therapist's *only* role. Freud's thinking evolved dramatically over the course of the first half of the twentieth century but in this belief he remained steadfast. The therapist's (analyst's) job is to interpret. Interpretation, like the obstetrician's forceps, drags reluctant unconscious material unwillingly from the womb-like protection of the unconscious into the light of day of the conscious. Interpretation was more than the therapist's tool, more than the therapist's *only* tool; it was the therapist's *raison d'être*.

It should be noted that Freud was not heavy-handed in his interpretations. He engaged the client (patient) in the process as much as possible. Freud would never (as some therapists do) listen to a patient's dream and then offer an interpretation. His protocol for dream interpretation was clear and unvarying: he would listen to a dream and then instruct the patient to free associate to the dream as a whole and to each and every detail of the dream. The *working through* of the dream material was as much the patient's responsibility as the analyst's.

It is thus profound and ironic that in modern psychodynamic theorizing interpretation has come under so much attack. Winnicott (1968a) said that as he matured as a therapist he used interpretation less and less, ruing his earlier use of the intervention, clearly believing that he had done his patients a disservice. In the same article he goes so far as to say that with "patients in a *certain classification category*" (p. 219, italics in original) interpretation should not be used at all. Among these certain types of patients, I assume that Winnicott includes both those firmly entrenched in the paranoid-schizoid position and those with severe False Self personalities.

As always, there is much wisdom in Winnicott's cautionary notes. With clients locked firmly in the paranoid-schizoid position it needs always to be remembered that they will hear from their therapists what they are programmed to hear, with little regard for what the therapist might actually be trying to say. If what is being projected onto the therapist in the moment is a critical parent internal object, then the interpretation will be experienced not as a helpful intervention but as a critical attack. If the *projection du jour* is the seductive parent, then the interpretation will be experienced not as an attempt at objective understanding but as a sexual come-on.

While I believe Winnicott's (and others') cautionary issues to be very well-founded, I nevertheless feel the need to add that this kind of distortion will occur in *all* of the client-therapist interactions, interpretations or otherwise, verbal and nonverbal as well. Winnicott (1968a) suggests that rather than providing interpretations, the therapist should focus on providing a holding environment in which growth will naturally occur. My caution is that the client in the paranoid-schizoid position will distort the attempts at holding to the same extent that he/she will distort verbal interpretations.

I struggled with Lucy for many months trying to form a "working alliance," trying to let her know that I cared about her, that I was on her side. In a moment of extreme frustration, I blurted out an ill-formed attempt: "Lucy, it makes me so sad that you are unable to find happiness in any part of yourself or any part of life." Rather than smiling at me gratefully, Lucy winced as though she had been slapped. Instantly, I realized how my well-intended words had been heard. The words spoken by me had been heard in the voice of Lucy's critical, rejecting mother. What Lucy had heard was [in a voice of disgust], "Well it's pretty *sad* [pathetic] that you can't even be happy [do anything right]."

Another client, Marilyn, reacted to my efforts to hold her as though she were being enveloped in the arms of a cactus. When Marilyn would say something with which I thoroughly agreed I would unconsciously murmur, "Yes, of course!" I eventually noticed that each time I did this, Marilyn, as did Lucy, reacted as though she had been slapped (Marilyn and Lucy had similar mothers). Marilyn did not hear what I had intended to convey which was, "Yes, I completely agree with you. I think you are absolutely right." What she heard was, "Well duh! That's pretty obvious, you dummy!"

As to clients with deeply seated False Self personalities, I have already written (Chapter 4) about the dangers of providing a "script" for them, even one more "accurate" or "functional" than the ones written for them in their childhoods. Clients with powerful False Self functioning need help (support, sometimes guidance) in discovering/creating a True Self. They do not need a newer/better False Self, created for them more to the liking of the therapist.

A young intern recently presented a case to me which she found extremely frustrating. The client indeed sounded very difficult and displayed numerous aspects of her functioning that would commonly be labeled "primitive." But without dismissing the level of the client's pathology, I was more struck by the quiet anger being generated out of my intern's frustration. "What is it you think your client needs?" I asked. "I think she needs insight," was the instantaneous answer. I tried to frame my response as gently as I could. "It sounds like you are saying that your client would be better off if she thought the way you think."

Again, while I strongly support Winnicott's cautionary note about providing a new script for a False Self personality type, I do not agree that we need to avoid interpretation altogether. I think (and this seems to be the current tactical consensus) that what is needed is caution in the way we phrase our interpretations. Interpretations that begin with "I wonder if there is a connection between . . ." are far preferable to those that begin with, "There seems to be a connection between . . ." Still better yet are those that attempt to engage the client in the process, those that begin with, "Do you think that there might be a connection between . . ."

This way of structuring interventions is in keeping with a more general approach to interventions which is that they should arise out of the experience of curiosity rather than out of an assumption of knowledge. The process of psychotherapy is a process of inquiry rather than an expository process. As early as 1920 Freud warned against psychoanalysis becoming a "pedagogic" process. The process of psychotherapy involves an exploration of what is unknown, not of what is known; of what doesn't make sense rather than of what does. Inexperienced therapists, perhaps needing to feel "useful" or "competent," will gleefully pounce on perceived "cognitive distortions," inconsistencies, or discrepancies between content and affect. But when these are triumphantly pointed out to the client the effect is frequently to leave the client feeling that he or she "didn't do it right," that they are even more inadequate than they had thought.

An attitude of curiosity is more likely to draw the client into the inquiry than make the client feel even more like a failure. "I am confused," I will say (a phrase I use frequently). "On one hand the story you just told breaks my heart. But on the other hand, the smile on your face and the flatness of your affect make me think that I should be amused. I am confused. Please help me understand." If (depending on the place we are in in the therapy) I decide that more of an interpretation is warranted than a simple question, that interpretation will still be framed in curiosity: "I wonder if what is happening here is that you are aware of the tragedies in your life but feel unable to bear the pain. What do you think?"

Still another modern objection to interpretation is informed by feminist concerns about "complementary relationships" (Benjamin, 1988, 1990, 1998, 2004). The potential complementary relationship in question is that between the "expert" and the "uninformed." On one hand this dichotomy makes sense. The initials after our names; the diplomas, certificates, and licenses on our walls; all serve an appropriate function in letting the clients know that they are not putting themselves into the hands of amateurs and quacks. But it is incumbent on us as therapists to know that our expertise is in the realm of facilitating a process rather than substituting for a process. Unfortunately, even the greatest of therapists sometimes forget this and the literature is full of case material showing therapists browbeating their clients into accepting their superior – and thus the client's inferior – positions. Albert Ellis, the founder of Rational Emotive Therapy, had the misfortune of being caught on tape doing just this. In his section of the well-known "Gloria" tapes, Ellis offers an interpretation to the "client," Gloria, who considers it and then politely but firmly rejects it. But Ellis does not appear to find this disagreement acceptable. He is the expert, he points out, reminding her that he, not she, is the one trained to "listen with the third ear." But even more subtle, less egregious, assertions of expertise can be detrimental to the client. I, for example, will never (even when requested by a client) pronounce a client's thoughts, feelings, behaviors, issues, to be "normal." This is because in doing so I would implicitly be reserving the right to declare those same things to be "abnormal," and that is a position I would never want to assume. What I might say instead would be something like, "Well, I don't know about 'normal' but I can easily see myself feeling or doing that." Or, to the contrary, "Well, as of this moment I'm having a hard time identifying with that, so help me understand better."

The problem with a complementary relationship is not that it feeds the narcissistic needs of the therapists to be revered as The Doctor or The Expert, but that it keeps – for as long as it lasts – the client in the role of The Sick One or The Uninformed One. And how can we help our clients grow and individuate when we are constantly reminding them of their inadequacy and their subordination?

But once again, let me plead for the preservation of a precious baby who is in danger of being thrown out after a very necessary scrubbing. In an earlier work (Brodie, 2007) I presented a simple interpretation and its potential beneficial consequences. I would like to re-present and re-discuss that interpretation here. The interpretation was one given to "Joe." Joe was the unrepentant bully, the self-described "bad kid" presented in Chapter 7. And, as I said earlier, Joe saw being a bad kid as fundamental to who he was, as if "A Bad Kid" had been printed on his birth certificate. My interpretation to Joe went something like this:

> So Joe, of course you are a bully. I would be a bully too if I had gone through what you went through. You got sick of being beaten up so you decided it is better to be the beater than the beaten. You may not like yourself as a bully, but it feels a hell of a lot better than being a victim. Let someone else play that role – and feel those feelings.

Let me assert first of all that this intervention is absolutely an interpretation. It is phrased like a statement of empathic identification and indeed it is (any interpretation that is not informed by empathy is a bad interpretation, however "correct" it might otherwise be). It is an interpretation because it suggests a *connection*, a connection that Joe is not aware of and is prone to resist. Joe was invested in seeing badness as an inherent part of who he was, something he was born with. My interpretation offered a different possibility: that being bad was something he had *become* and, furthermore, that he had become bad because of his life's experiences.

It should be noted that this interpretation is not offered from the position of an expert and it therefore implies no subordination of the client. There is no implied, "Joe, as an expert I deem your behavior to be 'normal.'" To the contrary, it is offered from the point of view of a peer. What I am saying is no more judgmental, no more out of a *superior* position, than, "Joe, if I had walked a mile in your shoes my feet would be as sore as yours."

As far as the potential for distortion through projection, that is always present. People in the paranoid-schizoid position project; that is their M.O. But while I cannot prevent projections, I can formulate my interventions in a way that make the projections more difficult to adhere to. As an authority figure (a doctor, a therapist, staff) Joe is prone to project onto me his abusive father and to react to me accordingly. But by making sure that all my interventions are empathically informed – that they come from my identification with Joe rather than my judgments about him – that projection is more difficult to sustain. At some point Joe might be tempted (as dwellers in the paranoid-schizoid position are wont to do) to flip the script and take my empathy as an excuse to project onto me his all-good mother, to make me the good rather than the bad object. But in my interpretation I acknowledged (unapologetically) my capacity for badness. I would, I said, have become as rotten a kid as he, had I experienced what he experienced. It is not in the nature of "good objects" to freely acknowledge their capacity for badness. I cannot prevent Joe, or anyone else who is determined to project, from doing just that. But I can make sure that my interventions, including my interpretations, do not feed or exacerbate that process.

Finally, there is the critique of interpretation that it may be replacing one False Self script with another, one more to the therapist's liking. This is certainly a complex issue but I think that, with fairness, I can say that my interpretation was not guilty of this. An important part of my reasoning is that my interpretation was not directly about Joe at all, it was about myself and how I would have behaved under his circumstances. To be sure, I was speaking of him indirectly, through my empathic identification with him. But I was not telling Joe who he was. I was offering myself as an object of identification and it was up to Joe to accept or reject that identification as he chose.

On a more subtle level, I was presenting to Joe a fundamental challenge to his script, one inherent to the way I think and anathema to the way Joe thinks: that I fundamentally believe that people are not born bad, that they become bad because of certain circumstances in their lives, circumstances that make sense and are intelligible as contributors to badness. This is a fundamental challenge to his script.

I would like to continue with this simple, empathically informed interpretation, one that at first glance doesn't even look like an interpretation, and elucidate some of the benefits should Joe be able to hear it.

The first thing the interpretation does is to place Joe in the context of a history. Joe was not born a bad kid; he became a bad kid because of the life events that constituted his personal history. Remember that in the paranoid-schizoid position there is no experience of history. In fact, the function of splitting is to undo history, to deny its relevance. The bad breast is not simply the good breast that has just been bitten. It is an entirely separate (part-) object that has no connection to the other, desired part-object. History makes connections: between the available-breast and the just-bitten-and-suddenly-withdrawn-breast, between the current bully Joe and the former victim Joe. The adoption of an historical perspective moves Joe out of the paranoid-schizoid position and into the depressive position. It undoes splitting.

Part and parcel of an historical perspective is the concept of cause and effect. A certain set of historical causes led to Joe's becoming what he is today. As these historical conditions change, a different outcome becomes possible. Joe is not inherently and forever locked into being a "bad kid." It is not simply *who he is*. Rather, it is *who he has become*, and he became this way for a certain set of reasons. As these reasons change, Joe too can change. As long as Joe remains in the paranoid-schizoid position he will remain that young child, struggling to cope with his abuse by identifying with his aggressor rather than with the victim. A sense of history – inherent in the interpretation – allows Joe to recognize himself as an emerging adult, one powerful enough to protect himself and without the need to forever attempt to flip the script on his childhood situation.

With cause and effect comes *choice*. Implicit in my interpretation is the issue of choice. "I would choose to be a bully too if I had gone through what you went through." The idea that the choice Joe made was an unconscious one does not make it any less a choice. Joe *chose* to identify with the aggressor rather than with the victim. He may not have experienced it as a choice. It may have felt like the only thing he could do. But in fact it was a choice. And because it was a choice he could at any time choose differently. And as, with the help of interpretations, his choices become conscious rather than unconscious, they become better choices.

The experience of choice is the experience of agency and the experience of agency is the hallmark of the depressive position. The paranoid-schizoid position is a world of "Shit happens!" "That's just who I am." "I'm a bad kid!" An historical perspective leads to a perception of choice and that leads to the experience of agency. With agency comes the experience of empowerment and with empowerment comes the acceptance of responsibility. In the old fable the scorpion convinces the frog to carry him on its back across the river by using the logic that the scorpion would never sting the frog en route because then they would both drown. Of course, the scorpion stings the frog anyway and, as they are both drowning, the frog asks, "Why?" To which the drowning scorpion replies, "It's my nature." As long as Joe denies history, he will not experience the power to choose, and as long as he has no experience of choice the issue of responsibility will be as meaningless to him as it was to the scorpion.

As Joe rejects splitting in favor of an historical perspective, he will cease to divide the world into part-objects. Joe expended an incredible amount of energy in trying to force all males of the species into one of two categories: bully or punk. To the extent that he is able to accept the interpretation I offered he is freed to see men for who they are: whole, complex, multifaceted people with strengths and weaknesses, virtues and shortcomings, areas of fear and areas of courage. He will be able to see others as whole objects; he will be able to see himself as a whole object.

With the perception of himself and of others as whole objects, Joe will move towards the experience of "ruth." As long as history remains undone by splitting, it makes little sense for Joe to be anything but "ruthless" towards his hated bad part-objects. Weaklings exist to be punked, to be bullied. They exist to carry for him the horrible feelings that he once bore himself, but that he could no longer bear to carry. Mercy and compassion (ruth) have no place with objects who are seen as being all-bad. Things are what they are, and what is bad is simply bad. It is only with the acceptance of history, with the perception of objects as whole rather than parts that Joe will be able to feel empathy and compassion for those whom he previously bullied. The perception of wholeness in others makes it much more difficult to be ruthless towards them. One cannot maintain the belief that someone "deserves" to be abused because he is weak (bad) if the perceived weakness is acknowledged to be part of a more complex collection of good and bad traits. And as he feels compassion for others, he will simultaneously feel compassion for himself.

Deserving compassion or ruth is not the only advantage of experiencing oneself as a whole object. A whole object is a *whole* thing: fuller, richer, more complex than a part-object. Joe's description of himself as, "I'm a bad kid. That's just who I am," was implicitly followed by, "and that's all that I am. That's all she wrote!" As long as Joe remains locked in the splitting world of the paranoid-schizoid position, *a bad kid* will be the beginning and the end of who he is (how he sees himself). A sense of history not only adds complexity to one's identity, it adds *fullness*. "That's just who I am" is replaced by "That is where I started. This is what happened to me on the way and how it has affected me. And this is where I am heading and what I hope to become."

Finally, the acceptance of wholeness in others leads to the acceptance of the *alterity*, the *otherness* of others. Joe's DSM diagnosis was indisputably Conduct Disorder. Nobody would have thought of him in terms of obsessive-compulsive functioning. Yet for Joe splitting had all the force of a compulsion. Joe needed to force people (men) into one of two molds: strong or weak, bully or punk. Men became pegs to be forced into round or square holes. Triangular or star shaped pegs were either unseen (as was I), or pounded into one of the ill-fitting holes until they screamed (as did his peers) or rebelled (as did his teacher). But as far as Joe was concerned, into one of those two holes they must go, their true shapes be damned. With the experience of wholeness comes the experience of alterity: things have shapes of their own; they have existence independent from our needs; they are not, as Winnicott puts it, bundles of projections.

All this potential growth from a simple intervention that is as much an expression of empathy as it is an interpretation! Of course, how much of the potential is realized depends on the client's ability to take the interpretation in. And this in turn depends on the immediate nature of the client-therapist relationship. A client deeply mired in the paranoid-schizoid position is unlikely to hear the intended meaning of any interpretation but will hear instead whatever in the moment is being projected onto the therapist. But the paranoid-schizoid position and the depressive position are not mutually exclusive. They are poles of a dialectical tension and most of our lives are lived in the harmonic interplay between those poles. An infant will, out of necessity, split its mother into the good breast and the bad breast, the good mother and the bad mother. But the infant needs simultaneously to be able to use the mother as a surrogate ego within the mother-infant unit. How well the infant is able to dance to these two different tunes at the same time depends on how well the mother negotiates the same harmonic counterpoint. When this dance is done between client and therapist it is called "psychotherapy."

Interpretation as recognition

So far, this chapter's discussion of interpretation (and especially the long example of "Joe") has focused on its utility in helping the client out of the paranoid-schizoid position and into the depressive position. But interpretation is at least as important – in intersubjective terms – as an essential component in the discovery of the self-as-subject. Benjamin (1988 and throughout her career) traces her theory of feminist psychoanalysis back to the German philosopher Hegel. Hegel (1807) argued that one cannot become aware of oneself as a subject until one sees oneself being seen by another, who is also seen as a subject.

This view is very similar to the argument that I have been making at various points throughout this book: that the concepts of self and other define each other dialectically. The concept of self makes no sense except in contrast to an other; and the concept of other can have no meaning except in distinction to self. Thus, the discovery of self and the discovery of other are not (cannot be) separate events, one preceding the other. They happen simultaneously. They are the same discovery, the same event.

Benjamin (1988) presents the self as existing in the dialectical tension between two seemingly contradictory poles: *the self is internally defined* (created through assertion)/*the self is externally defined* (discovered in recognition by an Other). The parallel to Winnicott's paradox of the transitional object is obvious: the transitional object had to be both created and discovered. And, as with Winnicott's paradox, the necessity of both poles is easily seen. Without the external, without recognition of the other, our sense of self is open to the whims of our Narcissistic self-deception. We can be whatever we fancy ourselves to be. Our self is captive to either our grandiosity or our shame.

Without the internal, self-assertion pole, our experience of self is completely subject to the view of others. We are either chameleons whose identity shifts with the company, or we become enslaved to some "master" whom we have granted the power to define us. Both poles are essential

But Benjamin points out a particular problem with this dialectic: there is only one of the two poles that we have any direct control over. The external pole is completely dependent on the ministrations of external subjects over whom we have no direct control. If we are unlucky, the other will see us as an object, and we will come to see ourselves as objects. Girls will grow up thinking that – because they are girls – they are highly emotional, limited in their logical abilities, and possess some powerful, innate "maternal instinct." Boys will grow up thinking that – because they are boys – they are tough and independent, not particularly interested in feelings or relationship, and inherently "assertive." If we are even more unlucky, we will not be seen at all, and we will go through life feeling wraith-like, invisible, constantly seeking some external recognition to validate our existence. To serve its function properly in this dialectic, the recognizing Other must be able and willing to see us as subjects: as whole, independently existing agents, not just as stereotypes or as bundles of their own projections. And unfortunately, this does not happen as often as we would hope.

In this sense, an interpretation is a kind of subjective *recognition* of, or *witnessing* of another, as a subject. When one offers an interpretation, one allows the other the experience of being seen as a subject. This is why a correct interpretation can be such an exhilarating experience for a client. Being truly, deeply witnessed means that one not only is *seen* but that one *exists* (as a subject).

> One session several years into my own therapy, I spent a good deal of time talking about how much I missed my wife and children who were on a long road trip across the country on which I had been unable to join them. At the end of the session I suddenly did something that I had never done before: I impulsively asked my therapist a personal question. "Do you have any children?" I blurted out. My therapist reacted to this impulsive and intrusive "doorknob" question with consummate grace. He smiled warmly and said, "You really do miss them." I floated the rest of the way out of his office in a state of elation.
>
> I felt that I had been truly seen and witnessed. First of all, he had seen and responded to my true – underlying but unspoken – question. What I had been asking him was not about his own family makeup, but whether he could himself feel or identify with my longing for my family. His response was an answer to this true, underlying question. And he did not answer with a cold "yes" or "no." Instead he answered with an expression of warm empathy that more completely answered my question than any concrete yes or no would have.
>
> Second, his response spoke directly to an issue I had been struggling with throughout my therapy. For my entire life I had (on an unconscious level) doubted my capacity for love and caring. When

I experienced my therapist witnessing how much I missed (loved and cared for) my family, I was more able to own a part of myself which I had previously doubted (from which I was self-alienated). Through that interaction I was able to experience myself as a fuller, more whole human being, as more fully a subject. Thirty years later, I can still feel the exhilaration.

13   Transference

As with interpretation, transference – the other foundational Freudian concept – has come under much recent attack. In this chapter I examine the controversy and try to extract from the debate a working definition of transference that I consider to be reasonable while justifying the notion that working in the transference is an essential part of any psychodynamic work. As in Chapter 8, I try to differentiate between Freudian and object relational conceptualizations of transference both in theory and in clinical application.

Transference, like interpretation, has come under much critical scrutiny in the modern psychodynamic discourse and, as with interpretation, I would like to argue that much of the criticism is valid and well-taken, but that any resulting reconceived concept of transference should be strengthened and enhanced rather than rejected or eviscerated.

Freud (1910a) listed transference as one of the pillars of psychoanalytic theory and as one of the essential components of psychoanalytic technique. When Freud first "discovered" transference he bemoaned it as an impediment to the therapeutic work. Why, he lamented, can't my patients see me as the well-meaning doctor (expert) that I am? Why do they insist on seeing me as their seductive father, as their abandoning mother, as the rival sibling? As is typical with Freud's brilliance, he quickly recognized transference as an invaluable asset to treatment rather than – and as well as – an interference. If, as Freud increasingly believed, neurotic symptoms relate to early childhood trauma and in particular to traumatic disruptions of normal Oedipal resolution, then some latter-day resolution needs to take place in the therapist's office. We are talking here of issues that happened decades, even scores of years, before the actual treatment. A male client may, at age four, have wanted to have sex with his mother and murder his father. But at age 40, when he is lying on the analytic couch, such issues will have long since retreated into unconscious inaccessibility. They may appear indirectly in dreams, slips of the tongue, free associations, in the neurotic symptoms themselves, but raising them to a level of consciousness would be like trying to raise Lazarus from the dead.

Enter transference! In transference the repressed affect is no longer buried and moldering in the grave, it is alive and well in the room. With transference the exploration of past lusts, of past hatreds, is no longer a dry, academic exercise. It is alive and well in the room. With transference, a parent who may have been dead for 20 years is no longer dead. He or she is alive and well in the room. Freud (1905) stated that in psychoanalysis the original neurosis is replaced by (is reconfigured as) the transference. With the transference the therapist has something immediate, tangible, real, and affectively alive to work with and that thing is right in the room, between the therapist and the client.

Freud's conceptualization of transference involves what he called a "repetition compulsion" (Freud, 1914b). People seem *compelled* to repeat over and over again past relationships, especially unhappy ones. A woman who had grown up with an alcoholic father may marry an alcoholic, divorce him, and marry another, and then perhaps another. When this woman enters therapy she may tend to see her therapist as weak and fragile and in need of some kind of rescue. It will be extremely difficult for her to trust her therapist with the depth of her emotional pain. A man who was the son of an abandoning mother may enter into a series of relationships all of which end with him being left. When this man enters therapy he may experience every therapist's vacation as a personal rejection and may even feel some aspect of quiet devastation at the end of each session.

For many years Freud struggled theoretically with the concept of transference as it seemed to violate another concept that was axiomatic to his world view, namely the Pleasure Principle (Freud, 1911). The Pleasure Principle states that it is human nature (animal nature, for that matter) to seek pleasure and to avoid pain. Transference seems to directly violate the Pleasure Principle. Indeed, transference seems to represent a compulsion to repeat painful experiences. The solution Freud (1920) eventually came to was the postulation that the repetition compulsion underlying transference represents an attempt to keep repeating a past trauma until a different outcome is achieved; that is to say, it is an attempt at mastery. This endless attempt to gain mastery requires the choice of an object – or the perception (distortion) of an object – that is like the original trauma-inducing object.

The hypothetical woman under discussion cannot simply go out and find a non-alcoholic mate and live happily ever after. This would not satisfy the fantasy she is trying to enact. The fantasy underlying her repetition compulsion is that she partners with a man who finally recognizes her worth to the extent that he finally renounces alcohol in favor of a relationship with her. Thus, the new object must be as close as possible to the original traumatizing object with the difference being that the new object must be judged to be worthy of some hope. The same is true with the hypothetical man in the earlier example. He too cannot go out and find a relationship-oriented woman and live happily ever after. He too must find a woman who approximates the original object, who is either commitment-phobic, perceived to be commitment-phobic, or subtly goaded into becoming relationship-phobic. The fantasy he is attempting to make true is that he is able to *transform* a relationship-phobic woman into a committed partner when he is finally able make her recognize his own inherent value. There is an apocryphal story that Einstein's definition of insanity was repeating the same behavior over and over again and hoping for a different outcome. Einstein probably never said it, but it is a pretty good statement of Freud's definition of transference.

This definition of transference – as a repetition compulsion driven by an unconscious need for mastery – is at variance with another phenomenon that is also frequently referred to as transference. Different writers refer to these different forms of transference by different names. Freud referred to the form of transference described previously as the "transference neurosis" or simply as "transference." Other writers have used the term "transference proper." This second form of transference is what I call a "transference reaction" although I am inclined to believe that we would be better off finding another name for it altogether.

> Let us create a hypothetical person – call him Sam – and postulate that Sam grew up with a sadistic, abusive father. Now imagine Sam driving along the highway and being pulled over for speeding. As the officer is writing up the ticket we can imagine Sam's seething rage. We can imagine how much Sam wants to scream obscenities at the officer, how much he fantasizes punching the officer in the face. If Sam is particularly "primitive" he may even indulge in fantasies of grabbing the officer's gun and "blowing the bastard away."

I present "Sam" as an example of someone enacting a "transference reaction" that fails to meet necessary criteria for "transference proper." There are important ways in which Sam's reaction corresponds to Freud's definition of transference. The *intensity* of the reaction is clearly disproportionate to the current situation and clearly represents the *transferring of affect* from an old, unresolved relationship to a current relationship where it (the intensity) is inappropriate. But the reason I call this a transference reaction rather than transference proper is that it lacks (or appears to lack) the definitive criterion of a repetition compulsion. If we were to add to the description of our hypothetical Sam that he is a chronic scofflaw who gives all appearances of (unconsciously) seeking out confrontations with the authorities, then Sam would clearly meet Freud's criteria for a transference or transference neurosis. But if what we are seeing is simply a characterological response to a random event, then what we are dealing with is *not* what Freud was talking about.

> When I was in graduate school I had a professor of "Behaviorism" who spoke smugly of Freud's "discovery" of transference. "Oh, we discovered that long ago," he said, "and we have studied it with much more scientific rigor than Freud ever dreamed of. It's called '*stimulus generalization.*'"

In terms of equating stimulus generalization with transference reactions, my professor was exactly correct. The original "stimulus" for our hypothetical Sam was his sadistic father and Sam placed his father in the stimulus category of "authority figures." Sam's "response" to his original stimulus was fear and rage. The more a second stimulus resembles the original stimulus, the more Sam's response will resemble his original response. There will be a "response gradient" that exactly corresponds to a "stimulus gradient." The less a new stimulus resembles the original stimulus, the less powerful will be Sam's response. It is exactly analogous to the pigeon which is conditioned to peck vigorously at a red target and will also be found to peck, but less vigorously, at a pink target.

My professor's error (an error commonly repeated even by practicing psychoanalysts) was in confabulating the transference reaction with transference proper. Stimulus generalization is a perfectly apt description for transference reaction, but it speaks nothing to the underlying repetition compulsion that defines the true transference. In a way, the two are opposites of each other. The unconscious experience of the transference reaction is something like, "You remind me of my abusive parent so get the hell out of my life." The unconscious experience of the transference proper may be something like, "You may be nothing like my abusive parent but I need to keep seeing you that way because I have unfinished business that needs to be finished on your bones." The great classical writers on transference (Bird (1972), Gill (1979)) were careful to distinguish between these two types of transference. Many modern writers, however, both defenders and critics of transference, tend to blur or ignore the distinction. I will speak to some of the implications of this later on in this chapter.

As with interpretation, controversy and critiques of transference have existed almost since its introduction into psychoanalytic/ psychodynamic theory. In a seminal article Hoffman (1983) critically reviewed not views of transference but critiques of transference. The central questions Hoffman addressed were, first, whether or not a pure form of transference exists. By this he referred to a pure fantasy projected onto the therapist that is unrelated to any "real" aspects of the therapist (Hoffman refers to this as the "asocial" model). His second question is (if the answer to the first question is negative) then does the concept of transference have any real value?

Hoffman has little trouble in arriving at a negative answer to his first question (indeed he almost takes it as a given): no pure form of transference exists. This suggests that some modification is needed in the description of transference proper that I just presented. In that description, I stated that in a transference proper a client will see you the way the client needs to see you, regardless of who you really are. This statement clearly needs to be modified. If Hoffman is correct, clients, at least clients in a non-psychotic transference, must be responding to at least something real in the therapist.

> The reader may remember how shocked I was when I finally realized that my client Lucy saw me as a maternal rather than a paternal transference figure. But this is not to say that Lucy was not responding to some of my very "real" behaviors. I was, after all, trying very hard (and in an often heavy-handed way) to relate to Lucy in a nurturing, supportive, loving (read *maternal*) sort of way. And, as Hoffman points out, there was another element of "truth" underlying her "transference": when I clumsily wished that she could be happy, I spoke out of frustration and impatience. And, to use Hoffman's phrase, Lucy was a Geiger Counter for frustration and impatience.

Hoffman goes so far as to suggest that rather than seeing transference as a kind of distortion (a break from reality) we should see transference as the opposite of distortion, that we see it as a "selective attention to and sensitivity to" (p. 59) certain realities of the therapist's presentation. This selective attention and sensitivity may allow the client not to distort reality but to "act as a kind of Geiger counter which picks up aspects of the analyst's personal responses in the analytic situation which might otherwise remain hidden" (p. 59). Seeing transference in this way, as a hypersensitivity to certain truths, Hoffman suggests that the view of transference as a distortion be rejected as inaccurate and misleading.

My own view is that Hoffman is here engaged in hyperbole and is in danger of creating a false dichotomy between "selective sensitivity" to reality and "distortion" of reality. Transference can be both at the same time. If I have a client who, out of a history of early sexual trauma, has a selective sensitivity to seduction and is therefore hypersensitive to subtle sexual messages that I, myself, have no conscious awareness of, and if this client identifies a dozen or even a score of such messages from me every session, I may have no dispute with the "reality" of her perceptions. But if she takes these collected perceptions and concludes from them that I, "like all men," am "only interested in one thing in a woman," then I would argue with some forcefulness that she is distorting who I am.

I can only guess that Hoffman is being polemical in choosing to dichotomize truth and distortion, writing as though something has to be one or the other. He writes critically of Greenson for his dichotomy between the "real relationship" and the "transference" (distorted) relationship. But Hoffman then seems to ridicule rather than laud Greenson's attempt to extricate himself from this dichotomy with the statement that, "in all transference reactions there is some germ of reality, and in all real relationships there is some element of transference. *All object relationships consist of different admixtures and blendings of real and transference components*" (Greenson, 1971, p. 218, italics in original).

I would go even further than Greenson, suggesting that some transference (distorted) relationships survive by absolutely submerging themselves in reality.

> Marion grew up in a family where she suffered occasional physical abuse and almost constant verbal and emotional abuse from both parents and older siblings.
>
> While in therapy with me, Marion went through a period where I became the good mother transference object (clearly a projection of a fantasy object) and every other authority figure seemed to become bad mother objects. To use Hoffman's phrase, Marion showed a "selective attention and sensitivity" to any abuse of power and the way she

described these incidents to me I could only agree that the other person in question seemed to be behaving badly.

Not only did her descriptions of these events sound convincing, but her attribution of the motives of the perpetrators sounded profoundly insightful. So-and-so was acting out of "wounded Narcissism," another out of "his insistence on being loved," and another out of "insecurity." She seemed empathic towards them even while she was holding them at fault.

Not only did I empathize with the injustices being done to her and admire her insight in the face of these injustices but I particularly admired her determination to stand up for herself. She would describe herself as calmly and rationally explaining to these people that she was not at fault and that they might want to look to themselves for someone to blame.

But Marion's confrontations did not go well. However calm and collected she attempted to be (one supervisor described her as becoming "lawyerly"), something of Marion's underlying contempt and rage was unconsciously communicated. It is here that these encounters become transference enactments. Marion's rage and contempt were clearly disproportionate to the actual situation (as she, herself, readily admitted) and I suggest that this kind of disproportionate reaction can fairly be called a "distortion."

Those transference enactments, those distortions, became injurious to Marion's career. Highly intelligent, Marion entered several work sites under high regard and left under what she considered to be a cloud (it was hard for me to evaluate this last perception. I suspected that Marion exaggerated (distorted) the degree of antipathy she produced).

I present Marion here as an example of a transference that is, in Greenson's term, an "*admixture*" of truth and distortion. But she also provides an extremely good example of the difference between transference proper and a transference reaction. This is a problem that I believe Hoffman and many of the "Modern Psychoanalytic," (or "relational psychoanalytic") writers share with my former professor: blurring the distinctions between transference reactions and transference proper. Marion certainly had a "selective sensitivity and attention" to abusive authorities. But she was also *driven* to expose and challenge the abuse that she perceived. This was a kind of (unconscious) *crusade* she was on. It was the acting out of a *repetition compulsion*.

In contrast to Marion is Rose.

> Rose was an adolescent girl in treatment at the locked, adolescent treatment center of which I have written. Rose was small, friendly, and outgoing, and well-liked by the staff and her peers. But the staff universally sensed something about Rose: she was dangerous. Rose had been severely physically abused as a child (much more so than had Marion), and consciously or unconsciously, Rose had made a sacred oath to herself (at who knows what age) that no one would ever put their hands on her again.
>
> As I have said, the Center worked with severely delinquent adolescents, many with long histories of violence, and while I believe that the staff did not abuse its power, physical restraints were not uncommon. Rose was a sweet girl, but she was not passive. She had what I would call a healthy degree of adolescent defiance.
>
> The problem was that whenever Rose became defiant she expected to be restrained (abused). And, in keeping with her oath to herself, when she felt threatened she became threatening. This initiated a vicious circle. The more Rose felt threatened, the more threatening she became. And the more threatening she became the closer the staff came to considering physical restraint. And the closer the staff came to considering physical restraint the more threatened Rose felt and thus the more dangerous she became.
>
> The difference between Rose and Marion is that Rose did not seek out confrontation. There was no element of repetition compulsion in her behavior. Her reaction was clearly an inappropriate transfer from earlier relationships to current relationships but without the compulsive element it must be classified as a transference reaction rather than transference proper. Had Rose been constantly provocative, my assessment would have been different.

Returning to the issue of distortion, I believe that Hoffman can be accused at most of hyperbole and this should not detract from the extreme importance of his thesis and especially the clinical implications of his views. The term "gaslighting" has become increasingly popular in discussions of clinical technique (ironically it is a term that comes from a movie that is over 70 years old). Gaslighting refers to an intervention on the part of the therapist that, however well meant, has the effect of making the client feel "crazy" (out of touch with reality). Nowhere is gaslighting more prevalent than in transference interpretations. A simple statement like, "No, I don't think you are talking about me right now. I think you are talking about your father (or mother, or sibling . . .)" is gaslighting. It informs the client that his or her reality is wrong (that he or she is crazy – out of touch with reality), and that the therapist's reality is the true reality. Neither is it much better to acknowledge the accuracy of a client's perceptions and then label the client's conclusion to be a "distortion." That is simply a more subtle form of gaslighting. To this dilemma, Hoffman (1983) offers the following solution:

> This is where the "objectivity" of the analyst enters and plays such an important role. It is not an objectivity that enables the analyst to demonstrate to the patient how his transference ideas and expectations distort reality. Instead, it is an objectivity that enables the analyst to work to create another kind of interpersonal experience which diverges from the one toward which the transference-countertransference interaction pulls.
>
> (p. 64)

In order to generate this new "kind of interpersonal experience" the therapists must avoid gaslighting.[1] Instead, the therapist needs to overtly acknowledge the potential accuracy of the client's observations and the logic behind their conclusions though not necessarily with a submissive agreement with those conclusions).

> A young female client I had been working with for several years suddenly noticed that I was staring at her chest. "Are you reading my tee-shirt," she challenged, "or are you looking at my boobs?" Startled back into consciousness by her challenge (I had actually been in a state of reverie), I thought for a moment and answered, "I'm not sure. Possibly a little of both." To her surprise my client found my answer appeasing. She said that she found it reassuring and comforting that I could be so honest and so comfortable with the sexual tension in the room.[2]

So, with Hoffman's cautionary notes taken to heart, the question still remains: what do we do with the transference in therapy? This is not an easy question to answer. In his seminal article Bird (1972) noted that, in spite of its universally acclaimed importance, very little had been written on how individual therapists actually use the transference in their work with clients. From my perspective, the situation has not changed much, a half-century later.

Freud's answer to the question of how to use the transference was the same as his answer to all such questions: interpret! While Freud saw transference as an essential tool in psychoanalytic work, he nevertheless never stopped seeing it as a form of resistance. Freud held the then current belief that action and memory followed entirely different neuropathways. The action then, that was inherent in the reenactments of transference, acted as a defense against remembering (as a way of keeping repressed material in the unconscious). He saw his task with transference therefore, to be the same as that with any other form of resistance: to attack it as quickly and as efficiently as possible.

Changes in our understanding of neurology have long since challenged Freud's understanding of the immediate function of transference. Even without such changes, observations such as those by Hoffman and others have suggested that a full frontal assault on transference via interpretation may be, at the very least, severely counterproductive.

Hoffman ends his critique by suggesting that one way we may use transference is to change the way a client views relationships by offering the client a different kind of relatedness – a kind of relatedness that is unafraid of self-scrutiny, accepting of self and of others, and willing to acknowledge and celebrate the client as Other.

I have already discussed in earlier parts of this book a number of different uses of transference. For clients who tend towards the paranoid-schizoid position, the transference enables the "metabolizing" of a wealth of projections. For clients with strong False Self personality structures, the transference allows the therapist to become a kind of more benevolent and accepting superego under which a more spontaneous True Self can be discovered/created.

But here I want to introduce a new, more specific use of transference, derived from my belief that the vast preponderance of the work in psychotherapy involves grieving (see Chapter 14). A few paragraphs ago I said that Freud viewed transference as a defense against remembering. I believe the first half of Freud's assertion is an invaluable contribution to our understanding. It is only the second half I disagree with. I see transference as a defense, but not against memory; it is a defense against grief. The logic is simple: if I can simply replace a lost object there is no need for me to grieve that object. Theoretically, this works very well in the paranoid-schizoid position where part-objects come and go randomly and no loss is permanent. But theory tells us also that none of us dwell exclusively in the paranoid-schizoid position. We all dwell somewhere in the dialectical tension between the paranoid-schizoid position and the depressive position.

Some of us may dwell closer to the paranoid-schizoid position than to the other, but none of us can ever completely avoid the possibility of, or the reality of, permanent object loss.

But on the flip side, none of us can ever completely avoid the *temptation* to deny permanent object loss. On one side of the dialectic we know that such loss is real, immutable, and inevitable. On the other side we play with the fantasy that loss is only temporary, that a new part-object will suddenly appear to take the place of the one that disappeared. When we are on that side of the harmonic we seek lost object substitutes, or we welcome them hungrily when they seem magically to appear.

I believe that there are two major things we, as human beings, need to grieve in our lives: the objects (people) we have lost and those that we should have had, but didn't, and never will have. This is not an either/or situation. I am speaking of two poles of a continuum. Those of us who have had meaningful relationships in our lives have nevertheless had moments in which those were wanting, hurtful, disappointing, or unsatisfying. And those of us whose lives have been largely alone and isolated have nevertheless had glimpses of, or moments of, a kind of connectedness that we recognize as a pearl of great price. So most of us fall somewhere in the continuum between these poles and it is sometimes difficult to know whether the loss of a real object or the loss of a fantasized object is the more difficult to grieve.

Another continuum – or harmonic – that we all live on is the harmonic between the paranoid-schizoid position and the depressive position. As I have discussed earlier (see Chapter 5), one of the main issues that keeps us perpetually attracted to the paranoid-schizoid position and wary of too firm a commitment to the depressive position is the issue of permanent object loss. The "depressive anxiety" stemming from either the potential for, or the reality of, permanent object loss keeps us forever under the seductive pull of the paranoid-schizoid position. In the paranoid-schizoid position we need never grieve because loss is always temporary. The "good object" is like a god with many avatars. When it disappears in one manifestation, we need only wait until it returns in another form.

In transference, lost objects, either real or fantasized, return in the avatar of the therapist. If the avatar is of a bad object, then it needs to be punished and abused until it admits its awfulness and makes a shamefaced retreat, making room for the return of the good object. If the avatar is of a good object it needs to be wooed and seduced, worshiped and adored, pleased sufficiently that it will decide to stay, so that mere mortals may bask under its warm and protective aegis.

Our job as therapists – the way we use the transference in therapy – is to allow ourselves to become these lost objects just enough to allow our clients to grieve them. In this task we are clearly walking a tightrope. If we allow ourselves to be seduced into the belief that we can actually be or become the parent the client never had, that our love can actually substitute for the love the client never received, that our love and goodness can actually compensate for all the pain and tragedy in the client's life, then we are setting up a dependency relationship that can only end disastrously in justifiable bitterness, disappointment, and recrimination. If, on the other hand, we err in the other direction, if we resist accepting the transferred relationships (identifying with the projections), if we too quickly interpret (and therefore reject) the transference, then we allow the client no space for feelings in the room, no immediate experience of a relationship to be valued. There is nothing in the room for the client to grieve.

> Karen was an intern at a training site at which I worked as both an individual supervisor and as leader of a "process group." Karen joined the process group a year before she was to become my individual supervisee. I quickly noticed that in the group Karen always made a point of sitting right next to me. I assumed that there was a transference going on and that my physical proximity was comforting to her. Midway through the first year she volunteered the real reason: the seat next to me was the only seat in the group circle in which she did not have to look at me. She had a powerful fantasy that if she looked at me she would burst into tears.
>
> At the end of the first year she became my individual supervisee, sat down in my office across from me, and immediately burst into tears. She spoke of a verbally and physically abusive stepfather and a mother who was unable or unwilling to protect her from the man's venom. I had quickly and powerfully become for her the father-she-had-never-had. Though not as powerful, my countertransference complemented her transference. I had two sons and had always wished for a daughter. And Karen was intelligent, an honest and courageous group member, an intuitive and insightful young therapist.
>
> Our quasi father-daughter relationship continued to our mutual satisfaction until 9/11/2001. Karen had grown up in New York City had had many happy memories of the World Trade Center. She was so devastated by its destruction that on that day she called her clients and cancelled all appointments. In our next session she told me that the Director of our clinic had called her into his office and threatened to

fire her. He had told her that she had abandoned her clients. She was the caretaker, he had said, and her clients may have been as upset as she was. It was her job to put her feelings aside and take care of her clients.

"Okay," she said to me through tears of bitterness. "I understand. It was my job to take care of them. But who takes care of me? Who puts their arms around me and comforts me?" It was here that the limits of our comfortable transference/countertransference relationship were reached. Rather than putting my arms around her and comforting her I responded firmly but empathically: "No one," I answered, feeling the pain of every word I said. "You will never get that. You should have gotten that when you were a child. It's too late for that now and I am so, so sorry." Karen spent most of the rest of the session weeping tears of genuine grief.

The pain of this grief is frequently perceived or experienced as unbearable.

Seth and Virginia were a couple in their mid-sixties, married for forty-plus years. Both were successful academics. Each had had years of individual therapy and together they had had some helpful couples therapy. Both looked upon their marriage as happy, rewarding, and loving. But they struggled together with a difficult, seeming at times to be intractable, marriage dynamic.

Seth's mother had been a driven, ambitious, self-absorbed professional for whom attention to her children had been fairly low down on her list of priorities. Virginia's father suffered from mood swings. On a good day he was restrained in his anger and criticism. On a bad day he would actively look for a fight, and in a fight he was relentless and merciless, until he had not just defeated, but humiliated, his opponent.

During periods when Virginia was preoccupied with her work, Seth's Abandoning Mother ORU would come into play and Seth would withdraw into a sad/angry pout, hoping on some unconscious level that his wife/mother would notice his unhappiness and come to comfort him. Instead, of course, Virginia would interpret her husband's behavior according to her Moody/Punishing Father ORU. In this interpretative schema, anger was random and unrelated to situational events. But instead of hiding as she and her siblings had done as children, Virginia would rail against Seth for being "angry and punitive." This would leave Seth feeling all the more abandoned and unseen, and the vicious cycle would escalate. Both Seth and Virginia had some conscious awareness of this dynamic. But, at the end of the day, each exhausted by the pressures of the day, disinhibited by a couple of glasses of wine, each would reenact the same dynamic. Why?

It is clear that in some way both Seth and Virginia were "transference objects" to each other. But what does this mean? I do not believe that this kind of transference can be defined – as did my old professor – as *stimulus generalization* or, for that matter, as does Hoffman as a *particular sensitivity and attention*. Seth and Virginia had been together too long (essentially their entire adult lives) and knew each other too well for this to have been simply an automatic or reflexive response. Rather, I submit that this response was – as Freud first described – *motivated*. But motivated by what? I believe the answers reflect two sides of the same coin. On one side is the maintenance of hope. Seth's perpetual hope was that his wife (mother) would come around: that she would recognize the error of her ways and see the pain she was causing her husband (son) and re-prioritize her life, placing her work in its "appropriately" lower place in comparison to her sad and needy husband (child). Virginia's hope was that by confronting her husband (father) in a way that she had never been able to do as a child, she would get him to recognize the injustice and cruelty of his ways and to have his eyes opened to the love and appreciation she so clearly deserved.

The flip side of the coin is pain. The giving up of this fruitless and counterproductive reenactment meant not just the abandonment of hope, but the acceptance of realities judged to be "unbearable." For Seth it was the acceptance of the reality that in his mother's mind/heart he was never more than a footnote in one of her legal briefs. For Virginia, it was the acceptance of the reality that her father never saw her as much more than a bull's-eye towards which he could hurl his darts.

These were hugely painful realities to be accepted, and one cannot fault either of them for being reluctant to do so, even at the cost of an endless series of frustrating and painful (though less painful) reenactments. The extent that Seth and Virginia were each able to progress out of this painful repetition compulsion and to see the other for who the other truly was (to move out of the paranoid-schizoid position and into the depressive position) was dependent on the extent to which each of them was able to bear "unbearable" pain and to grieve the loss of the (fantasied) parents that neither of them would ever have.

But before we finally leave this very long vignette, let us again give Hoffman his due. In both of these powerful and enduring "transferences," there was an important element of "truth," and coming to terms with that truth was an essential component of "resolving" the transference. Seth came to recognize and acknowledge that there was more than an element of truth in Virginia's perception of him: his withdrawal was *self-protective*, but it was also *punishing*. Seth liked to think of himself as a sweetheart, but he could be a jerk.

And Virginia came to realize and acknowledge that there was something objectifying in her treatment of her husband: he was something to be engaged with at her convenience and put on a shelf when she was through with him. She, too, could be a jerk.

And the recognition and acceptance of these *truths* took a great deal of pressure off the relationship. Seth and Virginia each recognized that they had more individual work to do and this was paradoxically empowering: each could do their own work rather than having to passively wait for the other to do his or her work first. And, again paradoxically, though seen in a less favorable light than they would have wished, each one felt seen more accurately, and consequently less like a bundle of projections.

The transference object is a substitute for a lost object, either real or fantasized. The transference object enables grieving by providing an immediately present object to mourn. But as long as the transference object remains a substitute for the lost object, grieving is inhibited. The "resolution" of the transference (the ability to see the transference object as who he or she really is rather than simply as a carrier of projections) either simultaneously or sequentially allows for grieving.

Jude was a married male in his early sixties. His mother has been a cold, self-absorbed scholar who worked out of her home. Jude remembered his mother saying hello when he got home from school, but never remembers her getting up from her desk and it was an unspoken rule that Mom was not to be really disturbed until Dad got home after five. Jude's experience of being warmly greeted was of his cageless pet parakeet which, as soon as Jude opened the door, would fly across the room and, with a loud "chirp!" alight on Jude's shoulder.

Jude married a woman who was also a scholar and, being well trained by his mother, was careful not to be too needy or demanding of his wife's time. But he consciously and explicitly made one demand of her: that she greet him when he got home. A smile from behind her desk and an "I'm almost done," would not do.

Across the course of over 30 years of marriage Jude grew as a person and he grew in his relationship with his wife. His wife had always been happy to give him what he demanded and over the years had never seemed to resent granting him this small indulgence. It was probably *because* Jude recognized that his wife really was happy to give him what he wanted that his attitude towards it began to change. He always enjoyed being greeted but he no longer experienced it as a demand or as a necessary ritual.

Jude reported that at a certain moment he was struck by a very clear thought. The thought was, "This greeting thing is very nice, but I don't really *need* it anymore. If she is busy with something when I get home that's fine. I can wait." As soon as Jude had this thought he began to cry, and he knew instantly that he was crying not for anything having to do with his wife, but for the relative indifference of his mother, a woman who had died nearly 20 years earlier.

Notes

1 Not a term used by Hoffman.
2 Obviously, I would only say this to a client with whom I had a sound working relationship.

14 Grieving

In this chapter I argue that while all psychodynamic theories have implicit or explicit focuses on loss and on dealing with loss, most treatises on clinical work tend to ignore or understate the role of grieving in psychotherapy. My position is that some form of grieving is an essential part or all clinical work, across all diagnostic categories.

The concept of grieving (or of unresolved grief) is central to the entire psychodynamic paradigm. In *Mourning and Melancholia* (1917), one of his most brilliant articles, Freud traces melancholia (depression) back to unresolved grief. The difference between normal grieving and depression, says Freud, is that normal grieving allows for the letting go of the lost object whereas in depression the lost object gets internalized as a haunting, torturing inner object. Ogden (1990, p. 134) sees this article as the origin of object relations theory since it is the first to introduce the concept of the *internal object*.

Grieving (object loss) is also central to Klein's theory. Klein's *positions* are defined by their particular kinds of anxiety. The anxiety of the depressive position (and that gives the depressive position its name) is the anxiety pertaining to *permanent object loss*. And it is the inability to deal with this anxiety – with the prospect of permanent object loss – that forces many to remain stuck in the paranoid-schizoid position.

Despite the centrality of object loss and grieving to many of the foundational psychodynamic theories (Freudian, Kleinian, and object relations) relatively little attention has been paid to the importance of the *facilitation of the grief process* in the clinical setting. Taking Freud one step further, I would assert that grieving is a factor not just in depression but is a factor, if not in the etiology of all disorders, at least in their treatment. This includes disorders such as anxiety.

Caitlin entered therapy with what would commonly be diagnosed as severe Generalized Anxiety Disorder with certain specific Social Phobias. The idea of speaking before a group, for example, produced so much anxiety that Caitlin delayed for years entering a graduate program where she knew that would be required.

Caitlin's mother sounds as though she suffered from a mixture of Bipolar Disorder and severe Borderline Personality. At best, the mother was able to function as a childlike companion to Caitlin. She was never able to function as a mother. When Caitlin was eight she received a phone call from her mother who said that she would not be coming home for a while because she had been psychiatrically hospitalized. Caitlin was to pack her things and an acquaintance (someone Caitlin hardly knew) would be by to pick her up. Caitlin says that something in her died in that moment.

Caitlin's father (who had never been much of a presence) disappeared shortly thereafter, and Caitlin was essentially left to raise herself. Along with her (double) abandonment, her unmet dependency needs, and some paranoid attitudes she gleaned from her mother, Caitlin grew up terrified. The world was overwhelming and dangerously unstable. And she was essentially alone in it.

As with many parentified children, Caitlin gained many competencies and, partly by dint of some extraordinarily hard work in therapy, she was able to use these competencies as the foundation for some real self-esteem and self-love. Her last remaining hurdle in therapy was to let go of her mother – both her real mother and her fantasized good mother – and this was no easy task. To give up her anxiety Caitlin had to come to terms with the fact that the world was not inherently dangerous and overwhelming. And to come to terms with this she had to come to terms with the fact that the world had been made to seem dangerous and overwhelming because of her mother's behavior and her mother's character. She had to mourn her mother as much as did any depressive, and her mourning had to include rage as much as sadness.

Another client with severe anxiety (along with some OCD features) was Caroline.

Caroline grew up with one of the few mothers I have heard about who sounded as dysfunctional as Caitlin's. Her mother's M.O., along with chronic screaming matches between herself and Caroline's father, was to make chronic suicide threats. Caroline reported a story from her early adolescence when she, as calmly and maturely as possible, had tried to confront her mother. "Mom," she had said, "I'm a kid. I need some stability in my life. I need some calmness. I can't deal with the chaos in this house." Her mother looked at her and replied, "Fine! I'll go kill myself."

As an adult Caroline constantly expected disaster, just as she had as a child. A successful professional, she had once noticed a slight billing irregularity in her business and had spent an entire night terrified, certain that she would end up in prison, her husband abandoned, and her children motherless.

Caroline had had ample opportunity to unlearn the lessons of her childhood but she appeared unable to do so. A previous therapist had diagnosed her with PTSD and essentially told her that she would have to learn to live with her fears, that she would never get over them. I saw it differently. I saw Caroline holding onto her fears as a way of holding onto her mother. To my mind she would let go of her fears when she let go of her mother.

The difficulty in this (to my mind) was not so much that her mother had been chronically suicidal. I believe Caroline would have been able to come to terms with this. The real problem was that her mother had *not* been suicidal. Despite all the suicide threats, she had never made a single attempt. Her indisputable craziness had coexisted with a cruel, calculated manipulativeness.

I presented this interpretation to Caroline. "It wasn't just that you grew up terrified," I said. "It was that the terror in your life wasn't real, it was fabricated. Your mother used terror to control you, to bend you to her will. For your whole childhood she manipulated you. She lied to you."

When I made this interpretation Caroline nodded in assent. Yes, she said, that made sense. But she was affectless when she said this. My suggestion made sense intellectually, it explained a lot, but she was unable to integrate it emotionally. To accept a chronically depressed, a chronically suicidal mother is hard enough. But to accept having a mother who would so abuse, so ill-use her child, that requires a lot more work.[1]

Unfortunately, if we look to the field of *grief counseling* for guidance in our role of facilitator of grieving in the psychotherapy process, we are not much helped. As is true with the practice of psychotherapy in general right now, current writings on grief counseling tend to focus on techniques and procedures, most with their own particular acronyms or sets of identifying initials. Object relations theory and intersubjectivity based treatments focus, as always, on *relationships*. The therapeutic relationship is important to all aspects of psychotherapy, but it is especially crucial in dealing with aspects of mourning.

The reader will note a considerable overlap in my discussion of the *facilitation of grief in psychotherapy* and my discussion of the *working in the transference*. To my mind these are essentially the same thing. Indeed, I would go so far as to claim that Freud's rather enigmatic concept of the "resolution" of the transference can best be understood as the completion of the mourning process. And, of course, as the mourning process is never completely finished, so too, as Freud (1937) argued, is the transference never completely resolved and the work of psychotherapy never completely done.

"Working in the transference" refers (in object relations theory) to the way therapists accept (contain) the internal objects that are projected onto them and to what they do with them until the client is ready to take them back. To my mind, the way the therapist accepts and handles the projections is the way the therapist facilitates the grieving. In this process therapists walk a tightrope. If they do not accept the projection enough, there will be nothing in the room to mourn. On the other hand, if they accept the projection too well, the client will have no motivation to change as he/she will have the fantasy of possessing everything he or she wants. A satisfactory substitution for the lost object will have been found and the client will remain happily in the paranoid-schizoid position where part-objects are easily substituted one for another.

If, for example, a client's mother is projected onto me and I fail to identify with (accept) the projection, then there will be no experience of the mother in the therapeutic relationship, no *feelings* that a client might associate with its mother: ether the warm/secure feelings that come with good maternal holding, nor the fear, rage, and despair that come with feeling abandoned or rejected by the mother.

If, on the other hand, I identify too much with the mother role, especially if I become too self-sacrificing, too selfless, too caretaking, then I will again be encouraging the client to regress to the paranoid-schizoid position and the client will believe that he or she has, at long last, found the sought-after part-object – the good breast – and, instead of having been helped by me, will become dependent on me. I must allow myself to become enough like the projected object so that the feelings related to the projected object are alive and powerful in the room. But I must not become so much like to projected object that the client can simply substitute me for the object. Grieving then would become unnecessary.

> When I returned from a three-week vacation, Caitlin exclaimed in the session that she was surprised to find herself amazed and delighted that I had returned "unchanged." The origin of this reaction was obvious to both of us. Caitlin's father had abandoned her when she was seven and the few times she had seen him thereafter he had changed from being warm and loving to paranoid and rejecting. Shortly before her father's abandonment her mother had become clinically depressed requiring psychiatric hospitalization. When she returned from the hospital she had changed from being fun-loving and alive to being a zombie-like invalid who sat unresponsive in her rocking chair all day. The interesting thing about this session was that Caitlin could not remember any feelings of "surprise" about her parents' changes. But the feeling of surprise was very powerful in the room with me that I was "unchanged."
>
> My three-week vacation made me sufficiently like Caitlin's abandoning parents so that abandonment feelings were alive and powerfully present in the room. (Therapists who cannot bear to be the bad object thus rob their clients of an opportunity to mourn.) But I was sufficiently unlike the original abandoning parents (I did not change) so that I could simultaneously facilitate grieving while being the object of the grief.

Along with the tightrope the therapist must walk between too much and too little identification with the projected object, therapists must also be careful to provide (be) a *whole object* for the client. This is not as simple or as easy as it sounds since we are saying that the therapist must identify (up to a point) with the client's projections and, by and large, what gets projected are *part-objects*. One of the most important of the myriad reasons that we do our clients no good if we allow ourselves to functions as part-objects for them is that (as we have seen in Chapter 5), part-objects do not get mourned. Part-objects come and go randomly (so their loss is never permanent) and they are easily substituted one for another. Only whole objects are mourned as only the loss of a whole object is permanent.

Thus, when a client projects the "good-mother" onto me I must accept the projection, but I must also "metabolize" it. I must become the good mother who fails. I must become the mother who understands but sometimes fails to understand. I must become the mother who is devoted but has a life of her own. I must become a mother who loves but has limits to her love. In short, I must be (become) a whole object. Only a whole object can be mourned.

If the "bad mother" is projected onto me I must again accept and then metabolize the projection. I must allow myself to be abandoning (as in ending the session on time, taking vacations, etc.), but I must be sensitive to the pain and anxiety that my abandonments cause. I must acknowledge that I frequently fail to understand (and sincerely empathize with the pain my misunderstanding causes), but make it clear that I am constantly working to understand. I must recognize and own my occasional impatience with my clients but acknowledge that my impatience is my issue and my problem and be ready with a genuine apology when my issues get dumped on my clients. In short, I must be (become) a whole object. Only a whole object can be mourned.

Only a whole object can be mourned. This brings me to an important aside. Therapists will frequently conspire with their clients to avoid mourning by encouraging splitting. This happens especially when the object being mourned is particularly repellent or loathsome. "Are you grieving your real mother or your fantasy mother?" a therapist will ask. But this question itself is based on splitting. The client did not have two mothers: a real mother and a fantasy mother. The client had a single, real mother who satisfied and disappointed. A fantasy mother may have been created in the client's mind to compensate for the disappointments, but the client in fact had only one mother. The relationship with that mother – as with all relationships – existed in neither the satisfaction nor the disappointment, but rather in the dialectic between them. Mourning must take place in the same dialectical space between reality and fantasy. To mourn the real mother, both the satisfactions and the disappointments must be mourned. If a fantasy mother has been created to avoid dealing with the disappointments, then that fantasy must be given up before the disappointments (along with the satisfactions) can be mourned. Only a whole object can be mourned.

Sometimes the process of mourning can be deceptively simple. As Freud (1925) noted in his article "Negation," sometimes the presence of something can be noted by its conspicuous absence.

> Anna was a 40-year-old woman whose mother had died five years prior to Anna's entering therapy. Anna had never grieved her mother's death. She hadn't needed to because she had become her mother. She had made "keeping the family together" her major role in life. She had taken over her mother's jobs in several charities that her mother had

been involved with. She had even forged friendships with many of her mother's old friends. When she spoke of her mother her only affect was of warm pride and admiration. She had never cried for her mother, not even at the funeral.

Our early work in therapy focused on grieving, but not for her mother. Rather, Anna was able to slowly and guardedly begin to grieve the loss of her former self and her former life. She had given up her career as a librarian in order to nurse her mother through a long bout with cancer and she was able to acknowledge and feel this as a loss. She admitted to missing her old friends and admitted to some impatience with the old people who now filled her life. But this grief work was clearly in conflict with and inhibited by her need to keep her mother alive by walking in her shoes.

In a session about a year into the therapy Anna was talking cheerfully about her mother and I found myself overwhelmed by sadness. I asked Anna to list all the feelings that came up when she thought of her mother. She immediately listed eight to ten feelings, all positive, including love, pride, warmth, respect, etc. Making no attempt to keep my own sadness out of my eyes or my voice, I said to Anna, "I am struck by the fact that in all the feelings you listed you did not include sadness." At this, her eyes filled with tears and she began to cry.

I suggest that two factors were operating here. First of all, Anna and I had been able to establish, in the months leading up to this session, an effective *holding environment*. Anna had been able to gradually let go of her need to be a mother herself and had allowed herself to feel mothered (held) by me. She had allowed herself to establish with me a kind of preverbal, empathy-based (mutual projective identification based) communication and mutual understanding. She had felt *held* by me and was thus able to relinquish her need to be the sole holder of the universe. Indeed, my intervention with her was a kind of holding. My intervention was not a "got-ya" moment in which she had been caught in a contradiction or an omission. Rather, it was a moment of empathic communication. It was what Ogden (1994) calls an "interpretive action." The complete intervention, verbal and non-verbal (communicated through eyes and voice) combined was:

I am struck by the fact that in all the feelings you listed you did not include sadness. But I understand that this is not because you do not feel sad. I understand that it is because you are afraid of being over-whelmed, devastated by your sadness, afraid that if you acknowledge your loss your world will crumble into chaos and anarchy. And I am happy to carry as much of your sadness for you, as long as I need to, until you are able to re-own it yourself.

The second aspect of my intervention that I think was salient was my use of the word, "I." I could just as easily have left myself out, have just said, "You did not include the word . . ." but unconsciously I chose to preface that clause with, "I am struck by the fact that." In doing so, I am introducing myself as a separate, external object, as an *alterity*. This brings us back to Winnicott's (1968a) somewhat odd description of the infant's epiphany, "I destroyed you. You survived my destruction. I love you!" Why does the infant love the object for surviving his attempt to destroy it? Because in surviving the infant's destruction, the object has demonstrated its externality, its reality. And in demonstrating its externality/reality, it has demonstrated its *usefulness* to the infant. In providing a successful holding environment for Anna, and in demonstrating the reality of that holding environment by surviving her attempts to destroy me (by making me useless and irrelevant as a caregiver), I had demonstrated to Anna that she did not need to be the sole maternal force in the universe: there are other mothers, there are other holding environments.

In psychotherapy, the process of grieving is rarely as simple as mourning the loss of a deceased loved one.

> Audrey grew up with a mother who was abandoning when she was not being physically or verbally and emotionally abusive. But there were occasional times when her mother would use her daughter for her own needs and the two would, momentarily, become best buddies. This was (as it is always) an extremely pernicious combination, and Audrey persisted well into her adult life in the vain pursuit of recapturing these blissful moments of parental approval and connection.
>
> For the first two years of therapy Audrey was severely depressed. Our sessions were marked by relentless self-hatred, punctuated by periodic expressions of fear that I would grow weary of her and kick her out of therapy. At the end of the second year her depression lifted significantly and she began to see herself, and our work together, in a very different light. She recognized that until then her work in therapy had been pretty much about keeping her head above water. Now she was ready and eager to "go deeper," to do some "real work" on herself.
>
> In a session a few months after this shift I suddenly saw a very different Audrey. In this session Audrey seemed relentlessly critical, hostile, and angry. Nothing I said seemed to be right or agreeable to her. In reviewing this session, the following week, Audrey asked me

what my experience was. I replied that I thought that she had identified with her inner mother and projected her worthless self onto me. "I felt as though nothing I did was right, that there was no way of pleasing or satisfying you. I thought that I must have been experiencing with you what it was like for you to be with your mother."

Without commenting on my interpretation, Audrey then offered her own. "I was mad at you for always pressuring me to leave my mother. You have no idea what she means to me. I know that I never *say* anything good about her, but that's the problem: you only listen to my words. I need your help in getting beneath my words. I need you to be more intuitive."

My first reaction was shock at how different our interpretations were of this event. But I quickly realized that our interpretations were different only at a superficial level of meaning. At a deeper level of meaning, we were saying almost exactly the same thing. I had interpreted Audrey as having attempted to engage me in a *direct communication* (Winnicott, 1971c, p. 54). A direct communication is a nonverbal communication (via projective identification) in which the communicator says, in effect, "I cannot tell you in words how I feel, so I will let you know how I feel by making you feel the exact same way." Audrey's interpretation (on a deeper level of meaning) was almost exactly the same thing. She was saying, "We are communicating too much on a verbal (symbolic) level. We need to communicate on a more preverbal, intuitive level (via projective identification) so that I can process preverbal experiences."

I believe what Audrey was telling me was, "We need to go back to the kind of preverbal communication that a mother has with her infant: a holding environment. I need to experience a holding environment with you so that I can know, in immediate experience, what I got from my mother and what I did not get. That is the only way I can grieve. If I never know what I got and what I didn't get I can only wander in confusion and doubt. If I know what I got I can appreciate my mother for it and be sad at having lost it. If I know what I missed out on I can be sad about that and then move on. In either case, I have to know. I have to have the experience of saying, "Ya, that's it!" or "No, that's not it!". Otherwise I am lost.

Note

1 Recently Caroline reported to me that in moments of severe fear or anxiety she forces herself to rage and swear in fantasy at her mother. This is a start!

15 Identification

As Chapters 9 and 10 focused on the work of Ogden and Chapter 11 focused on Winnicott, Chapter 15 is derived primarily from the work of Jessica Benjamin. Benjamin argues (persuasively, to my mind) that we can help our clients only to the extent that we can identify with them. This represents a fairly radical departure from the traditional view in which a therapist's identification with the client was greeted with fear and innumerable cautionary notes.

Thomas Ogden has made a lifelong study of projective identification. Jessica Benjamin has made a similar study of identification. Their conceptions of these terms are both very similar and very different.

Identification is one of those problematic psychoanalytic terms that seems to have a different meaning for each user. Benjamin's use of the term is essentially the same as Winnicott's (see Chapter 3). Benjamin writes of identification as a kind of seeking commonality with another object, similar to Ogden's projective identification in that it appears to involve a fantasy of projecting an aspect of oneself into another object. But it comes from an entirely different psychological space. Projective identification involves projecting an aspect of oneself into another for the purpose of safekeeping. A negative aspect of the self is projected into another so that it is less of a danger to the self. A positive aspect of the self is projected into another to protect it from the negative aspects of the self. In either case, the projected material is safer – less threatening or less threatened – when contained in another object.

With identification *per se*, an aspect of the self is projected into another for the purpose of seeking commonality. When someone tells us that he cannot sleep without a light on, then we seek to make sense out of this behavior by projecting our own fear of the dark, or our living memory of our childhood fear of the dark, into the other. "That's why I needed a night-light. Is it the same with you?" When identification is a purely unconscious process it runs the risk of serious distortion. If I unconsciously assume that your need of a light comes from a fear of the dark then I may be oblivious to other possible explanations, such as your history of bedwetting and your need for a clear path to the bathroom. But to the extent that it is conscious, it can be checked out, and to that extent it can be the basis for interpersonal communication and understanding.

I have already discussed identification (see Chapter 1) in the context of the holding environment. Winnicott discusses identification as an essential mechanism by which the mother is able to provide an adequate holding environment for her infant. In the context of psychotherapy, Benjamin sees identification as inhibiting our tendency to *pathologise* our clients. Benjamin says that if she had to err, it would be on the side of over-identification rather than under-identification. Benjamin goes on to severely criticize Freud for his unwillingness/inability to identify with his early hysterical patients, especially including Dora, Freud's pseudonym for Bertha Poppenheim who later went on to some renown as a pioneering social worker and Jewish feminist. Poppenheim's hysterical symptomology, Benjamin asserts, was a preverbal expression of rebelliousness against gender oppression. When she finally found her voice, says Benjamin, she went on to become an articulate crusader against such oppression. Because he had equated the feminine with passivity, Freud was unable or unwilling to identify with Poppenheim's position and was thus unable to see the inchoate, healthy defiance and rebelliousness in her symptomology. Hysterical symptomology, says Benjamin, is an *action* and, as such, it falls midway between passive helplessness and symbolic (verbal) expression. But given that Victorian women were struggling against a gender system that worked to keep them helpless and passive, an action – any action – was a positive step forward.

Benjamin further asserts that Freud's failure of identification with his clients led to his failure to fully appreciate the positive, healthy aspects of another of his major discoveries: resistance. Resistance, says Benjamin, like hysterical symptoms, represents a healthy refusal to submit passively (as an object) to the will of an external authority. Benjamin cites the story of Poppenheim's famous act of rebellion (resistance) when, in a certain session, she could not be (would not allow herself to be) hypnotized (an hypnotic trance being a state of almost complete passive submission). Instead, she asked Freud simply to allow her to talk. Freud was wise enough to let her do this and thus (so the story goes) out of this act of defiance (resistance) was born Freud's "discovery" of his primary psychoanalytic technique: *free association.*

In Benjamin's approach, identification is one of the primary ways in which therapists come to understand their clients. It is essentially the same process (without the element of "almost an illness") that Winnicott describes in the "primary maternal preoccupation." Therapists must *feel themselves into their clients' places, and so meet their (ego) needs.* I agree with Benjamin that without some kind of identification, a therapist's understanding of his or her client is incomplete. Any understanding of a client that lacks an element of identification is purely "textbook" understanding and, even if accurate, useless to the client (useless at best! At worst a "textbook" understanding makes the client feel further objectified). Benjamin (1998, p. 15) quotes Gallop (1985) as saying "Nobody wants to be unlocked with a skeleton key."

In the early 1970's I was offered a position working in a locked, residential treatment center with delinquent teenagers. I had grown up in an isolated, white, upper-middle class suburb and had literally never known a person of color, a delinquent, or even a poor person. Furthermore, my parents, though not analysts themselves, were involved in the heady Los Angeles psychoanalytic community of the time, and I had heard countless (unethically told) dinner party stories recounted by analysts about their work with their famous Hollywood clients. How, I wondered, could I function in such a setting? I took the job, immediately fell in love with my new clients, and stayed for nearly 20 years. This was because, to my great surprise, I identified with my delinquent adolescent clients. How?

Both of my parents were highly successful academics, both internationally famous in their own fields. Between them they wrote a dozen books and both have had biographies written about them. As a child, the bar of success set for me looked astronomically out of reach. I had always assumed that I would graduate from college and go on to get a post-graduate degree. That was simply expected. But unconsciously I felt that no matter how much I achieved in life, I would always be, by my family standards, an abject failure.

So when I went to the treatment center I met one hundred kindred spirits. These were children who (obviously for very different reasons) also felt doomed to failure. All of them knew that no matter how much they excelled in school or on an athletic team, they would never leave the ghetto, they would never escape the violence, they would never leave poverty. They were doomed to failure.

So I knew something of how they felt. Other members of the treatment staff knew what they thought, knew how they saw the world, but

> I felt a unique bond with these kids because I identified with them: I felt something akin to what they felt. This bond enabled – empowered – my therapeutic work with them. They saw me (correctly) as being from a different world than theirs, but they felt connected to me nonetheless. They felt respected by me. They opened up to me in ways they did not with other staff. Intuitively they felt and accepted the paradox: I was from a different world, but I was one of them.

As an intersubjective theorist, Benjamin also emphasizes the *mutuality* of identifications. Clients, she says, cannot identify with (identify with in the sense of internalize) their therapists if their therapists cannot identify with (feel themselves into) their clients. I would go what might be a step further and assert that clients cannot identify with their therapists unless they *know*, on some level, that their therapists identify with them.

> Hester, a client in her early thirties, had been depressed her entire life. So chronic was her depression that it wasn't until her early twenties that she realized that she was depressed. Prior to that, depression had simply been her *normal*. After an heroic effort in high school she had gotten herself into a good college where she immediately found herself unable (because of the depression) to do her work. Despite anti-depressant medications, she dropped out of college, went back a year later and dropped out again. She entered art school and dropped out of that. She was pursued by a young man in art school, entered into a volatile relationship with him until he was tragically killed in a motorcycle accident.
>
> When she entered into therapy with me she was severely withdrawn and semi-vegetative. Our early sessions were marked by long silences in which see seemed to forget that I was in the room and would give a startle response if I broke the silence.
>
> Hester worked hard in therapy and made much progress. She made friends (she had never before had a friend), lost them, and made new ones. She maintained a job working with young children who she loved and who gave her a reason to live. She enrolled in the local community college and got straight A's. Hester terminated with me when she was admitted to a four-year college on the East Coast. In our goodbye sessions I was amazed by the woman sitting across from me. She said that she was "sure" that she would do well academically, that she was "looking forward to making new friends," and that she even expected to be "happy." These were words and concepts that had never been part of Hester's vocabulary.

Yet I felt that our work was unfinished. It was unfinished in that Hester had never let herself identify with me, nor to accept that I identified with her (that we shared a common humanity). Hester had always seen me as a kind of saint-like person and had dismissed any of my suggestions that I might in any way identify with her. She needed to protect me – and herself – by keeping me on a pedestal where I could be admired but not touched. The result was that she left therapy without the sense of shared humanity with me that I so powerfully felt with her. She had made friends and was looking forward to making new ones. But she hadn't quite given up the (protective) illusion that she was somewhat different from other people, that she did not share normal human needs, normal human feelings.

Mutual identification – by which I mean the mutual, conscious or unconscious awareness, by both therapist and client, that each, in fundamental ways, identifies with the other – is essential for the therapeutic couple's emergence out of what Benjamin calls the complementary therapist/client relationship, namely, that of healer and sick one, expert and novice, authority and ignorant one. In a larger sense, however, it is essential for a client to be able to experience identification with the larger world. As long as Hester resisted awareness of my identification with her, she was able to maintain the illusion of her separateness from the rest of humanity, of her fundamental pathology. Mutual identification opens the door to the experience of *relatedness;* it provides a middle ground between the polar pathologies of fusion and existential isolation. With mutual identification one can, at the same time, be both separate-and-autonomous and connected.

This leads to the hoary issue of self-disclosure. Current psychoanalytic theories, especially intersubjective theories, tend to downplay the classic psychoanalytic juncture against therapist self-disclosure, though cautionary notes about the practice continue to abound. Aron (1991) boldly announces, "Self-revelation is not an option; it is an inevitability" (p. 255).

I have supervised interns for over 30 years. I am used to them coming to me anxious, sometimes guilt ridden, over the same issue: "I self-disclosed! Did I do wrong?" And each time I give the same answer:

That depends on the needs of your client. If I felt it was in the best interest of my client I would self-disclose my masturbation fantasies. If I felt it was in the best interest of my client to remain unseen, I would be a clam. It all depends on what is in the best interest of your client.

By and large I have found this a helpful response. It eases the intern's guilt and anxiety and it refocuses the intern on the best interest of the client rather than on blind rule following ("do this." "Don't do that").

> I was extremely perplexed when I found myself self-disclosing to a client without any sense that I was doing it "in the best interest of the client." The case was as follows:
>
> The client, who had been referred to me by a colleague, was a tall, muscular young man in his late twenties. When I asked for some history he immediately began by describing his history with rowing. He had rowed in college and then moved into the national team. He had gone as far as the Olympic trials. I listened quietly to his impassioned description of this period of his life, and then I asked a question which I knew would lead to my self-disclosure. "So what college did you row for," I asked. "Stanford," he replied. "Oh," I said casually, "I rowed for Cal."
>
> The client leaned back in his chair, his eyes got big, and he said, "Woah! Go Bears!" at the end of the session I gave my standard first-session spiel: "I strongly advise you to interview two or three different therapists. Therapy is an issue of chemistry. It doesn't matter what a therapist's credentials are, or how highly he or she is recommended. What matters is the chemistry between you and your therapist." "Oh no," he replied. "You rowed for Cal. You are my therapist."

I have since told this story to several of my colleagues hoping, mostly, I think, to assuage my guilt but also hoping for some insight into my behavior. To my surprise, none of my colleagues found fault with my behavior and some even lauded it. While I am not yet convinced that my intervention was "laudatory," I have nevertheless come to the following understanding:

> What I believe I was trying to say to my young client was, "I can identify with you. I know what it is like to prepare for hours for a race that no spectators will attend. I know what it is like to win or lose a race by half a length (a respectable victory) and know that the margin of victory (or loss) represents the losing team rowing at 99.95% of the speed of the winning team. I know what it feels like to be on a splinter of a boat where eight bodies are moving as one. I know what it feels like to work for countless hours to perfect a single, simple, coordinated motion of arms, legs, and back. I know the exhilaration of victory and the heartbreak of defeat. I can identify with you."

And to this my new client responded positively, affirmatively, and with certainty.

Aron quickly follows his clarion statement about the inevitability of therapist self-disclosure with several paragraphs of cautionary disclaimers. His cautionary notes are extremely important, though I lack the space here to go into all of them in detail. Perhaps the most important is the summation in which he cautions that,

> The danger of any approach that focuses on analysts' subjectivity is that analysts may insist on asserting their own subjectivity. In the need to establish themselves as separate subjects, analysts may impose this on the patient, thus forcing the patient to assume the role of object. Analyst's imposition of their own subjectivity onto their patients is not "intersubjectivity"; it is simply an instrumental relationship in which the subject-object polarities have been reversed.
>
> (p. 256)

Certainly, intersubjectivity cannot consist of the *imposition* of one subjectivity onto another. Intersubjectivity is the *mutual discovery* of another's subjectivity. How can the therapist facilitate this mutual discovery and not impede it? Certainly, the therapist cannot simply *assert* his or her subjectivity and expect the client to receive it. My attempts to simply *tell* Hester how much I identified with her were met by a blank stare, a polite smile, and utter disregard. On the other hand, my attempts to *show* her how she and I were alike bore more fruit.

> In one session Hester talked about a classmate who made her very uncomfortable. The source of this discomfort was this classmate's apparent total lack of self-awareness. Rather than following the usual protocol of exploring why this characteristic was so upsetting to Hester, I purposefully interjected my own similar reaction. "Oh yes," I said, "when I'm around someone like that I get totally paranoid. I suddenly wonder if I have spinach between my teeth, if my fly is open and nobody dares tell me, or if I am farting and completely unaware of it. It is my worst nightmare!" Hester's eyes got wide and she leaned forward excitedly: "Yes," she exclaimed, "that's exactly how I feel."
>
> Hester's experience was not simply one of feeling *seen* or *understood*, it was one of feeling *connected*. Another human being shared a reaction she had. She was not a freak; she was not unique or alone in her feelings. She was connected to another person by a common

reaction. I could identify with her and therefore she was enabled to identify with me.

Without mutual identification we are stuck in complementary relationships: doctor/patient, guru/acolyte, friend/foe.

Arnold was a medical student engaged to Juliette, a graduate student in clinical psychology. Arnold's father valued intelligence, achievement, and rationality above all else. Emotions were deemed "feminine" and scorned. Arnold described growing up with his father as involving a "circle." To be inside the circle was to be in his father's esteem and to adhere to his father's values. Showing emotion, irrationality, or anything less than unimpeachable success resulted in being excluded from the circle. Being outside the circle was a kind of purgatory, but not one without the possibility of redemption. Admitting the error of one's ways, begging forgiveness, and rededicating oneself to absolute rationality allowed for reentry into the circle.

Unsurprisingly, Arnold was very insecure in his relationships, and was easily wounded. In fact, his skin seemed to be so thin that, though he loved Juliette and knew that she loved him, his description of the relationship sounded like almost perpetual torture. If, for whatever reason, she became self-preoccupied or withdrawn, Arnold would feel rejected and abandoned (kicked out of the "circle"). This was so painful to him that he felt that he had "no choice" but to withdraw into a cold, unloving, self-protecting state (perhaps in identification with the father?). In this state he reasoned that if she had hurt him (even unintentionally) she must not love him and that she must therefore prove her love by acknowledging her mistake, sincerely apologizing for the pain she had caused him, and promising never to make that mistake again. When he was satisfied that she had met these criteria, she would be readmitted into the circle of his good graces.

I noted, but did not point out to him, that his behavior (withdrawal) was the same as the behavior he has found so unforgivable in her. I judged that to do so would simply provoke a huge shame reaction in him (he had been "irrational") following which he would have struggled to get back into my "circle." I also noted but did not interpret to him his having acted exactly as his father had: punishment by ostracism and withdrawal of love.

Either of the previously mentioned tacks might have led to important work in the long term. But neither addressed the immediate pain he complained about (nor, for that matter, the retaliatory pain he was inflicting on his fiancée). So instead I refocused our work on how dangerous the world was to him, especially people and relationships, and subsequently how difficult it was for him to trust. His repetitive demands for proof (proof after proof after proof) of her love for him was, I suggested, the opposite of trust. He seemed to be incapable of trust.

Arnold accepted this interpretation readily and proceeded to try and work on this "lack." If he could just correct this personal inadequacy he would be a better person and would be admitted back into my "circle." Obviously, this work went nowhere (again, I could have worked on his father-transference with me, but this did not seem to be the work at hand). No matter how hard he tried, Arnold could not will himself to become more trusting person.

After some struggle with this issue I (we) realized that my interpretation had been off base. Arnold could not *will* himself to be more trusting because his lack of trust was not a "lack" at all: it was a logical consequence of his view of the world as inherently dangerous. It was as if he had been trying (at my urging) to get himself to be able to trust a rattlesnake.

Arnold's "problem" (what caused him so much pain) was not a lack of anything; it was his certainty that the world and everyone in it was dangerous. And this certainty, in turn, came from his inability or unwillingness to identify with anyone except his father. Arnold loved his fiancée and he knew (cognitively) that she loved him in return. But she was an alien species to him: she was a female. Arnold *felt* nothing in common with her and that made her unknowable and dangerous. He experienced his withdrawal from her as being totally unrelated to her withdrawal from him because he experienced himself as being totally different from her: he had no *identification* with her.

Arnold had grown up severely isolated. His peers bullied him and picked on him for being a "nerd." And when they were not picking on him they exploited him for homework answers. And his family, who were themselves isolated through their common defense of arrogance, provided no help. Arnold had some (ambivalently held) identification with his father, but that was it. He described his mother as kind, warm, and comforting, but she was one of those "emotional females" and any identification with her would have severely threatened his tenuous identification with his father.

And now he was in a relationship with another kind, warm, comforting, and emotional woman whom he knew he loved. He was generally successful (though with great effort) in warding off the impulse to have contempt for her as his father had had for his mother. But he could not yet identify with her.

For a person to experience another person as a subject (as an Other), that other person has to be seen as both different and similar. If the Other is experienced as entirely different (no identification), then it will be seen as an alien about which nothing can be known and, therefore, upon which projections must be hurled if any sense is to be made of it. It has to be an object. Similarly, if an Other is perceived as entirely similar (over-identification), it too must be an object. Indeed, if the identification is too great then the Other is not really even seen as an Other; it is a clone of, or an extension of, the self. A subject – an alterity – is perceived as both different and same. The perceived similarities (identifications) are a source of security, connectedness, comfort. The perceived differences are a source of stimulation, excitement, a potential for growth. For much of the time Arnold was able to see the differences in Juliette in this positive light. He recognized in her a strength in her emotionality that intrigued him and that he coveted. His father had taught him that such a thing could not exist. But Arnold could not deal with any emotionality that was less than perfectly loving. At the slightest hint of emotional withdrawal (to which he was acutely sensitive) he would retreat to the paranoid-schizoid position and project onto her all of his father's sadistic rejection. Interestingly, when he was in this tortured position the only way he could see out of it was not in seeing her for who she really was (a return do the depressive position), but in insisting that she become his good, all-loving mother instead of his punitive, rejecting father.

Arnold could see Juliette's differences. Sometimes they intrigued him and sometimes they terrified him. What he could not see was the similarities they shared. He was unable to see even that they both withdrew emotionally for the exact same reasons: self-protection. He knew that his own withdrawal was self-protective, but could only see hers as being punishing and rejecting. His developmental task – and his task in the relationship – was to allow himself to identify with Juliette. This was an enormously challenging task as it involved accepting on an emotional level what he already knew on an intellectual level: that his father was wrong, that emotionality did not imply emasculation and loss of worth.

At the beginning of this chapter I discussed Jessica Benjamin's damning critique of Freud for his failure (refusal? inability?) to identify with his hysterical clients. While Benjamin's argument seemed radical to me when I first read it, I now recognize that the great majority of my therapeutic failures have come from failures in my ability to identify with my clients, and that as long as I am able to maintain an identification with my clients, I am able to provide basically competent therapy.

Linda was a successful professional who nevertheless presented as emotionally primitive due to a failure of the holding environment and the mother-infant unit. Linda's parents were traumatized refugees who had themselves been successful professionals in the old country, but who had been emotionally destroyed by the traumatic events in their lives, leaving them childlike, dependent, and paranoid (Linda had been told as a child to play indoors rather than in her yard because if she played in her yard she was sure to be kidnapped).

I had decided, early in our work, that most of Linda's issues were due to developmental deficits rather than to more classic neurotic struggles and as a result I had adopted a therapeutic stance that involved a lot of "re-parenting." One danger in this is, of course, that the parent/child relationship is inherently complementary. I was aware that in my work with Linda I was constantly on the edge of condescension.

For some time, Linda had been working on her guilt at not taking better care of her parents. This guilt was determined by personal, familial, and cultural forces. She recounted her uncle telling her that she did not really need to buy a home of her own because she would eventually marry and move into her husband's home. She "knew" (and I had no reason to doubt her) that what her uncle was really saying was, "You shouldn't be spending money on yourself. You should be spending it on your parents." Ironically, her parents disagreed with her uncle. They wanted her to buy a house or condo and were less than subtle in expressing their anticipation that when she did get married and move in with her husband, they themselves would move into her vacated place.

I had listened to such stories with a mixture of sympathy and outrage. How can any parents, how can any family, how can any culture, be so abusive of their children? I was generous in expressing my sympathy, and more guarded in expressing my outrage. But in neither was I identifying with Linda.

Then a certain session was different. Linda had always asked, in a plaintive, childlike voice, "What should I do?" And I had always responded, "I can't decide that for you. You have to decide that for yourself." But my response had always been formulaic. I was the "good parent," trying to encourage my client/daughter to grow up and make decisions on her own. In this particular session, Linda continued with her questions. What was different was that instead of sounding helpless and dependent, she sounded grief-stricken. And, as she wept, I softened. And as I softened, the barrier I had erected between myself and her dissolved. I was suddenly able (willing?) to will myself into her psyche and see the world though her eyes.

And through Linda's eyes the world looked hopeless and bleak. To remove the burden that her parents represented Linda would have to reject her parents, reject her extended family, and reject the values and community that she had grown up with and continued to be a part of. And even if she were able to (or wanted to) do all that, she would still have her internal objects and closely held values to deal with. Linda strongly believed that it was her responsibility to take care of her desperate parents and who was I to tell her she was wrong?

For the rest of the session I sat mostly quietly as Linda wept. But my quietness had a different quality. I was no longer waiting with practiced patience for Linda to "grow up" and "own her power." Instead, I was listening with intense sadness to someone who was truly in a terrible, unwinnable situation.

At the end of the session Linda dried her tears but did not relent in her questioning: "I still want you to tell me what to do," she said. My answer was subtly but significantly different from answers I had given in the past. I did not say, as I so often had, "I cannot decide for you. You have to make your own decisions." Instead, I said more thoughtfully (and more emphatically), "I really don't know. There seems to be no good way out; no way out without terrible pain and loss. All I can really say is that if you do decide to separate from your parents I, for one, won't blame you."

For most of our work together I had functioned with Linda as Benjamin had described Freud as functioning with Dora. I had approached her with a kind of benevolent arrogance. She was the child-like adult who had been inadequately parented and I was the parental adult who would help her overcome past deficits.

Linda did, of course, have serious developmental deficits. But in allowing myself to become locked into a complementary parent/child relationship with Linda I cut myself off from identifying with her and therefore failed to recognize the reality of her dilemma and the intensity of her pain. When Linda began to weep I was finally able to identify with her pain and to recognize the terrible grief she was dealing with. The complementarity of our relationship was broken and each of us came closer to recognizing the subjectivity of the other.

16 Depressive position struggles
The False Self

While previous chapters have focused on the process of getting from the paranoid-schizoid position to the depressive position, this chapter focuses on struggles of the depressive position: what Winnicott called "False Self pathology." I argue that, as with so many of Winnicott's concepts, the concepts of the True Self and the False Self are frequently misunderstood and misapplied. I also argue that these are extremely important concepts and that the recognition and abandonment of False Self functioning and the discovery/creation of the True Self is an inherent part of all psychotherapy.

Are we there yet? No, not by a long shot!

In normal childhood development one can expect a gradual shift in functioning from the paranoid-schizoid position to the depressive position. This shift is never linear, and it is never complete. But it is significant. As I have said earlier, the functioning of the paranoid-schizoid position, in its purest state, epitomizes what is generally referred to as the Borderline Character Disorder. In the depressive position, or as close as we can come to it, we see people for who they really are (as opposed to seeing our own internal objects projected onto them), we have a sense of our own subjectivity and agency (rather than experiencing ourselves as objects to whom things simply "happen"), and we recognize ourselves as the creators of meaning in our lives (rather than passively believing that things simply "are what they are"). But there are pathologies of the depressive position, serious pathologies that tax the skill of any therapist. We may have gotten out of the paranoid-schizoid position and into the depressive position, but we are not home yet.

If splitting is the defining defense in the paranoid-schizoid position, then repression is the correspondingly characteristic defense of the depressive position. Repression does not happen in paranoid-schizoid functioning because there is no reason for it. If, to use the classic Freudian model, I suddenly find myself sexually lusting after the mother who had up until then always been nurturing and comforting to me and if I suddenly find myself threatened by and competitive with the father who had up until then always been kindly and protective, then in the paranoid-schizoid position there is no problem: I simply split. There is the sexy mother and the nurturing mother, and they are unrelated to each other. And there is the competitive father and the protective father, and they, too, are unrelated to each other. It is only when I no longer split, when I recognize that these would-be disparate part objects are, in fact, facets of the same whole object, that a defense like repression becomes necessary. I can no longer simply act "as if" I had two mothers, Sexy Mommy and Nurturing Mommy. In order to preserve and protect the relationship with the one mother I really do have, I have to bury (repress) the sexual longings I have for her.

If disorders of the paranoid-schizoid position are disorders of splitting, disorders of the depressive position are disorders of repression. But this statement immediately needs to be qualified. There are many theorists, particularly in the object relations school, who describe repression as simply another kind of splitting. These theorists distinguish between what they call a "vertical split" and a "horizontal split." A vertical split is what is commonly referred to simply as splitting. An aspect of an Other, and a corresponding aspect of the self, are split into two aspects each, one good and one bad. What happens next is that one or more of these split-off aspects are projected onto another object, either through simple projection or projective identification. In horizontal splitting (repression) a part of the ego is also split-off, but instead of being projected out, it is simply buried. Thus, if in the paranoid-schizoid position I judge my aggressive impulses to be unacceptable, I will project them onto someone else who I will then identify as a bully or aggressor. If, in the depressive position, I find my aggressive impulses unacceptable I will bury them into my unconscious and perhaps adopt some kind of "reaction formation" by becoming a vegan and a pacifist.

It is easy to see here why Otto Kernberg (1976) says that object relations theory and Freudian psychoanalysis are complementary rather than competing theories. Object relations theory, he says, with its emphasis on the primitive defense mechanisms of splitting, denial, identification, projection, and projective identification, is better suited to explaining disorders of the paranoid-schizoid position (character disorders) while Freudian theory provides the best explanation for disorders of the depressive position (neurotic disorders).

I believe that there is a great deal of wisdom in Kernberg's formulation, but there is also a danger of overlooking Winnicott's enormous contributions to our understanding of depressive position struggles. This contribution has to do primarily with Winnicott's formulation of the distinction between True Self functioning and False Self functioning.

Winnicott's "True Self" and "False Self" functioning

D.W. Winnicott's concept of the True Self and the False Self offers a simple and extremely elegant alternative (supplement) to Freud's theory of drive and repression. Winnicott starts out with the notion of a True Self. The True Self is what one truly is: it is our true thoughts, our real feelings, our impulses, our interests, our likes and dislikes, our fears, our longings. Winnicott says that the True Self is what is unique about a person but, as I shall argue later, surely this definition is too narrow. The True Self must also include what is universal in us: our need for love, our childhood fear of the dark, our fear of abandonment, our longings for physical touch.

In any case, Winnicott suggests that in each of us some of these personal qualities are not accepted by our primary caregivers. He calls this an "impingement." Impingements are hurtful because they are when those who mean the most to us do not appear to accept who we really are. Some impingements are so small as to be hardly noticed at the time, but they can have a cumulative effect. Other impingements are devastating. In either case, the psyche acts to prevent future pain by burying the True Self under a protective blanket called the False Self. Thus, Winnicott says that the False Self protects the True Self, by protecting the psyche from the pain caused by impingement, by the rejection of some aspect of the True Self.

The similarity to Freud's concepts of repression and the unconscious is obvious. In both theories some aspect of the self is not accepted because it is considered threatening or unacceptable. This aspect of the self is then denied/buried, pushed down into some place in the psyche that is unavailable to conscious awareness and therefore impervious to future threat or hurt.

But there is a huge and important difference between Freud's theory of repression and the unconscious and Winnicott's theory of True Self and False Self functioning. Freud's is a drive theory and drives (in Freudian theory) cannot be stopped. Even when repressed, they constantly seek discharge and will eventually find expression in one form or another. If primary libido is blocked (via repression), then libido will be expressed through sublimation. If sublimated libido is blocked, it will be expressed through symptom formation, dreams, slips, etc. But it will always find some (however indirect) avenue of expression.

Winnicott's is not primarily a drive theory, although some needs (such as the need for object relatedness) may assume drive-like proportions. In Winnicott's schema, when an aspect of the self experiences impingement it simply disappears under the protective cover of the False Self and, rather than finding a circuitous route to expression, it may simply atrophy there.

> A child is playing creatively with crayons and a coloring book. His mother comes along and gently and lovingly says, "That's great, Honey, but try and stay within the lines. Some moments later his father comes by and gently and lovingly says, "That's great, Honey, but the sky is blue not green."

These impingements are kindly and lovingly made and certainly well intended. The child himself may not even notice the pain of the implicit rejection, but the cumulative effects will be that he will eventually learn that his artistic or creative side is not valued or accepted by those he loves most, and that what is valued is his ability to "stay within the lines" and to "get it right." This young child may grow up to be an accountant or an engineer rather than an artist. More importantly, the child may well deny ever having had an artistic or creative impulse, that part having been systematically effaced by the loving but unaccepting ministrations of parents. And indeed, it may be possible that in fact the child's creative side has disappeared. Although the False Self is presented as a protective blanket designed to insulate the True Self from further hurt (impingement), if left under that blanket long enough, aspects of the True Self may simply suffocate and die.

Impingements may be subtle, well intended, and cumulative in their effect. They may also be catastrophic.

> When Caitlin was eight her father, who had always been in and out of her life, left for good. When her mother tried to comfort her, Caitlin angrily rejected her mother's ministrations. "No," she said defiantly, "I don't care. I never cared about him." Caitlin, who had always adored her father, buried her True Self love under the protective False Self protective blanket of indifference.
>
> And her False Self functioning continued to "protect" her through her life. Pretty and vivacious, Caitlin would easily enter into romantic relationships. But at the first sign of trouble in the relationship she

would wash her hands of it. "Oh well," she would exclaim, "that one didn't work out. Maybe the next one will work out better."

This False Self indifference served her well (protected her from pain) until her mid-thirties. Then time caught up with her. Her "biological clock" was running out. She was afraid she was losing her youthful good looks. She had done a lot of good grief work of her father in her therapy. And so, up through the protective False Self blanket of indifference a True Self feeling began to percolate: loneliness.

In spite of its simplicity (or perhaps because of its simplicity) and because of Winnicott's characteristic reluctance to dull the potential impact of a concept by over-defining it, the concept of the True Self and False Self is open to confusion and misunderstanding. Certainly, some aspects of the False Self correspond quite simply to what in current culture would be called being "fake." Winnicott (1960b) himself suggests this meaning of the term when he suggests that an early form of False Self acquisition occurs when the toddler is constantly reminded to say "thank you" long before being developmentally capable of experiencing any true feeling remotely akin to *gratitude*.

In this view, the False Self is simply a set of socially acceptable behaviors that can and do change with the particular situation. I smile at people, including strangers, even though those people give me no pleasure. I say, "Have a nice day!" even though I don't really care what kind of day someone has. I'll say, "No, that's okay. You have the last piece," even when I really want to eat more. In some cases, this kind of behavior is simply being polite. With some people, however, particularly with those with a strong need to "fit in," such behavior can be highly problematic. The teenagers I worked with for years at the residential treatment center were particularly outraged by excessive "fakeness." "If you are a gangster that's fine," they would say. "And if you are not a gangster that's fine too. Just don't pretend to be something you are not!"

Mitchell (1993) presents a long and thoughtful critique of the True Self/False Self concept, listing numerous problems with it. What, for example, is really "true" about the True Self? Does "true" mean that it is something we are born with, some part of our biology? Or can true be learned? And if it can be learned, then whose "truth" are we dealing with: one's own or one's teachers'?

In an earlier work (Brodie, 2007) I presented as an example of True Self/False Self functioning a case presented to me by a student. The client in this case did not have a strong False Self presentation. Indeed, he seemed to have no sense of self at all. The student/therapist would find him in the clinic waiting room staring at the floor in fear, he later explained to her, that someone would say "Hello!" to him and he wouldn't have a clue how to respond.

This client had been raised, as he put it, "like the family dog: out in the back yard." His mother had kept him there not out of her own sadism, but rather in an effort to protect him from his father's constant and vicious sadism. The client reported a memory of having come into the house to ask for a drink of water. His father had slapped him hard enough to knock him across the room and had snarlingly demanded, "Did I ask you if you were thirsty?"

So here we are presented with a client who grew up not even knowing if being thirsty was an acceptable part of himself. His young therapist, in a particularly creative moment, brought into a session three different kinds of cookies and asked him to taste each one and tell her which he preferred. He did as requested, discovered that he liked the peanut butter cookie the best, and he started to cry. His tears had nothing directly to do with cookies; he had discovered something True in himself.

In keeping with Mitchel's objections, the concept of True Self needs further clarification. One may well wonder what is "true" about a preference for peanut butter cookies. If this client had been born in China, or India, or among the Inuit, he might have gagged at the taste of a peanut butter anything, let alone a peanut butter cookie. So it is too facile to say that a preference for a particular kind of food represents anything "true," including the sudden discovery of the joys of peanut butter. What was important for this client, what brought him to tears, was not an American style cookie. The tears of joy that came with the discovery of True Self Functioning came with the discovery that he had *preferences*, that he was not indifferent to whatever slop was put in front of him, that he had *likes* and he had *dislikes*, whatever those likes and dislikes might be. Exactly what his likes and dislikes were was secondary to the fact that he had them.

Mitchell (1993) suggested that the terms True Self and False Self be abandoned and that we substitute for them the terms "authentic" and "inauthentic." There is much to be said for this. When I say that I am not hungry when I am hungry I am being polite but inauthentic. When I ignore someone whom I have no interest in I am being rude but authentic. When I say to a client, "Your words tell a story of great tragedy but when I listen to your voice I feel absolutely nothing," I risk hurting that client's feelings but I am speaking form a position of authenticity.

But Mitchell's objections make sense *only* if the False Self is seen as a conscious, choice-available function. But others, like Ogden (1990), see the False Self as being primarily an *unconscious* function, unavailable to conscious decision-making.

> When one of the adolescent gangsters I used to work with would reach out as a child for love and affection only to have his gestures time and time again painfully rejected, that child would eventually develop a False Self protection. His True Self needs would be buried under a False Self blanket of denial. "No," he would tell himself, "I don't need love. I'm hard. I'm down. Love is for sissies and momma's boys." And in order for this defense to work, in order for the potential pain of rejection to be avoided, the False Self words of denial *have to be believed* and the True Self needs *cannot be felt*.

Thus, however valuable Mitchell's concepts of authentic and inauthentic functioning, they cannot mean the same thing as Winnicott's concepts of True Self and False Self functioning. When a gangster says that he doesn't need love, even though this is what Winnicott calls a "False Self presentation," he is speaking authentically: he really believes it. Similarly, were this same gangster to say (because he knows that it is what his therapist wants to hear), "of course I know that I need love," he would be speaking inauthentically although he would be speaking (unknowingly) about a quality of himself that is part of his True Self.

So the task set by Winnicott is far more difficult, and far more complex, than the task Mitchell sets for therapists. Mitchell would have us speak authentically to our clients and help them develop the courage to speak authentically to us. This is without doubt an invaluable and daunting component to any psychotherapy. But the task Winnicott gives the therapist is more daunting still. He would have us help clients get in touch with disowned and disavowed parts of themselves and reject parts of themselves that they have long held to be true (authentic).

> Hester began her first session with me with the words, "I don't think my mother was capable of love; and I don't think she even liked me very much." This was said with a wry smile, more sardonic than sad. She dealt with this situation by developing a powerful False Self. "I don't need love," she told herself. "I don't even need to be liked.

I don't need friends. I don't need people." She would make it through life, she decided, on her anger and her determination. [When I first started working with Hester I was reminded of the Rudyard Kipling's *Just So Story*, "I am the cat that walks alone, and all places are the same to me."]

A year into therapy Hester told me the following story. "I first went into therapy in my early twenties and was placed on antidepressant medications. At one point I made what must have been one last attempt to get my mother's attention. I took about three months' worth of my medication and then told my mother that I had overdosed. My mother simply looked at me and said, 'Maybe you should end your therapy. It doesn't seem to be helping you.' And then she walked away.'" Sputtering with my own indignation and horror, I stammered out something like, "My God! You must have been devastated."

The next session Hester gently and patiently told me that I had missed the point of her story. She hadn't been devastated. She couldn't remember having any emotional reaction at all. She had simply gotten the response she had expected.

This is how the False Self protects the psyche from pain. In the face of one of the coldest and cruelest maternal rejections that I have ever heard of, Hester herself didn't bat an eyelash. She had long ago convinced herself that she neither deserved not needed love. There must, of course, have been some last-gasp glimmer of the True Self (a true need for maternal love) that sparked the suicide gesture itself (the attempt to get mother's attention). But the False Self was well enough entrenched that when this last spark of True Self functioning was cruelly doused, Hester felt no pain. This was just who her mother was; this was just who she was (and what she deserved); and this was just the way the world was.

So what?

So here is the therapist faced with an enormous dilemma (or series of dilemmas). How do we therapists "treat" something about which we have no concrete evidence, and of which our clients not only have no awareness but would also likely experience as "inauthentic" if we were able to point it out to them?

The Freudian therapist has it relatively easy. The Freudian unconscious leaves marks. In fact, it is known by its marks. It expresses itself through dreams, through slips, through neurotic symptoms, and through the transference. Indeed, Freud was sufficiently steeped in nineteenth century science that he never would have postulated a construct that could not somehow be *seen* (even if only indirectly seen) and measured.

But Winnicott's (buried) True Self leaves no such observable marks. It does not express itself indirectly; it does not express itself at all. It is buried and in the process of atrophying, and perhaps dying. Yet it is in this process of *atrophy* and *deadness* that the therapist is able to identify the presence of the False Self. Winnicott (1960b) says that the False Self is marked by the experience of "deadness." Something of my True Self, something that was once true, alive, and vital in me is now dead or dying, suffocated or suffocating under the thick (supposedly protective) blanket of the False Self. Where I used to feel alive and vital, I now feel dead.

To take a rather extreme Freudian example, a client who as a child repressed a powerful murderous rage at the subsequent siblings who "stole" his mother's love from him may, through reaction formation, proclaim himself the defender of "unborn innocents." But Freud would say that his aggression has to come out somewhere, and would not be surprised to see this person murderously targeting (or at least having murderous fantasies of targeting) doctors who perform abortions.

In contrast, the hypothetical child with the coloring book presented earlier would not be expected to become a sublimated or even neurotic artist. That child might well grow up to be someone who experienced pleasure in engineering work and who professed no understanding of, nor interest in, art *per se*. But Winnicott would expect that there would be some lingering though vague awareness of something that was but that is no longer, something that was alive and vital but is now dead, something that he/she might dimly recognize in others as creativity or spontaneity, and know that he/she lacks it, in short, a sense of *deadness*.

The word "spontaneity" is crucial to understanding the concept of the True Self. Winnicott purposefully says very little about the nature of the True Self: "There is but little point in formulating a True Self idea except for the purpose of trying to understand the False Self, because it does no more than collect together the details of the experience of aliveness" (1960b, p. 148). So the True Self is nothing more than an aggregate of the experiences of aliveness. This is why, as I indicated in the example of the client who was presented different cookies to taste, the True Self does not consist of a preference for peanut butter cookies over chocolate chip, or sugar cookies over oatmeal cookies. The True Self is the experience of noticing that different foods affect the taste buds differently, and that one has a preference for one taste over another. It is also why, if the True Self is the experience of aliveness, the False Self is experienced as a kind of deadness.

One of the few specific things Winnicott (1960b) does say about the True Self is that it is "linked" with "the spontaneous gesture" (p. 145). Winnicott says that it is always the "spontaneous gesture" that is the object of impingement. This linkage between the spontaneous gesture and the True Self may at first be somewhat confusing. It may be clearer if one looks at the flip side of the equation, at the False Self. The False Self, developing as an alternative to the True Self, develops at moments of impingement, moments where the True Self, expressed through spontaneous gestures, is rejected. It happens when the child is told that its spontaneous decision to draw the sky green instead of blue is unacceptable. So instead of spontaneous gestures, the child learns rule-following, learns to be robotic. The sky is blue, leaves are green, and tree trunks are brown. That's the rule. That's just the way it is. There is no room for spontaneity when one is playing by the rules. To the extent that one is spontaneous, one is functioning in accordance with one's True Self. To the extent that one is functioning according to some pre-defined set of rules, one is functioning in accordance with a False Self, and one is functioning robotically. And to the extent that one functions like a robot, one cannot have the experience of aliveness.

Along with functioning robotically, the other metaphor I use to describe False Self functioning is reading a script (see Chapter 4). Clients with False Self Personalities go through their lives as though they are reading from a script. The script may have been co-written by the clients themselves and their significant caretakers. The script may contain many things that are "true." But it is still a script. And the *truths* that the script may contain are not what Winnicott is talking about as True Self functioning any more than a truth found in a book can be an example of True Self functioning. The "truth" in True Self functioning is marked by spontaneity – it cannot be scripted.

> The hypothetical child in the vignette given earlier in this chapter has had a script written for him in which skies are blue. Much of the time this may be perfectly true. But though False Self functioning may contain truths, the truths are all part of a script. The boy with a powerful False Self may look up and observe, "Yup! The sky is blue today." The comparable response from somebody in touch with True Self spontaneity is more likely to be something like, "Wow! Look at the color of that sky!"

Clients frequently enter therapy feeling that they need to protect their False Self scripts. "My parents," they will say defensively, "were good and loving people." And saying that they will look anxiously at the therapist, expecting their script to be rejected. "That's not true," they half expect to hear, "your parents were judgmental, cruel, and abandoning."

In this case the client's script is probably truer than the therapist's substitute script. Most parents (I would like to believe) are good and loving people. But even good and loving people are human and, as humans, are capable of unintended impingements on the True Self functioning of their well-loved children. The job of the therapist is not to write a substitute script to replace the client's script. It is to help the client feel (spontaneously) and deal with the pain caused by the impingements from those good and loving people.

When clients with predominantly False Self functioning (clients with what Winnicott (1960b, p. 143) calls "False Personalities") show up for therapy, it is usually because of some powerful but poorly identified malaise. They are frequently in professional jobs that they are good at but from which they derive no particular pleasure. They will be in conflict-free marriages and they will have children whose soccer games they attend. But they will tell you that they are unsatisfied with themselves and with their lives, that "something is missing," that they are not depressed but neither are they particularly happy. They will rarely use the word "deadness," at least in the early sessions of treatment, but when the therapist introduces the word the client will respond with surprising agreement.

By and large, False Self functioning is *sensed* and *intuited* rather than being objectively observed and measured. This is one more area where it is especially important for the therapist to be able to adopt what Freud (1909) called a state of "hovering attention" or "evenly-suspended attention," an ability to attend to both what the client is saying and what the client is not saying, to the client's emotions and to the therapist's emotional reaction, to the content of the work and to the process underlying the work. Therapists working with False Personalities will frequently notice a "deadness in the room" or even feelings of deadness in themselves in relation to those clients before the clients consciously take note of it in themselves.

An intern I supervised was extremely upset with herself because of a powerful reaction she had in sessions with a young schizophrenic client. "I dread seeing her," she said. "Every time I see her I feel drugged.

It is everything I can do to stay awake. I feel like putting toothpicks under my eyelids." I suggested that maybe what she was experiencing was a "direct communication" of a deadness in the client herself, an otherwise amiable young woman.

When the intern graduated from the program the client was transferred to another young intern. A few months into this second intern's program she came to me as agitated and guilt-ridden as had been her predecessor, and for the exact same reason. What struck me was not just that her reaction to this client was the same, but that she even used some of the same words to describe it: "I feel like putting toothpicks under my eyelids."

The *deadness* that each of these young therapists experienced in the presence of this very disturbed client was not a sign of any fault in the therapists themselves. To the contrary! It came from their sensitivities to something profoundly important in the client who functioned entirely on a False Self level. Whether there was a True Self still there, struggling to breathe under the False Self protective blanket, or whether it had long since suffocated and died, no one could yet say.

Sometimes False Self functioning can be obvious. When I worked with young delinquents my attention would be caught by the abused girl who claimed to have no fear or by the abandoned boy who claimed to be indifferent to love. Both fear in the face of danger and a need for the love of a nurturing figure are, I believe, hardwired into our human nature. Without them Homo sapiens would have become extinct millennia ago.

But therapists must often rely on their own intuitions to detect False Self functioning. Something in what a client says or does simply does not *feel* right. Yalom (2002) describes one client as being "always bubbly and enthusiastic and reminds me of a lively tour guide or an adorable tail-wagging puppy" (p. 121). Many clients will tell personal stories of incredible tragedy and loss in a way that leaves the therapist feeling as though listening to a story about someone the client barely knows, as though the client's emotional reactivity itself has shut down and been buried.

Although the True Self is considered to be buried under the False Self, the depth of the interment fluctuates widely; the True Self may still be more or less visible beneath the surface.

I noticed that one particularly cheerful and "upbeat" young psychology intern I supervised consistently avoided dealing with potentially depressing issues with her clients and would even steer them away from feelings of sadness. When I confronted her on this her face became suddenly sober. She had suffered deep depressions as a child and adolescent and had, with great effort, pulled herself out of them. She was terrified, she acknowledged, that if she got too close to her clients' depression she would be sucked back into her own.

With other clients the False Self may so completely obliterate the True Self that it is experienced as entirely ego-syntonic and "authentic." I find this to be frequently true of clients we label as "passive aggressive."

One superficially amiable young client was constantly hurt or amazed that people seemed to be so frequently angry with him. The problem, as he saw it, was his memory and his "inability" to get organized. When I suggested to him that his propensity to arrive at our sessions ten to fifteen minutes late, and to occasionally not show up at all, might be a sign of a lack of respect for me or our work together, he appeared hurt and betrayed. Surely I, of all people, knew about his memory problem! The same was true when he would "forget" to bring his checkbook to sessions for weeks at a time. Yet this young man genuinely *felt* neither disrespect nor animosity towards me. He was intelligent enough to see that his behavior might be interpreted as such, but he insisted that such interpretations were in error. "I don't *feel* angry or hostile towards you," he would protest, and I could only believe him.

So how do we access the inaccessible?

Let's start to answer that question by going back to Hester.

Hester's True Self was buried as deeply as any I have seen. She had spent her childhood and adolescence genuinely convinced that she had neither need of, nor interest in, any other human being. And this was not just a cognitive certainty; Hester did not *feel* any such need either.

One of the things that always amazed me in listening to Hester's history was her insistence that no one ever reached out to her, no teacher, relative, neighbor, or mother of a friend; recognizing her as a sad little girl in need of a hug. Now Hester was an attractive young woman and must have been a very pretty little girl. Yet no one seemed to have recognized her sadness nor responded to it. In retrospect, I believe that Hester had so completely and deeply buried her fundamental need for human warmth and contact that she never exuded any such need.

What *began* to crack Hester's thick layer of False Self was a relationship. In her mid-twenties Hester was pursued, wooed, and (partially) won. I say partially because although Hester allowed herself to enter into a relationship with a young man, she never really allowed herself to feel love for him. To the contrary, she reported that she found nothing but fault with him. He could do or say nothing right. He was a fool for loving her. She could only make him unhappy. And then, three years into their relationship, he was tragically killed in an accident.

Hester's initial reaction was grief mixed with relief. They had not been right for each other anyway. He, ironically, was better off than she. He was free of the burdens of this dreary world while she was left to deal with it.

But then something unexpected happened. Her feelings of relief faded, but her grief intensified. She missed him. She missed him more than she would have thought possible. This was not "right." This was not in accordance with her lifelong False Self functioning. Something True in her had been touched and resurrected. And it refused to be buried again.

So Hester went into therapy. She entered therapy with a compassionate and gifted young therapist who adored her. And, as had Hester's boyfriend, her therapist pursued her, wooed her, and won her. Hester felt her therapist's love and responded to it. To be sure, it was still far from being entirely welcome. Hester would talk about how *painful* it was to feel loved. The pain came from the reminder of how horribly unloved she had felt as a child. Thus, this was the exact same pain that had contributed to the formation of the False Self in the first place. The difference was that in the presence of the loving therapist the pain was bearable. In the original presence of the unloving mother, the pain of feeling unloved had been unbearable, and therefore the need for love itself had been denied and buried under a "needless," schizoid, False Self.

Again, tragically, two years into therapy Hester's therapist was forced to terminate her practice and referred Hester to me. Fortunately, I too, had no trouble finding Hester lovable. So by now Hester had had three different experiences with being loved. The early cracks in her False Self had at that point developed into fissures. And as her True Self need for love and connection began to emerge, so accordingly did her self-concept begin to change. Since she no longer had to convince herself that she didn't need love, she no longer had to convince herself that she was unlovable. Difficult as it was, she began to *like* herself rather than despise herself. She began to recognize and appreciate her own intelligence, as opposed to her previous belief that all of her success had been due to sheer, bull-headed stubbornness. And Hester began to develop something that she had never previously had or even dreamed of having: friendships.

I suggest that there are two basic rules for working with False Personality clients. Do not be seduced or fooled into thinking that the False Self presentation is true. And, when you do see signs of True Self, go after it relentlessly. The decision the therapist makes to *not* respond to the False Self as if it were True can sometimes appear harsh or cruel, especially with clients who experience their False Selves as authentic.

> Celeste, a client in her mid-forties with a powerful False Self presentation, reported the following important learning experience from her childhood. She had, she told me, always been confused by her older sister's choice of clothing (sweat suits and jeans) which got her sister no attention. Celeste herself had quickly learned that if she let her hair grow long and straight, if she wore long dresses, and if she looked adults in the face and smiled broadly at them, the adults would smile back and shower her with attention.
>
> As I heard this story I immediately resolved that whenever Celeste would flash me one of her sweet, winsome smiles, I would not smile back. As I was formulating this decision I questioned myself as to whether or not I was being cruel. But it seemed clear to me that to willfully reinforce her already powerful False Self would be far crueler.
>
> Celeste was referred to me for couples therapy by another of my clients who was very fond of her. I remember, when Celeste first called to make an appointment, thinking that I immediately understood my other client's fondness for Celeste. She sounded so sweet and so pleasant on the phone. This initial impression was redoubled in our first session. She seemed so loving, so attentive to her husband. She smiled at him sweetly. She listened attentively to what he said and was careful to respect his point of view even when she disagreed. She would touch his arm reassuringly when he began to get upset. She seemed the perfect wife.
>
> As the sessions progressed, my impression of her as the perfect wife only grew, but my emotional reaction to her shifted from being very positive to being quite negative. There was something in her perfection

I began to find stultifying. She was too perfect. At last I was finally able to put a name on it: she was a "Stepford Wife." She was a robot.

A month into couples therapy Celeste called me to say that she had discovered that her husband was cheating on her, that she had ordered him out of the house, and that she was beginning steps to dissolve the marriage. I agreed to continue seeing her in individual therapy.

It turned out that for many years her husband had been subject to violent rage attacks, that he had frequently been verbally abusive to her and occasionally physically abusive. She reported all of this in a very matter-of-fact way, with the only affect expressed being one of puzzlement and curiosity. She said that she, herself, did not experience anger and it always puzzled her to see people who did. She talked about her husband as though he were some kind of specimen under a microscope, and of her years of abuse as though it were something she just had to endure.

The emergence of Celeste's True Self was a slow and gradual process, with no watershed or "aha!" moments. It was facilitated by Celeste's husband, who remained true to form – antagonistic and abusive – throughout the divorce proceedings. But Celeste now had more distance from him and she had weekly sessions with me. In those sessions I tried simply to adhere to the two rules I mentioned previously. I did not respond to her "understanding and compassionate" attitude towards her husband and, whenever I glimpsed some hint of anger or frustration with him – anything that felt "true" – I explored these with empathy and compassion.

A year into the divorce proceedings Celeste sat in my office and said, with genuine feeling, "I hate him! I wish he would get out of my life forever. But he is the father of my children so I know he never will. But I wish he would!" This was not her prettiest moment. She was not the pretty little girl with the long hair and the winsome smile. This was not the Stepford Wife. This was a human being talking, and I had never felt more warmly towards her nor more fond of her.

Winnicott (1960b) advocates that, in cases of severe False Personality, the False Self be identified and labeled directly and that the deadness associated with it be unabashedly interpreted:

In one case, a man patient who had had a considerable amount of analysis before coming to me, my work really started with him when

I made it clear to him that I recognized his nonexistence. He made the remark that over the years all the good work done with him had been futile because it had been done on the basis that he existed, whereas he had only existed falsely. When I had said that I recognized his nonexistence he felt that he had been communicated with for the first time.

(p. 151)

Winnicott then quotes another client as saying, "The only time I felt hope was when you told me you could see no hope, and you continued with the analysis" (p. 152)

To tell a client that he does not exist, to tell another client that you see no hope for him, may seem beyond the courage of even the most experienced therapist, let alone the novice. And the reader may be forgiven too if he or she is a bit skeptical of the positive results Winnicott claims for these interventions. Yet at times I, too, have been as daring and I can testify that the results can be as Winnicott describes.

> I supervised a young female intern who was extraordinarily bright, but, due to a profound False Personality structure, was characterologically incapable of doing the kind of therapy that I teach. This young woman had once shared with me a fantasy she had of me, in the telling of which it became clear that this was not her own fantasy, but rather one she had borrowed verbatim from her best friend who was also an intern of mine. Thus, what might have been the ultimate spontaneous gesture (an intimate fantasy) turned out to be a script she had borrowed from a friend.
>
> I was trying to tell her, as kindly and as gently as I could, that she needed to learn to do a different kind of therapy, one that did not rely so heavily on the therapist's self-awareness and self-understanding. "But I do understand myself," she said defensively. "I have a lot of self-awareness." I immediately countered in a way that surprised myself. "Oh no you don't," I said. "You have as little self-awareness as anyone I have ever known. You know nothing about yourself. You don't even know how you feel."
>
> These words were spoken firmly, but with more empathy than anger or criticism and when she began to weep softly, she did not look like someone who had just been slapped. I let her cry for a minute and then asked her what she was feeling. "I feel seen," she said with what appeared to be genuine appreciation.

Despite these stories of treatment successes, I personally find the False Personality clients to be among the most difficult to treat, and my own treatment failures easily rival my successes with such clients.

> Kim was a high-level media executive in her early thirties. An Asian-American, Kim had grown up with more than the stereotypical "tiger" parents. "No, my dad was crazy!" she emphasized, describing a history of both verbal and physical abuse. But although recognizing both his brutality and his sadism, Kim had nevertheless adopted the False Self persona that he had insisted upon. Her entire life focus was on success, and success was defined entirely in monetary terms. She needed to make a lot of money, and nothing else in life seemed to matter.
>
> Kim did not enter therapy because she experienced any dissatisfaction with herself or her life. Rather, she had been urged into therapy by a supervisor who had cautioned her about how brutally critical she could be with her subordinates. She attended therapy regularly, but never appeared to derive any comfort or satisfaction from it. It seemed to be a penance she had to go through because of her past failures. Most clients eventually express some pleasure at feeling seen, feeling supported, even being challenged. But Kim did not. She did what she was supposed to do in therapy, but did it robotically.
>
> An apparent turning point came not with any change in our relationship but with a new boyfriend. He was a young man whom all of her high-powered friends and colleagues warned her against. "He was too nice. He lacked ambition. He wasn't hungry enough. He wasn't ruthless enough. He would never get anywhere." Kim was very troubled by these comments, all of which she agreed with, but nevertheless found herself very drawn to this man.
>
> I pressed her to explore what he meant to her, how he made her feel, what attracted her to him. The answers were that he softened her. He humanized her. He brought warmth to an otherwise cold existence. But these answers discomforted her more than they gave her any pleasure. She finally decided that he was "unworthy" of her and she dropped him. Shortly after that, she abruptly terminated therapy.

Working with False Self personalities – dream analysis

If, as Winnicott says, the True Self resides in the spontaneous gesture, then few phenomena can be more spontaneous than dreams. As Freud (1900) pointed out over a hundred years ago, there is censorship even in dreams.

The "dream work" that the psyche undertakes to disguise the "latent content" under the "manifest content" is an act of censorship. Notwithstanding, Freud labeled dreams the "royal road to the unconscious" and we might equally see them as the royal road to the True Self. Ogden (1994) offers a modification of Freud's (1900) theory that all dreams represent the fulfillment of a wish. Sometimes, suggests Ogden, the wish may be one split-off part of the psyche that needs to be heard by another part of the psyche.

> Tiffany, an African American teenager I worked with in the locked residential setting, was one of the angriest human beings I have ever known. She got along with neither staff nor her peers. Her affect ranged from barely controlled, simmering rage to explosive outbursts of fury. The clinical staff and I tried every trick in our repertoires to reach her, but without success.
>
> Tiffany would sometimes ask to work in therapy group but her "work" was always the same: a repetitive diatribe against a particular staff member with whom she had had an incident which made her label the staff member "racist." So perseverative and so unproductive was this use of the group's time that at a certain point the treatment team asked her not to work in group until she had gained more self-control.
>
> A few months later Tiffany asked in group if she could work. She had definitely mastered some self-control so I nodded in agreement. She began to give an almost exact rereading of her old diatribe, about the same incident and the same staff member, clearly working herself towards a crescendo of rage and injured angst. I considered stopping her but decided to let her vent.
>
> That night I dreamed about the Hetch Hetchy Dam. By way of background, the Hetch Hetchy Valley was a glacial valley that John Muir called the second most beautiful valley in the Sierras, after the Yosemite Valley. But in the 1910s the city of San Francisco decided it needed a steady water supply, the Tuolumne River was dammed, and the Hetch Hetchy Valley is now underwater. Almost since the moment of its completion there has been talk of tearing the dam down and restoring the valley.
>
> My dream was unusual in that there were no visuals: it consisted entirely of thoughts. "What an enormous undertaking," I thought, "it would be to tear down a dam that big. And even if they were able to tear it down all that water would have to go somewhere. And if they removed the water there would be a valley floor covered by sediment

and muck scores of feet deep. And if they were able to clean out all the sediment and muck then there would be nothing left: all vegetation had died a hundred years ago. The valley would be dead."

When I awoke from the dream I knew instantly that the dream was about Tiffany or, more precisely, about my true feelings towards Tiffany: despair and hopelessness. Tiffany's defenses (the dam) were too strong. And even if we were able to penetrate those defenses there would be nothing but pain and anger and sadness (the sediment and muck). And if we were able to work through all the feelings, there would be nothing left, no life. Tiffany was by now nothing but rage. There was no other life there.

Rightly or wrongly, these were my true feelings; this was my True Self needing to be heard and seeking expression through my barely censored (but still spontaneous) dream. The False Self that had tried to repress these feelings was my Professional Self which had believed (at least I had believed so back then) that therapists needed to remain positive and hopeful at all costs.

Still, a powerful False Self personality structure can put up daunting barriers even to the use of dream analysis. Clients with strong False Self presentations will frequently show little curiosity or interest in rich dream material, shrugging off dreams as "just weird" (c.f. Yalom's (1989) chapter, *In Search of the Dreamer*).

Abby, highly intelligent and well versed in psychology, brought dream material into therapy from the onset. But this appeared to be more out of a sense that this was what she was *supposed to do* than out of any genuine curiosity. When I would ask for her associations she would reply, "Well, I think that Freud would say . . ." or, "Jung says that this symbolizes . . ." Abby even reported having an "app" for dream interpretation.

Dreams may be inherently *spontaneous gestures*, but there is nothing inherently spontaneous in our ability or willingness to work with them. Lacking that, we are left with our one, fallback tool in our toolbox: the psychotherapy relationship.

Bibliography

Aledort, S. (2002). The omnipotent child syndrome: The role of passionately held bad fits in the formation of identity. *International Journal of Group Psychotherapy*, *52*(1), 67–87.

Aledort, S. (2014). Excitement in shame: The price we pay. *International Journal of Group Psychotherapy*, *64*(1), 91–103.

Aron, L. (1991). The patient's experience of the analyst's subjectivity. In S. Mitchell & L. Aron (Eds.), *Relational psychoanalysis: The emergence of a tradition* (pp. 243–268). Hillsdale, NJ: Analytic Press.

Aron, L. (1996). *A meeting of minds: Mutuality in psychoanalysis.* Hillsdale, NJ: Analytic Press.

Beck, A. (1979). *Cognitive therapy and the emotional disorders.* New York: Meridian Books.

Benjamin, J. (1988). *The bonds of love: Psychoanalysis, feminism, and the problem of domination.* New York: Pantheon Books.

Benjamin, J. (1990). Recognition and destruction: An outline of intersubjectivity. In S. Mitchell & L. Aron (Eds.), *Relational psychoanalysis: The emergence of a tradition.* Hillsdale, NJ: Analytic Press.

Benjamin, J. (1998). *Shadow of the object.* London: Routledge.

Benjamin, J. (2004). Beyond doer and done to: An intersubjective view of thirdness. *Psychoanalytic Quarterly*, *73*, 5–46.

Bion, W. (1952). Group dynamics: A review. In *Experiences in groups* (pp. 141–192). New York: Basic Books, 1959.

Bion, W. (1956). Development of schizophrenic thought. In *Second thoughts* (pp. 36–42). New York: Jason Aronson, 1967.

Bion, W. (1957). Differentiation of the psychotic from the non-psychotic personalities. In *Second thoughts* (pp. 43–64). New York: Jason Aronson, 1967.

Bion, W. (1961). *Experiences in groups.* London: Tavistock.

Bion, W. (1967). Notes on memory and desire. *Psychoanalytic Forum*, *II*(3), 271–280.

Bird, B. (1972). Notes on transference: Universal phenomenon and hardest part of analysis. *Journal of the American Psychoanalytic Association*, *20*, 267–301.

Bowlby, J. (1988). *A Secure Base: Parent-child attachment and healthy human development.* New York, Basic Books.

Brodie, B. (2007). *Adolescence and delinquency: An object relations approach.* New York: Jason Aronson.

Brown, L. (2011). *Intersubjective processes and the unconscious: An integration of Freudian, Kleinian and Bionian perspectives*. New York: Routledge.

Carnes, P. (2010). *The betrayal bond: Breaking free of exploitive relationships*. Health Communications, Incorporated. ISBN 978-0-7573-9719-6.

Casement, P. (2014). *Further learning from the patient: The analytic space and process*. London: Routledge Mental Health Classics.

Cohen, J., Mannarino, A., & Deblinger, E. (2006). *Treating trauma and traumatic grief in children and adolescents*. New York: Guilford Press. ISBN 978-1-60623-848-6.

Fairbairn, W. R. D. (1952). *Psychoanalytic studies of personality*. London: Routledge.

Fenichel, O. (1945). *The psychoanalytic theory of neurosis*. New York: W. W. Norton & Co.

Freud, A. (1936). *The ego and the mechanisms of defense*. New York: International Universities Press.

Freud, S. (1900). *Interpretation of dreams* (Standard ed., Vol. IV, pp. 1–630).

Freud, S. (1905). *Fragment of an analysis of a case of hysteria* (Standard ed., Vol. VII, pp. 3–124).

Freud, S. (1909). *Analysis of a phobia in a five-year-old boy* (Standard ed., Vol. X, pp. 3–152).

Freud, S. (1910a). *Five lectures on psycho-analysis*. Fifth lecture: Transference and resistance (Standard ed., Vol. XI, pp. 49–58).

Freud, S. (1910b). *The future prospects of psycho-analytic therapy* (Standard ed., Vol. XI, pp. 139–151).

Freud, S. (1911). *Formulation on the two principles of mental functioning* (Standard ed., Vol. XII, pp. 215–226).

Freud, S. (1912). *The dynamics of transference* (Standard ed., Vol. XII, pp. 99–108).

Freud, S. (1914a). *History of the psycho-analytic movement* (Standard ed., Vol. XIV).

Freud, S. (1914b). *Papers on technique Remembering, repeating and working-through: Further recommendations on the technique of psycho-analysis* (Standard ed., Vol. XII).

Freud, S. (1916–1917). *Introductory lectures on psycho-analysis* (Standard ed., Vol. XV).

Freud, S. (1917). *Papers on metapsychology (1915): Mourning and melancholia (1917)* (Standard ed., Vol. XIV, pp. 237–260).

Freud, S. (1918). *From the history of an infantile neurosis* (Standard ed., Vol. XVII, pp. 7–124).

Freud, S. (1920). *Beyond the pleasure principal* (Standard ed., Vol. XVIII, pp. 3–66).

Freud, S. (1923). *The ego and the id* (Standard ed., Vol. XIX, pp. 3–68).

Freud, S. (1925). *Negation* (Standard ed., Vol. XIX, pp. 235–242).

Freud, S. (1937). *Analysis terminable and interminable* (Standard ed., Vol. XXII, pp. 211–254).

Freud, S. (1940). *An outline of psychoanalysis* (Standard ed., Vol. XXIII, pp. 141–208).

Gendlin, E. (1971). *Lecture*. Chicago, IL: University of Chicago.

Gill, M. (1979). The analysis of the transference. *Journal of the American Psychoanalytic Association*, *27*, 263–288.

Green, A. (2004). Thirdness and psychoanalytic concepts. *Psychoanalytic Quarterly*, *73*, 99–136.

Greenberg, J. (1986). Theoretical models and the analyst's neutrality. In S. Mitchell & L. Aron (Eds.), *Relational psychoanalysis: The emergence of a tradition*. Hillsdale, NJ: Analytic Press.

Greenson, R. (1971). The real relationship between the patient and the psychoanalyst. In M. Kanzer (Ed.), *The unconscious today*. New York: International Universities Press.

Grosskurth, P. (1986). *Melanie Klein: Her life and her work*. New York: Alfred A. Knopf, Inc.

Hegel, G. W. F. (1807). *Phänomenologie des Geistes (Phenomenology of mind)* Trans. A. V. Miller, London: Oxford University Press, 1977.

Hoffman, I. (1983). The patient as interpreter of the analyst's experience. In S. Mitchell & L. Aron (Eds.), *Relational psychoanalysis: The emergence of a tradition*. Hillsdale, NJ: Analytic Press.

Jung, C. (1963). *Memories, dreams, reflections*. New York: Pantheon Press and Random Houses.

Kalsched, D. (1996). *The inner world of trauma: Archetypal defenses of the personal spirit*. New York: Routledge.

Kernberg, O. (1976, 1984). *Object-relations theory and clinical psychoanalysis*. New York: Jason Aronson.

Kohut, H. (1971). *The analysis of the self: A systematic approach to the psychoanalytic treatment of narcissistic personality disorders*. Chicago, IL: University of Chicago Press.

Kushner, H. (1981). *When bad things happen to good people*. New York: Schocken Press.

Levenson, E. (1972). *The fallacy of understanding*. New York: International Universities Press.

Lewin, K. (1947, June). Frontiers in group dynamics: Concept, method and reality in social science; social equilibria and social change. *Human Relations, 1*, 36. doi:10.1177/001872674700100103.

Lewis, C. S. (1976). *A grief observed*. New York: Bantam Books.

Mahler, M. (1972). On the first three subphases of the separation-individuation process. *International Journal of Psychoanalysis, 53*(3), 333–338.

Miller, A. (1981). *The drama of the gifted child: How narcissistic parents form and deform the emotional lives of their talented children*. New York: Basis Books.

Mitchell, S. (1988). *Relational concepts in psychoanalysis*. Cambridge, MA: Harvard University Press.

Mitchell, S. (1991). Contemporary perspectives on self: Toward an integration. *Psychoanalytic Dialogs, 1*, 121–147.

Mitchell, S. (1993). *Hope and dread in psychoanalysis*. New York: Basic Books.

Mitchell, S. (1997). *Influence and autonomy in psychoanalysis*. Hillsdale, NJ: Analytic Press.

Mitchell, S. (2000). *Relationality: From attachment to intersubjectivity*. Hillsdale, NJ: Analytic Press.

Mitchell, S. A., & Black, M. J. (1995). *Freud and beyond: A history of modern psychoanalytic thought*. New York: Basic Books.

Moore, B., & Fine, B. (Eds.). (1990). *Psychoanalytic terms and concepts*. New Haven: American Psychoanalytic Society and Yale University Press.

Nussbaum, M. C. (2001). *Upheavals of thought: The intelligence of emotion*. Cambridge: Cambridge University Press.

Ogden, T. (1984). *Projective identification and psychotherapeutic technique*. New York: Jason Aronson.

Ogden, T. (1990, 1986). *The matrix of the mind: Object relations and the psychoanalytic dialog*. New York: Jason Aronson.

Ogden, T. (1994). *Subjects of analysis*. New York: Jason Aronson.

Ogden, T. (1999). The analytic third: An overview. In S. Mitchell & L. Aron (Eds.), *Relational psychoanalysis: The emergence of a tradition*. Hillsdale, NJ: Analytic Press.

Ogden, T. (2004). The analytic third: Implications for psychoanalytic theory and technique. *Psychoanalytic Quarterly, 73*, 167–195.

Ogden, T. (2013, December 2). [Letter to Bruce R. Brodie]. Copy in possession of Bruce R. Brodie.

Racker, H. (1968). *Transference and countertransference*. New York: International Universities Press.

Renik, O. (1993). Analytic interaction: Conceptualizing technique in light of the analyst's irreducible subjectivity. In S. Mitchell & L. Aron (Eds.), *Relational psychoanalysis: The emergence of a tradition*. Hillsdale, NJ: Analytic Press.

Rodman, F. R. (2003). *Winnicott: Life and work*. Cambridge, MA: Perseus Publishing.

Sandler, J. (1976). Countertransference and role-responsiveness. *International Review of Psycho-Analysis*, *3*, 43–37.

Schedler, J. (2010). The efficacy of psychodynamic psychotherapy. *American Psychologist*, *65*(2), 98–109.

Searles, H. (1965). *Collected papers on schizophrenia and related subjects*. New York: International Universities Press.

Searles, H. (1979). *Countertransference and related subjects*. New York: International Universities Press.

Stark, M. (1999). *Modes of therapeutic action: Enhancement of knowledge, provision of experience, and engagement in relationship*. New York: Jason Aronson.

Stern, D. B. (1983). Unformulated experience: From familiar chaos to creative disorder. In S. Mitchell & L. Aron (Eds.), *Relational psychoanalysis: The emergence of a tradition* (pp. 77–108). Hillsdale, NJ: The Analytic Press.

Stolorow, R. (1997). Principles of dynamic systems, intersubjectivity, and the obsolete distinction between one-person and two-person psychologies: A meeting of the minds: Mutuality in psychoanalysis by Lewis Aron (Hillsdale, NJ: The Analytic Press, 1996). *Psychoanalytic Dialogs*, *7*, 859–868.

Stolorow, R. (2013). Intersubjective systems theory: A phenomenological-contextualist psychoanalytic perspective. *Psychoanalytic Dialogs*, *23*, 383–389. doi:10.1080/10481 885.2013.810846.

Stolorow, R., & Atwood, G. (1992). Three realms of the unconscious. In S. Mitchell & L. Aron (Eds.), *Relational psychoanalysis: The emergence of a tradition* (pp. 365–378). Hillsdale, NJ: The Analytic Press.

Stolorow, R., Brandshaft, B., & Atwood, G. (1983). Intersubjectivity in psychoanalytic treatment: With special reference to archaic states. *Bulletin of the Menninger Clinic*, *47*(2), 117–1128. doi:0025-9284/83/0117-0128$01.20/0.

Summers, F. (2005). Creation and discovery in the psychoanalytic process. In *Relational and intersubjective perspectives in psychoanalysis* (pp. 131–151). New York: Jason Aronson.

Tuber, S. (2008). *Attachment, play, and authenticity: A Winnicott primer*. New York: Jason Aronson.

Wachtel, P. (1997). *Psychoanalysis, behavior therapy, and the relational world*. Washington, DC: American Psychoanalytic Association.

Wachtel, P. (2008). *Relational theory and the practice of psychotherapy*. New York: Guilford Press.

Winnicott, D. (1949). Hate in the countertransference. *International Journal of Psychoanalysis*, *30*, 69–74.

Winnicott, D. (1950). Aggression in relation to emotional development. In *Through pediatrics to psycho-analysis: Collected papers* (pp. 204–218). New York: Basic Books.

Winnicott, D. (1954). The family affected by depressive illness in one or both parents. In *The family and individual development*. London: Tavistock and Routledge, 1965.

Winnicott, D. (1956). The primary maternal preoccupation. In *Through pediatrics to psycho-analysis: Collected papers* (pp. 300–305). New York: Basic Books.

Winnicott, D. (1960a). The theory of the parent-infant relationship. In *The maturational process and the facilitating environment* (pp. 37–56). New York: Karnac.

Winnicott, D. (1960b). Ego distortion in terms of true and false self. In *The maturational process and the facilitating environment* (pp. 140–152). New York: Karnac.

Winnicott, D. (1968a). The use of an object and relating through identifications. In C. Winnicott, R. Shepard, & M. Davis (Eds.), *Psychoanalytic explorations* (pp. 218–227). Cambridge, MA: Harvard University Press.

Winnicott, D. (1968b). The use of the word use. In C. Winnicott, R. Shepard, & M. Davis (Eds.), *Psychoanalytic explorations* (pp. 233–235). Cambridge, MA: Harvard University Press.

Winnicott, D. (1968c). Roots of aggression. In C. Winnicott, R. Shepard, & M. Davis (Eds.), *Psychoanalytic explorations* (pp. 458–461). Cambridge, MA: Harvard University Press.

Winnicott, D. (1971a). Mirror-role of mother and family in child development. In *Playing and reality* (pp. 111–118). New York: Tavistock and Routledge.

Winnicott, D. (1971b). Playing: A theoretical statement. In *Playing and reality* (pp. 38–52). New York: Tavistock and Routledge.

Winnicott, D. (1971c). Playing: Creative activity and the search or the self. In *Playing and reality* (pp. 53–64). New York: Tavistock and Routledge.

Winnicott, D. (1971d). The place where we live. In *Playing and reality* (pp. 104–110). New York: Tavistock and Routledge.

Winnicott, D. (1971e). Dreaming, fantasying, and living. In *Playing and reality* (pp. 26–37). New York: Basic Books.

Winnicott, D. (1971f). Transitional Objects and Transitional Phenomena. In Playing and reality (pp. 1–25). New York: Basic Books.

Yalom, I. (1989). *Love's Executioner: & other tales of psychotherapy*. New York: Harper Perennial.

Yalom, E. (1997). *Lying on the couch*. New York: Harper Perennial.

Yalom, E. (2002). *The gift of therapy: An open letter to a new generation of therapists and their patients*. New York: Harper Perennial.

Index

For Product Safety Concerns and Information please contact our EU
representative GPSR@taylorandfrancis.com
Taylor & Francis Verlag GmbH, Kaufingerstraße 24, 80331 München, Germany

www.ingramcontent.com/pod-product-compliance
Lightning Source LLC
Chambersburg PA
CBHW060150280326
41932CB00012B/1705